Guide to Software Development

T0192207

Arthur M. Langer

Guide to Software Development

Designing and Managing the Life Cycle

 Springer

Dr. Arthur M. Langer
Columbia University
School of Continuing Education
Lewisohn Hall 510A
10027 New York
NY, USA
al261@columbia.edu

ISBN 978-1-4471-6169-1   ISBN 978-1-4471-2300-2 (eBook)
DOI 10.1007/978-1-4471-2300-2
Springer London Dordrecht Heidelberg New York

British Library Cataloguing in Publication Data
A catalogue record for this book is available from the British Library

Printed on acid-free paper

Springer is part of Springer Science+Business Media (www.springer.com)

Preface

How to improve the quality and process of implementing enterprise software remains a most challenging topic at conferences on information development and business process reengineering. Over the past few decades the question of how to do this has only become more complex, especially with the growth of sophisticated package software products in the market such as SAP and Oracle Financials. These products, called enterprise resource planning (ERP), claim to provide a quicker and more cost-effective way to fully integrate software applications in all parts of the business. Yet, so many of them fail to be either cheaper or faster by the time they are put into production. Furthermore, the decision to make or buy software is not simple and in many cases organizations now need to consider some combination of both. Therefore, the problem that this book addresses is to how best determine to make such decisions and what effect such decisions have on the software development life cycle (SDLC). Although there are many different SDLC methodologies, this book offers an integrated approach that includes the management and decision practices that are critical for success. Accordingly, the role of the analyst and the project manager needs to be linked throughout the SDLC. The objective; however, continues to be how information technology professionals can create automated solutions that fit user and customer needs. By suggesting that professionals may find success in mixing methodologies, this book breaks important new ground.

Many books written on this subject tend to focus too much on the mechanics of how to do analysis or how to do project management, rather than on the art of performing both functions successfully. As I have stated in previous books, the most successful implementers are not necessarily the best technicians, but rather are gifted individuals who have the ability and insight to extract information from users and transfer their knowledge into logical solutions. But today even accurate requirements do not ensure success without quality management. The field of information technology is no longer new, and the time has come for education to focus on producing quality products faster and cheaper. Thus, this book seeks to develop the skills and insights that distinguish successful software implementations.

The book identifies many new alternatives for how to manage and model a system using sophisticated analysis tools and advanced management practices. It emphasizes how and when professionals can best apply them and what benefits can be derived from their application. The book's approach is to recommend that analysts and managers be agile and to not over commit to using any one methodology, rather learn to deal within the constraints of the political and cultural realities of their organizations. It may come as a surprise to many lay readers to learn that this approach is unique among many textbooks. Yet, the fact is that most books teach only a single method and advocate the use of that method alone in all projects.

The Aim of This Book

The risks involved when making decisions about enterprise software solutions are substantial: those projects that involve reengineering activities have a failure rate of over 50%. Obviously, then, the stakes are very high, and identifying the sources of failure can be invaluable. In general, I have found that project failures can be attributed to two major issues: (1) those that have difficulty defining accurate business requirements and (2) those that have problems with managing change. Both of these major challenges can be overcome by following many of the steps I have outlined in this book. This book is therefore meant to be a "how to" guide taking theory and applying it to the realities of practice.

The book recognizes that there are few off-the-shelf products that can provide a complete solution for any organization. Thus, most enterprise-level solutions will be a combination of packaged and custom-developed software. This "hybrid" realism has changed the way professionals undertake the SDLC, particularly, as it relates to selection of third-party vendors and the legal ramifications of working with outside consultants. For this reason, the book includes subjects like build vs. buy, searching for vendor solutions, and vendor contract considerations.

My enthusiasm for writing this book was supported by many of my students at Columbia University who found that existing books on software development to be

- *Very hypothetical*: Although they explain the methodologies and management concepts, they do not provide enough concrete examples.
- *Too technical*: They do not deal with the political and cultural realities of how things get done in organizations. Indeed, the objective of providing software solutions is to service business units in organizations. The management side of developing software solutions is as important as the technical side.
- *Lacking modest but effective cases*: The examples do not provide an understanding of the technical and management concepts effectively or are too simplistic for practice implementation.

The Intended Audience for This Book

This book assumes a reasonable understanding of computer and business concepts. The material is presented to be used for an introductory project management class or analysis and design course in a university program. In addition, it can be used by practicing information technology professionals or executives who are managing software projects and need an in-depth understanding of the principles of the analysis and design and project management processes. Furthermore, many business managers who are also responsible for ERP-type projects may find this book a way of developing a useful understanding of the requirements process as well as the entire SDLC.

Acknowledgments

I want to thank all the staff at Workforce Opportunity Services for their great work in establishing a new supply of IT workers from the inner-city and rural poor areas around the world. Your contributions are well deserved. Of course I want to acknowledge all of my students at Columbia University for their dedication and inspiration and certainly for keeping me on my toes in class.

A very special thanks to Cali Grace Caprio, my first grandchild who brings me joy every day.

New York   Arthur M. Langer

Contents

Introduction

1

After decades of writing about the field of analysis and design, I write this book to focus on the evolution of software in the world. We have seen over the past 40 years, the continual expansion of the library of software applications that are used in common workplace as well as in the personal lives of people throughout the world. Indeed, software applications continue to change the world and as a result the challenge of managing the advent of huge application libraries has become of paramount importance. In addition, the advent of social networking has also had a salient impact on the uses and effects of applications over the Internet and the expansion of open source has now created an environment of applications that can be used on demand and across multiple platforms.

The purpose of this book is to provide professionals and academics with a guide to manage the life cycle of placing software applications into production. This book breaks new ground because of this narrow focus, which is more on implementation than on engineering per se. This book provides guidance on how to determine whether to make or buy and allows readers to determine sections that are fitting for their use. Technical readers, that is, those engaged in analysis and design will find chapters that provide the approach and tools on how to create an architecture of system needs. Business users can become more educated in the system development life cycle for both package software and customized applications. Business and IT people will also get a better understanding of project management methods and contract consideration in the relationships they have with vendors and independent consultants.

What Is, Is

Over 40 years of developing requirements for systems has taught us that the only successful approach to developing software applications is to accept what exists in the user's environment, however far from ideal those conditions may be, and work within those limitations. It may be very tempting to use analysis time to try to refocus on how the user does business. Yet efforts to redesign or reengineer,

A.M. Langer, *Guide to Software Development*,
DOI 10.1007/978-1-4471-2300-2_1, © Springer-Verlag London Limited 2012

unless specifically requested by the user, will typically be a waste. Although your assessment may be correct and your suggestions potentially useful, being correct is less important in this situation than being wise and understanding the ability of your users to successfully implement and utilize what they need. Analysts tend to ignore this simple wisdom, much to their own distress and that of their clients.

Looking at a typical example of an analysis situation will help to illustrate this point. Let us assume that an enterprise needs a relational database model to gather information about a subject area of the business. There are 200 offices that will need to connect into a nationally provided service. Users disagree on the mission of the applications and cannot determine what reports or query information they want. Some offices are automated, but they do not have the same software and hardware. There is little expertise in the user community to determine the data requirements and file layouts (identifying elements in each file). Management has requested that the analyst establish a specification which identifies the requirements of the system as well as the necessary hardware and software.

Faced with so unwieldy a task, many analysts will adopt the following approach in an attempt to impose order on a disorderly situation:
1. Force users to define all requirements. Since they are unable to do so, this insistence will probably result in their guessing or providing incomplete information.
2. Determine the hardware and software configuration, despite having inaccurate or incomplete requirements.
3. Ignore the political environment.
4. Establish a project plan that everyone knows will fail, but push ahead with it anyway.

It should be clear that this approach is the wrong one, on a number of different counts. Yet, such an approach is all too typical for analysts confronted with a less-than-ideal working environment. Happily, there is a better approach for all concerned, one that recognizes and responds to the conditions actually present at the user's site. In this case it is evident that the users are not positioned to provide the requirements for a system, largely because they do not fully understand their own needs and because they do not agree among themselves. What the analyst needs to understand in such a situation is that because of this lack of knowledge and organization, user needs will tend to change during the process of product analysis and design. Such changes are to be expected; they are simply part of the life cycle for this particular implementation. To ignore the situation and try to implement a system is to invite failure. Put simply then, what is, is. The task of the analyst is to work with what is, rather than trying to change it or—even worse—simply denying it. Once you as an analyst understand that reality, you understand that your solution must accommodate what will inevitably occur.

Here is a more sensible approach to the situation described above:
1. Focus on designing a model that can provide the users with the capability they want. Create a project plan that assumes that the database will be incomplete during Phase I because of the user's inability to define the correct information. The process will therefore be an iterative one and thus will be finalized during the later parts of the development life cycle.

2. Do not try to identify hardware before it is clear what the usage requirements are, such as peak-time processing and number of users. It will be more beneficial to establish the operating system or architectural environment that you want to support, pending the results of the analysis.
3. Utilize a software system or tool that will allow users to generate new scenarios such that they can see how these scenarios relate to the entire system.
4. Set up a pilot program. This will require that certain offices agree to be test sites for the early versions of the software. The function of the pilot is to provide feedback on the effectiveness and shortfalls of the product. It is important to state clearly the objectives of the pilot and the format of the feedback in order to ensure the success of the exercise.
5. Formulate a plan that depicts a schedule for getting the entire enterprise implemented and live on the new system. Be sensitive to the politics of the situation, and use a realistic approach that will not require a cultural change in order to implement software in the existing environment.

The essence of this approach is to develop a strategy that fits the reality of the environment, rather than force the environment to change. Throughout this book, we will explore this simple but crucial concept. No two system development projects are identical, and the more familiar the analyst is with the environment, the more successful the project will be. This book will also argue against the conventional wisdom that suggests using an approach based on only a single methodology (e.g., Yourdon, Martin, and Booch). The mixing of methodologies allows the analyst a wider range of tools. Hands-on experience shows that this kind of mixing of methodologies can be done quite successfully and that it is appropriate in a large number of analysis situations.

Most important to the purpose of this book is the evolution of the application development world over the last 20 years. We have gone from solely an in-house build it yourself focus to what is commonly known as "commercial-off-the-shelf (COTS)" solutions. This book will integrate the classic approaches of developing applications to specifically meet user needs with the unique conditions of going with the "best-fit" approach of COTS. But the decisions today are not at all binary—build vs. buy, etc. With the expansion of software modules, programs that provide specific tasks, pieces of code can be brought together to build applications, but yet are bought. Furthermore, there is the impact of open source, which has slowly changed the way organizations pursue using reusable code that no one owns.

Finally, and what I feel sets this book apart from others, is its commitment to an IT and user integration. Too many books still discuss how IT can save the day or lead the implementation. Leadership is a tricky thing, and it certainly does not suggest control as a solution. IT must become better leaders by displaying the ability to influence management and users, not to tell them what needs to be done. Thus, this book speaks to both IT and non-IT personnel and hopefully provides a provocative approach to ensuring better success when determining why, what, and how of providing application solutions.

Just What Is a Complex Project?

Most analysts, project team members, and users worry about the complexity of their projects. Their requirements seem entirely unique to them, and therefore a very special approach seems to be required. How many times have you heard: "the tools and approaches used elsewhere just won't work in this environment?"

The truth, however, is very different: the only truly complex projects are those that people make so! It is important for the analyst to recognize that the procedures utilized, regardless of the size of the project, should remain fundamentally the same. As we have discussed above, the analyst's approach to the implementation of each project should be tailored individually; however, the procedures for this implementation should remain constant. Very often the organization of interviews, the utilization of techniques such as Joint Application Development, discussed later in this chapter, or the simple addition of more analysts to the project can solve what appear to be insurmountable problems.

In fact, most of the myriad problems that arise in product development can be traced to two fundamental issues:

1. People are trying to solve the wrong problem, i.e., the identified problem is not really what is wrong.
2. The solution to the real problem is often much simpler than that it first appears to be.

Because we have failed to recognize these issues, the industry's frustration with developing appropriate software solutions has been chronic, and this situation has not really improved over the last 25 years! The question is why?

To put it bluntly, analysts often fail to do their jobs properly! We tend to put together plans and schedules that are doomed from the start to fail, an issue treated in more detail later. The ultimate goal of the analyst must take into account the reality of the environment in which the work is occurring. Remember, work within the environment. Let users decide what degree of change is appropriate for their own operation; do not take it upon yourself to demand that they change.

For example, how many times have you seen a Gantt Chart[1] for a project schedule that resembles the one in Fig. 1.1.

It looks nice, but in reality the plan it depicts could never happen. Focus in particular on the intersection of development and quality assurance (QA) activities. The plan shows that once development is finished, the materials are forwarded to QA for testing. The sequence assumes, however, that QA will never find an error and that, therefore, the materials will never be returned to development! Any analyst knows that this scenario is very unlikely to occur. Such poor planning results in deficient allocation of resources to the project. Should the development schedule be met, programming resources most probably will be allocated to other projects. Thus, if QA finds errors, which they undoubtedly will, reallocating these programming

---

[1] A Gantt Chart is a tool that depicts progress of tasks against time. It was developed by Henry L. Gantt in 1917.

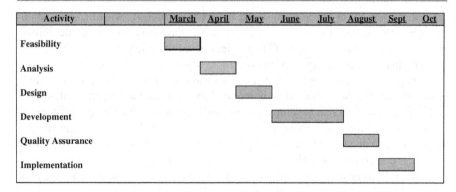

Fig. 1.1 Sample Gantt Chart

resources becomes difficult and problematic. And remember: programmers do not like returning to an "old" program to do maintenance or error fixing.

Figure 1.2 reflects a more realistic view of the life cycle of the project.

The difference in approach is striking. The question is, as sensible as this plan appears to be, why don't we always do it this way? Quite frankly, this plan does not look as nice—as neat and tidy—as the previous plan. But of course simply denying the pain of reality—the inevitable inconveniences and delays—does not make that reality go away. In defense of the previous configuration, some developers might suggest that the iterations of efforts between testing and fixing the software are assumed to be included in the QA time. Maybe, but don't count on it! Just look at the second schedule and you will see how the results of this proper allocation added to the delivery time of the project. It is clear that the original plan was simply incorrect.

There is absolutely no reason why a schedule should not reflect the reality of what will most probably occur. The results are clear: realistic planning provides a more reliable schedule. Among the many benefits of such a schedule are the confidence and respect gained by both the users and the development staff. There is nothing like producing a schedule that reflects what everyone is confident will occur.

Activity		March	April	May	June	July	August	Sept	Oct
Feasibility									
Analysis									
Design									
Development									
Quality Assurance									
Implementation									

Fig. 1.2 Modified Gantt Chart reflecting realistic project activity behavior

At this point, experienced analysts are no doubt wondering: what happens when management dictates to us how much time we have and shows no flexibility about running behind schedule? This problem is unfortunately not uncommon and typically fits into one of three scenarios:

1. Management is ignorant about the analysis and construction of systems and simply has no idea how much time is required to complete the project. In this case the analyst will need to develop a convincing presentation for management about the details of how systems are designed and developed. The presentation should be carefully documented to refer to the industry statistics for similar projects in similar companies. This kind of documentation adds much credibility to the discussion. You can also consider having an independent source, such as a respected consulting firm, to support your position.

2. Management has little confidence in development. They feel that picking a date and sticking to it is the best method of getting the project finished. Yes, this is the bully technique! It usually results from bad experiences, probably from looking at those unrealistic Gantt Charts. In this situation, the analyst must take steps to gain management's confidence. Using the suggestions above would be a good start. In addition, you will need to research and understand the history of what your predecessors did to encourage this type of distrusting and dictatorial attitude on the part of management and find a tactful way to address those issues.

3. Unfortunately, bad management does exist. If you cannot win any concessions or understanding from management, you may have reached what is known as the "no-win scenario." Management is simply unwilling to allot adequate time for the completion of the project and they are unwilling to be persuaded otherwise. When this situation exists in the workplace, the advice is straightforward: you can leave, or you can find some way to deal with this constraint. In either case, be aware that under the no-win scenario there is little hope that the project will result in the development of quality software. This perspective is not cynical, but rather realistic: some projects are doomed to fail before they begin. What is important is that the analyst recognize as early in the life cycle as possible that the project cannot be successful.

Because this book represents more about selection and management of software applications, it is necessary to modify the systems development life cycle (SDLC).

The *traditional SDLC* is most commonly used to design products in three major parts:

1. Requirements analysis
2. Data modeling
3. Normalization

During the first phase, requirements analysis, the development and design team conduct interviews in order to capture all the business needs as related to the proposed system. The data modeling phase consists of the creation of the logical data model that will later be used to define the physical data model or database structures. After the database has been modeled and designed, the normalization phase is implemented to help eliminate or reduce as much as possible any redundant data. All of the specifics of how this is accomplished will be detailed in

Chapters 7 and 8. Below is a more specific description of what activities are included in the development, testing, and production cycles of the SDLC.

Development

The development life cycle includes four overall components. Using this perspective, "development" would consist of all the necessary steps to accomplish the creation of the application. This includes feasibility, analysis, design, and the actual coding. Feasibility represents the tasks necessary to determine whether the software project makes business sense. Most organizations would integrate the process of return-on-investment (ROI) during this step. ROI consists of the financial steps that determine mathematically whether the project will provide the necessary monetary returns to the business. Focusing solely on monetary returns can be a serious pitfall, since there are many benefits that can be realized via non-monetary returns (Langer, 2011). Feasibility often contains what is known as a high-level forecast or budget. The "high" would represent the "worst-case" scenario on cost and the "low," the best case or lowest cost. The hope of course is that the actual cost and timetable would fall somewhere in between the high and the low. But feasibility goes beyond just the budget; it also represents whether the business feels that the project is attainable within a specific timetable as well. So, feasibility is statement of both financial and business objectives and an overall belief that the cost is worth the payback.

Analysis is the ultimate step of creating the detailed logical requirements or the architecture of the applications and database. Ultimately, the analyst creates a requirements document that outlines all of the needs for the coders to work from, without going back to the users directly for clarification. Analysis, as an architectural responsibility, is very much based on a mathematical progression of predictable steps. These steps are quite iterative in nature, which requires practitioners to understand the gradual nature of completion of this vital step in development. Another aspect of the mathematics of analysis is decomposition. Decomposition as we will see establishes the creation of the smaller components that make-up the whole. It is like the bones, blood, and muscles of the human body that ultimately make-up what we physically see in a person. Once a system is decomposed, the analyst can be confident that the "parts" that comprise the whole are identified and can be reused throughout the system as necessary. These decomposed parts are called "objects" and comprise the study and application of object-oriented analysis and design. So the basis of working with users ultimately leads to the creation of parts known as objects that act as interchangeable components that can be used whenever needed. One should think of objects like interchangeable parts of a car. They sometimes are called "standard" parts that can be reused in multiple models. The benefits are obvious. Such is the same objective with software: the more reusable, the more efficient and cost effective.

Design is far less logical than analysis but a far more creative step. Design is the phase that requires the physical decisions about the system, from what programming language to use, which vendor database to select (for example, Oracle, Sybase,

DB2), to how screens and reports will be identified. The design phase can also include decisions about hardware and network communications or the *topology*. Unlike analysis, design requires less of a mathematical and engineering focus, to one that actually serves the user view. The design process is perhaps the most iterative, which could require multiple sessions with users using a trial and error approach until the correct user interface and product selection has been completed. Design often requires "experts" in database design, screen architecture experts as well as those professionals who understand performance needs of network servers and other hardware components required by the system.

Coding represents another architectural as well as mathematical approach. However, I would suggest that mathematics is not the most accurate description of a coding structure, rather it's about understanding how logic operates. This component of mathematics is known as "Boolean" algebra or the mathematics of logic. Boolean algebra is the basis of how software communicates with the real machine. Software is the physical abstraction that allows us to talk with the hardware machine. Coding is then the best way to actually develop the structure of the program. Much has been written about coding styles and formats. The best known is called "structured" programming. Structured programming was originally developed so that programmers would create code that would be cohesive, that is, would be self-reliant. Self-reliance in coding means that the program is self-contained because all of the logic relating to its tasks is within the program. The opposite of cohesion is coupling. Coupling is the logic of programs that are reliant on each other, meaning that a change to one program necessitates a change in another program. Coupling is viewed as being dangerous from a maintenance and quality perspective, simply because changes cause problems in other reliant or "coupled" systems. The relationship to coding to analysis can be critical given that the decision on what code will comprise a module may be determined during analysis as opposed to coding.

Testing

Testing can have a number of components. The first form of testing is called program debugging. Debugging is the process of a programmer ensuring that his/her code in a program executes as designed. Debugging, therefore, should be carried out by the programmer, as opposed to a separate quality assurance group. However, it is important to recognize that debugging does not ensure that the program is performing as required by end users, rather only confirms that the code executes and does not abort during program execution. What does this mean? Simply that a programmer should never pass a program to quality assurance that does not execute, at least showing that it does perform under all conditions. Once again, this process does not ensure that the results produced by the program are correct or meet the original requirements set forth by users.

Once a program has been "debugged" it should then be sent through the quality assurance process. Today, most large organizations recognize that quality assurance needs to be performed by non-programming individuals. As a result organizations create separate quality assurance organizations that do nothing but test the correctness and accuracy of programs. Quality assurance organizations typically accomplish this by designing what is known as acceptance test planning. Acceptance test plans are designed from the original requirements, which allow quality assurance personnel to develop assurance testing based on the users' original requirements as opposed to what might have been interpreted. For this reason acceptance test planning is typically implemented during the analysis and design phases of the life cycle but executed during the testing phase. Acceptance test planning also includes system-type testing activities such as stress and load checking (ensuring that the application can handle larger demands or users) or integration testing (whether the application communicates and operates appropriately with other programs in the system) as well as compatibility testing, such as ensuring that applications operate on types of browsers or computer systems. Testing, by its very nature, is an iterative process that can often create "loops" of redesign and programming. It is important to recognize that acceptance testing has two distinct components: first, the design of the test plans, and second, the execution of those acceptance plans.

Production

Production is synonymous with the "going live" phases. Ultimately, production must ensure the successful execution of all aspects of a systems performance. During production, there is the need to establish how problems will be serviced, what support staff will be available, and when and how inquiries will be responded to and scheduled for fixing. This component of production may initiate new development and testing cycles because of redesign needs (or misinterpreted user needs). This means that the original requirements were not properly translated into system realities.

On the other hand, production as a life cycle includes other complex issues:
- Backup, recovery, and archival
- Change control
- Performance fine-tuning and statistics
- Audit and new requirements

Backup, Recovery, and Archiving
Operational backup should be defined during the development phases; however, there are inevitable backup requirements that need to be modified during production. This occurs because the time it takes to complete data backup is difficult to predict. The speed in which data can be placed on another media is not an exact science and is based on the complexity of how data are selected and the method of placement on another location and/or media. The speed also heavily relies on factors such as disk input/output speed, network throughput (speed of communication network), database backup algorithms, and the actual intervals between backup cycles. Why does this matter? It matters because backups require systems to be "off-line" until they complete, meaning that the system is in-effect not operational. Thus, the longer

the backup process, the longer the system is off-line. A most popular example of the potential backup dilemma is overnight processes that must complete by the beginning of the next morning. If the process of backup will take longer than the allowed time, then analysts/designers need to determine a way that can condense the timeline. The alternatives might typically include limiting the actual data used to backup or multiple devices to increase throughput

Recovery, on the other hand, is more about testing the quality of the backed up data and to determine whether the data stored can be recovered in the operational system. So, the first aspect is to see whether the necessary data needed to bring the system "back" can be accomplished. One hopes that recovery will never be necessary, but the most glaring exposure on quality assurance is to not really know whether the data we think we have can actually be restored back to operational forms. For example, it is one thing to backup a complex database; it is another to restore that data so that the key fields and indexes are working appropriately after restoration. The only assurance for this is to actually perform a restore in a simulation. Simulations take analysis and design talent and need to be conducted on some intervals that ensure that backup data integrity is preserved.

Restoration and backup become even more comprehensive when portions are what is called "archived." Archived data are data that are deemed no longer necessary in the "live" system, but data that may be required under some circumstances. So, data that are determined to be ready for archival need to be backed up in such a way that it can be restored, not to the live system, but rather a special system that will allow for the data to be queried and accessed as if it were live. The most relevant example that I can provide here is accounting data from past periods that are no longer needed in the operations system but may need to be accessed for audit purposes. In this example it might be necessary to restore a prior year's accounting data to a special system that simulates a prior year in question, but that has no effect on the current system.

This traditional SDLC is no longer applicable to most development projects that might start with an existing package—especially a third-party vendor-developed product. Thus a modified SDLC is required for package software development that comprises 12 complex steps:

1. Assessing business requirements
2. Build vs. buy issues
3. Establishing requirements (RFI, RFP)
4. Searching for solutions
5. Controlling costs and realistic budgeting
6. Creating requirement documents using analysis tools
7. The data
8. Legacy systems and data conversion
9. Business process reengineering
10. Data analytics and data warehouses
11. Documentation and acceptance testing
12. Going live and conclusions

Figure 1.3 graphically shows the flow from one stage of the SDLC to another.

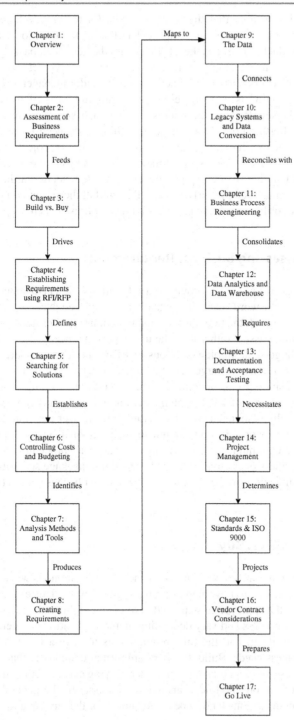

Fig. 1.3 Diagram of chapter flow

It is interesting to note that the *integrated* SDLCs for predeveloped software applications are actually far more complex than that of the traditional SDLCs for undeveloped products. This can be attributed to the fact that package software products require both development-related activities and project management—management that covers both internal activities and vendor management. Each step of this modified SDLC is defined below and forms the basis of the chapters to follow—each chapter defining the details of how each step can ensure a higher rate of success. Furthermore there are generic things that need to be done while the SDLC is occurring, including analysis tools to be used, project management, standards, and vendor contract considerations. These subjects are often addressed outside the SDLC rather than being parallel concepts that can derail the success of the project if not integrated properly. To avoid this pitfall these four components are embedded in the forthcoming chapters. A brief description of each chapter follows.

Chapter 2: Assessing Business Requirements

The first and most critical step in providing a software solution is to understand what users really want. The word "user" has actually been replaced over the years with the word "business." Indeed, the target for most application solutions needs to be geared to solving a business issue, rather than the user's personal needs. This point is very relevant to the large-scale implementations of ERP (enterprise resource planning) solutions. ERP solutions are large organizational products that essentially link all aspects of the business to an integrated system—certainly a complex application. Historically, almost half of ERP implementations fail as it succeed. ERP project failures are typically associated with the inability of the user community to accept the way the system works in comparison to their personal business preferences. That is, the user community is not willing to change its procedures to meet the more generic business operations that are designed into package software products. Thus heavy modifications to the existing product inevitably cause project delays and potential failures.

Chapter 3: Build vs. Buy

The classic question that has challenged business organizations is whether to build applications in-house or to buy them as prepackage software. This chapter will provide guidance on the appropriate steps to determine the right choice. Obviously, the decisions can be complex and vary depending on the application, the generic nature of the application itself, and the time requirements to have a functional application to meet business needs. Build decisions are further complex in that they can be developed in-house or by an outsource provider. Buying can also come with choices on the amount of custom modifications that are necessary—the general rule being that over 20% modifications tend to be a bad choice for the buy equation.

Chapter 4: Establishing Requirements Using RFP and RFI

Once decisions have been made for build vs. buy and appropriate specifications have been completed, organizations need to create a document that can be examined by third-party vendors or product suppliers so that an estimate of "fit" can be assessed—fit meaning the amount of customization required or development time necessary. Two such documents can be used: request for information (RFI) or a request for proposal (RFP).

This chapter seeks to define the similarities and differences between the two types of documents and when one type might be preferred over the other. In either situation, the main focus of the documents is to provide potential vendors or developers with enough information so that they can determine the scope of the effort and the associated costs for providing a solution. The documents also provide the selection group to be able to compare bids because the requirements are consistent, that is, the document itself requires a standard format of response thus allowing each solution to be compared, as they say—apples-to-apples.

Chapter 5: Searching for Solutions

This chapter sets forth the strategy for obtaining bids from the best sources that match the requirements. There are challenges to determine what types of vendor and/or consulting firms need to be selected and what preliminary steps firms should exercise before asking for a formal bid. This chapter also addresses the types of searches that can be done, from hiring a third-party consulting firm, an independent contractor, to a more public forum. Levels of searches are also addressed, including having decision points where certain vendors get eliminated and narrowed to a final group of acceptable solutions. The chapter also covers the ways to contact potential solution firms and the procedures for doing the necessary due diligence of not only the product, but also the firm itself. That is, too many firms may not be as dependable as its marketing materials suggest. Solutions also include hybrid approaches where both third-party-developed and internally developed software can be integrated.

Chapter 6: Controlling Costs and Realistic Budgeting

Costs are always a huge factor when undertaking major application projects. We know from experience that application projects typically are late and over budget. The question is why? The problem often relates to underestimating the complexity of the project and the time it takes to get organizations to properly define what they need. And let's not forget the role of politics, which inevitably affects the way things get done. It is also very difficult to define what you need and to obtain consensus across departments and organizations. Today, any software application will likely touch multiple parts of the organization and require retrofitting of other "legacy" applications. This chapter will address ways in which costs can be properly forecasted and how to develop realistic budgets that are attainable during the life of the project.

Chapter 7: Analysis Methods and Tools

This chapter provides an overview of the tools or core concepts that analysts use to create specifications or the logical equivalences of what the system needs to do to provide answers for users. The chapter defines each type of structured diagramming technique and what each diagramming method provides to completing the logical architecture of the system. Regardless of whether a package software system is required or the system is to be developed internally, the organization must create logical analysis before it can truly understand the needs of the business.

Chapter 8: Creating Requirement Documents Using Analysis Tools

This chapter builds on Chapter 7 and outlines a step-by-step procedure for designing and developing specifications that reflect the engineering requirements for building systems. This portion of the book provides the necessary tools that analysts and designers need to provide program developers with detailed, yet creative technical specifications toward the "processing" portion of the requirements document including data flow diagrams, process flow diagrams, building a data dictionary, writing algorithms, state transition diagrams, and an introduction to entity relational diagrams. Validating that an application meets requirements is a most difficult process. This chapter discusses alternative ways of accomplishing this task, including creating check lists, quality assurance procedures, group review sessions, and product simulations. The approach is to focus more on what the software does not do, as opposed to its features and functions. The chapter also emphasizes a review of mathematical calculations, that is, the way in which the system handles formulas and produces results. Results also encompass analysis alternatives, types of outputs, and open systems compatibilities.

Chapter 9: The Data

This chapter covers how the back-end database engine is designed. The process of logic data modeling to produce a complete entity relational diagram is covered as well as methods of transferring data to multiple data storage facilities. Creation of data repositories is also discussed. The chapter effectively completes the data portion of the requirements document.

Chapter 10: Legacy Systems and Integration

This chapter outlines the process of interfacing the new system with preexisting applications called *legacies*. Issues of product fulfillment, connectivity of legacy databases and processes, and integration of multiple systems architecture are covered. This chapter combines many of the suggested approaches to user interface and application specifications development that are covered in previous chapters.

Chapter 11: Business Process Reengineering

This chapter identifies a way of *changing* rather than interfacing with legacy systems using a technique called business process reengineering (BPR). BPR examines the entire ways in which data are used and processed and takes a holistic approach to how a packaged solution can replace many of the preexisting applications. In other words, BPR seeks to replace rather than interface which requires organizations to rethink how this would change their processes to meet the ways a package software would make the business more efficient.

Chapter 12: Data Analytics and Data Warehouses

In this chapter the process of engineering data query and reporting options are discussed, especially to allow organizations to effectively report and analyze the operation. The chapter shows alternative data storage methods to enhance reporting performance and covers the recording, storage, and analysis of transactions that occur across enterprise systems. There is particular focus on decision support systems development, end user query development, and reconciliation of reporting through data warehousing.

Chapter 13: Documentation and Acceptance Testing

New systems must be documented and tested to ensure they comply with the requirements document. Thus, this chapter addresses the role of documentation and how acceptance test plans are developed and put into operation before the system is deemed usable and ready for implementation. The approach is to focus more on what the software does not do, as opposed to its features and functions. The chapter also emphasizes a review of mathematical calculations, that is, the way in which the system handles formulas and produces results. When changes are made to any application package there are also a series of steps that must be undertaken to ensure that the quality of the package is maintained. This process can be very convoluted, since the customizations could affect other aspects of the original package. The approach to solving this dilemma usually requires a close partnership among the stakeholders, including the software vendor, the vendor who made the modifications, and the internal organization.

Chapter 14: Project Management

This chapter presents a definition and description of the duties and responsibilities of the project manager. The project manager is the most important individual in the application software process. Overall, the project manager must have both soft skills and hard skills. Hard skills are defined as the technical skills necessary to converse with development personnel and soft skills cover such management abilities as leadership, integrity, intuition, mentoring, creativity, and compassion. The chapter also provides the necessary processes, recommended procedures, and reporting techniques that tend to support higher rates of project success. Furthermore, many projects have suffered because the management was not able to appropriately manage the contracted vendors. Organizations make the mistake of assuming that outsourced development and management is a safeguard for successful project completion. Organizations must understand that third-party vendors are not a panacea for comfort and that rigorous management processes must be in place in order to ensure a successful project. The "squeaky wheel gets oiled" phrase is very applicable when managing your vendors. This chapter offers best practices that keep vendors on their toes!

Chapter 15: ISO 9000 and the Software Development Life Cycle

New software systems need to comply with general standards for them to be useful, especially if they are integrating with legacy applications or part of a complete redesign using BPR. ISO 9000 is an international concept of standardization of quality that should be adopted in any major software development or implementation of a package software solution.

Chapter 16: Contract Considerations

Once vendors have been selected, organizations need to have contracts that protect their corporate interests, while at the same time are fare to the vendors. Vendors typically have standard contracts or skeleton agreements for organizations to work from, but there are significant issues that must be covered such as indemnity, access to source code, process of communication if there are problems, warrantees and guarantees, and support.

Chapter 17: Going Live and Conclusions

User training usually requires a phased approach paralleling the life cycle of the new product. Some parts of training can take place early, but a huge portion will likely occur as the system approaches the go live phase. Training may also need to be repetitive and completed among different management and staff users. Training can be shared, that is, some being done by internal users, others by the third-party vendors or by the product company. There is also the concept of "train-the-trainer," where third-party trainers train internal users to take on the major parts of training among the user staffs. The chapter also covers the documentation, often considered part of the training process. The contribution of the organization's IT department is always one of debate. Many organizations consider the IT department as the "owner" of the effort and expect that IT personnel will act as the main department handling every aspect of the implementation. Other organizations adopt a user-controlled effort, where the IT department is essentially used to accomplish specific tasks. The latter approach has a major advantage in that the business becomes the owner, and effectively should be, since they are the beneficiaries of the application software product. In yet another approach, the IT executive takes on a leadership role, where IT is responsible from an executive level, but the business department still owns the responsibility to get the product implemented and absorbed by the organization. This chapter represents the pinnacle of the project completion. Sections cover key issues to be coordinated among the stakeholders, business partners, and vendors to ensure that everything is ready for production. The go live step should also consider the handling of problems, including application bugs that need to be fixed or worked around (finding an alternative way of doing something in the system). The go live phase must also address final sign off with vendors and stakeholders.

Reference

Langer, A. M. (2011). *Information technology and organizational learning: Managing behavioral change through technology and education* (2nd ed.). New York: CRC Press.

Part I
Determining Needs

Assessing Business Requirements

So how does one assess the needs of a system before seeking a solution in the market? The most valuable step is to create a requirements document that depicts the needs of the system you are seeking. It also provides a platform for the businesses affected by the software solution to agree-to-agree before starting the process of selection. The first aspect of understanding business requirements is the tiers of software development.

The Tiers of Software Development

The life cycle of software development continues to evolve, particularly with the advent of the object paradigm. The life cycle of development inevitably affects the way analysis and design is accomplished. Indeed, it only seems natural that the rapid changes in software methodologies would be accompanied by parallel development in analysis and design. Unfortunately, such is not the case, and the advances in software development continue to overshadow the importance of analysis and design.

As the software industry focuses on integrated software solutions through robust web-based package software, it becomes vitally important for the analyst to use the appropriate sequence of tiers to arrive at requirements. Developers cannot expect good results from taking shortcuts, tempting as it may be to do so. The recommended sequence of tiers is outlined below.

User Interface

Regardless of the type of software applications being developed, systems cannot be effectively designed without an appropriate user interface. The user interface tier acts as the foundation for the project: without a solid foundation at this level, the project is at risk of collapsing at some point during development. Despite its importance, the user interface tier is often overlooked: many software projects today move

A.M. Langer, *Guide to Software Development*,
DOI 10.1007/978-1-4471-2300-2_2, © Springer-Verlag London Limited 2012

too quickly into development without the effort having been spent to determine what is really needed from the user community. Successful analysts are aware of the critical importance of the user interface phase of any project. Chapter 1 focuses on methods of formulating user interfaces that can significantly improve software development.

Tools

Software systems require that analysts have the appropriate tools to do their job. Furthermore, and an even more significant challenge, is understanding which of the many available tools to use at any given point. Software development tools are often designed for specialized use rather than for general application, and using the wrong tool can potentially cause significant damage. Finally, the sequence of use for each specialized tool is also critical to success. Indeed, the order of operation, as well as the relationship among specialized analysis tools, must be mastered to ensure success.

Productivity Through Automation

Having the appropriate tools and knowing how and when to use them is only part of the formula for success. Analysts must also be productive and productivity can be accomplished only through the use of automation. Automation is implemented using integrated computer-aided software engineering (CASE) products. These products provide the analyst with an automated and integrated toolbox of features that are centralized through a core data dictionary and repository.

Object Orientation

Successful projects employ the concepts of object orientation (OO). Whether or not software systems are OO compliant, analyzing systems using the object method builds better systems that are more cohesive, reusable, and maintainable. More cohesive code is "tighter" code and is more easily fixed and maintained. It is also the foundation of the reusable components that can be incorporated into other applications later. Without the OO construct, systems tend to have pieces that are recoded and hard to maintain. With the advent of the enterprise solutions and e-commerce transactions that will be vital to the survival of corporate business strategy, building object-based systems has become more a requirement than an option. However, as this book will show, businesses and organizations cannot just jump into OO, but rather they must create the foundations first through the previous tiers of development. Put another way, it is more important to understand the concepts of OO during analysis and design than it is to have the OO scheme actually programmed.

Client/Server

Today's software is still governed by the concept of client/server processing. While client/server has become more widespread, it has not necessarily become better understood. As with the OO paradigm, client/server software development is often confused with network hardware strategy. While client/server hardware topology is an important issue in itself, it has little to do with the process of deciding how software modules should interact across the network and where such modules should be placed. Such decisions will be driven by issues that arise during the process of analysis. Client/server software processing, in its true implementation, involves the interaction of objects and defining the way in which they will communicate with each other. Thus, analysts must first be versed in the laws governing OO if they are to pursue the client/server model. Incidentally, almost all web-based applications that use JAVA, Active-X, and other controls are designed essentially under the guidelines of interaction objects in a client/server environment.

Internet/Intranet

The advent of web-based technology, sometimes known as Internet/Intranet processing, has led the industry to the use of a new breed of software applications. This new breed requires more robust processing and involves careful design and placement of pictures that provide users with a true "cafeteria" style of operation. These new applications bring new challenges to analysts and designers. Increasingly, it is not programmers who are designing the interface; rather, analysts themselves are beginning to work with commercial advertisers and marketing departments to create a "look and feel" that will be critical to the survival of many businesses. Web-based systems, a result of the Internet/Intranet boom, represent another level of analysis. I believe that in the future, e-business will exert the strongest shaping influence on the analyst's profession—a profession destined to become tomorrow's integrators of systems development. Indeed, programming tools will continue to become easier to develop and more abundant in precoded forms. There will, undoubtedly, be less distribution of development teams, that is, companies will find more and more outsourced solutions to fill their needs. Notwithstanding the "automation" of code, the need for integrators who can communicate with executives, line management, and operations personnel will ultimately be the most significant forces in the development of strategic-based systems over the Internet.

Internet/Intranet processing requires that analysts have mastered the client/server paradigm. Indeed, many professionals have dubbed Internet development as "client/server grown-up." While this may or may not be the best definition of Internet/Intranet development, it is another statement that supports the tier concept, the concept that underlies the approach of this book.

The tiers of software development are focused on presenting the steps necessary to be successful as a professional analyst. I call each of these steps tier because of their building block nature and their dependencies on each other. I believe, therefore, that to learn to become an effective analyst, the specifics within each of these tiers must be mastered and must pass critical information to the next level. Rather than

Tier	Analyst Application
6	Internet/Intranet – Web based transaction processing, media, and graphics
5	Client/Server – breaking down objects to their client and server applications
4	Object orientation – selection of objects and classes
3	CASE – automation and productivity of Tier 2
2	Structured Tools – DFD, PFD, ERD, STD, process specification, data repository
1	User Interface – interviewing skills, JAD, RAD

Fig. 2.1 Tiers of analysis and software application development

looking at analysis sequentially, I would present the steps as levels as depicted in Fig. 2.1.

Figure 2.1 shows how each tier must be dependent on the other. There is a profound message in this diagram which suggests that no tier can be developed or exist without the previous one. To ensure success on a project, everyone involved in the design and development of application software must fully understand the interdependent nature of these tiers. Analysts must be able to convey to their colleagues that to go Internet/Intranet development, organizations must first have excellent user interfaces, mastery of a structured toolset, a vehicle for automation so that the process will be productive, an understanding of the concept of objects, and a way to deploy these objects in a client/server environment. It all sounds so simple, and in many ways it is. The question answered by this new edition is *how?*

The following sections provide a step-by-step process of gathering the data that you need to create a requirements document.

Establishing User Interfaces

The success factors in analysis start with the established interfaces from day 1. What does this mean? You must start the process by meeting with the right people in the organization. In the best projects, the process is as follows:

1. *Executive interface*: There needs to be an executive level supporter of the project. Without such a supporter, you risk not being able to keep the project on schedule. Most importantly, you need a supporter for the political issues that you may need to handle during the project (discussed in detail later). The executive supporter, sometimes known as a sponsor should provide a preliminary schedule advising the organization of what is expected and the objectives of the project. The executive supporter should attach a letter to the preliminary schedule and send it to the project team members. The letter must put the importance of the project into perspective. Therefore, it is strongly recommended that you draft this letter yourself or at least have influence over its content, since doing so can ensure that the message is delivered appropriately. The executive supporter should also establish regular reviews with the analyst and the user community to ensure that objectives are being met.

Fig. 2.2 Established interface layers

2. *Department head or line manager interface*: If appropriate, the department head
   should provide guidance about which individuals should represent the department needs. If there are several people involved, the analyst should consider a
   JAD-like approach. Depending on the size of the organization, the department
   head might also establish review sessions to ensure compliance.
3. *Functional user interface*: Perhaps the most important people are the ones who
   can provide the step-by-step needs of the system. Figure 2.2 shows a typical
   organization interface structure.

Forming an Interview Approach

The primary mission of an analyst or systems designer is to extract the physical
requirements of the users and convert each to its logical equivalent. The most critical step in this mission is the actual interview, in which you must establish a rapport
with the user(s) who will facilitate your obtaining the information you need. Your
approach will dramatically change based on the level and category of the individual
being interviewed. Therefore, prior to meeting with any user, it is critical to understand the culture of the company, its past experiences with automation, and most
important its organization structure.

The following five-step procedure will help guide you more smoothly through
the interview process.

Step 1: Get the organization chart: There are few things that are more useful in
   understanding the chain of command and areas of responsibility. Depending on
   the size of the enterprise and the scope of the project, the organization chart
   should start at the executive supporter level and work down to the operational
   users.

Step 2: Understand everyone's role in the organization chart: If there are any individuals not involved in the project (who should be, given their position in the
   organization), first ask why, then make a notation for yourself that they are not
   to be included. Management may assume an individual or role should not be
   included and may often overlook their importance. Do not be afraid to ask why
   a person is not deemed necessary for the analysis of the system and determine

if you are satisfied with the reasons for their exclusion. Remember, you can still control and change the approach at this point, and management will probably respect you for doing so.

Step 3: Assume the situation is political: Be sure you understand the personalities that you will have to deal with. In almost any implementation, politics among people becomes part of the process. To ignore its existence—and the constraints it is likely to impose—is to invite failure. The question is how to obtain information about internal politics. The best approach is to start as high up in the organization as possible, typically at the executive supporter level. You might be surprised at the amount of information they have. Of course, you should not ask explicitly about the politics, but rather phrase your question as follows: "Can you give me some perspective on potential department and personnel conflicts that may occur during the interview cycle and that I should be aware of?" You may not always get the answer you need, but if you keep asking the question during every interview, you will discover a great deal about the way the organization functions. And remember, only people make projects complex!

Step 4: Obtain information about user skill sets: To start an interview without knowledge of the user's technical skills puts the analyst at a huge disadvantage. Having this information will allow you to formulate a plan of questions and determine the best approach to the interview. If the user has no knowledge, the questions should be tailored to include a minimum of technical content. The following guidelines for preparing for interviews reflect a common sense approach, yet it is amazing how many analysts fail even to consider such strategies!

1. Gather information before the session to allow the user—as well as yourself—to be prepared and to give you both a much clearer understanding of what will be covered during the interview.
2. Develop a questionnaire. Technical questions should be phrased differently depending on the level of knowledge possessed by the user.
3. Determine whether the interview will provide enough input to obtain the necessary information. This is not always the case; however, it happens more often than you might think. Understanding user capabilities before the interview may change not only the scope of the meeting, but may also suggest who, in addition to the user, may need to be in attendance at the interview.

Step 5: Arrange for a pre-meeting with the user: A pre-meeting may not always be possible, and in any case it must be a short meeting, perhaps half an hour. The session should be designed to be high level and provide a general idea of what will be covered during the actual interview. But more important, it will allow you to get a snapshot of the user. You might say you are obtaining a "comfort level" (or "discomfort level") for that user, and such meetings can provide you with an idea of what to expect and how to finalize your approach. What do you look for? Here is some direction:

1. The pre-meeting should give you enough feedback to place or confirm the user's technical level.
2. Look at everything in the user's office or their environment. Is it sloppy? Is it tidy and organized? The state of the user's environment will often be consistent

with the way they provide information. The insight you gain from observing the environment should give you guidance about the types of questions to ask this individual.

3. Look for signs of attitude. The user's level of interest should be evident. Do they view the upcoming session as a waste of time or are they excited about the meeting?

4. The information gleaned in the pre-meeting can provide you with helpful hints about what to expect from the interview and from the user in general.

Dealing with Political Factions

The importance of internal politics at the user's site should never be underestimated. Perhaps the most common question raised by both professionals and student analysts is how to provide quality analysis when office politics get in the way. Here are some guidelines:

1. First, assess whether you are in the no-win scenario. Many of us hate to admit that the no-win scenario does indeed exist in many environments, but you should be on the lookout for the signs. If your manager will not support you, if the company is underpaying you, if the users hate you, if there are no automated tools to do the analysis, and if upper management doesn't care, then you are in a difficult position. If you cannot change the situation, you must inform management that the results of your analysis will be significantly impaired by the lack of support and tools to complete the project properly. The techniques offered in this book assume that all parties are interested in providing the best solution possible, not in providing a system that is barely adequate.

2. On the other hand, do not be too quick to assume that you are in the no-win scenario. Most politically hampered projects need some strategy to get them on course, and most problems can be overcome if you know how to approach them. Here is a typical example of such a problem and some ideas you can apply to solve it:

   Problem: The users who currently operate the system won't talk to me. They are afraid either that the new system might replace them or that their jobs will significantly change. In short, they fear change.

   Recommended solution: Most operational users are managed by a supervisor or "In-Charge." Sometimes even a line manager can be directly responsible for production workers. In any event, you must determine who is responsible and meet with that person. The purpose of the meeting is to gain their support. This support is significant since you might find that the supervisor was once in operations and will be able to understand the problems you may encounter. If the meeting is successful, the supervisor may be able to offer a strategy. This strategy can vary from a general meeting with the users, to individual discipline, to escalation to upper management. Whatever you do, do not allow such a situation to continue and do not accept abuse; to do so will ultimately reflect on you and your abilities.

Obviously, if the supervisor is also a problem, then you have no choice but to go to upper management. However, this option is not a desirable one from the analyst's viewpoint. Upper management's reaction may not be helpful, and it could be damaging. For example, they might be indifferent to your problem and instruct you to deal with it yourself or they might simply send the supervisor a letter. In some cases you may be fortunate and the supervisor's responsibilities regarding the system will be given to another manager. Consider, though, how unpleasant the consequences may be if you appeal to upper management and get no support: you may be left working with an already-unhelpful supervisor who has been made even more so by your complaint. It is important to remember that once you go to upper management, the line has been drawn. Supervisors typically are responsible for the day-to-day operation. They usually know more about the entire operation than anyone else, and therefore you are well advised to find a way to get them on your side. A supportive supervisor can be invaluable in helping you overcome problems, as long as you are not shy about suggesting ways to get the users comfortable.

Categories and Levels of Users

Establishing user interfaces represents the vehicle to formulate much of the interview approach. It is necessary, however, to go further into the characteristics of the people, particularly with respect to the *category* and *level* they have within the organization. Figure 2.2 established the three general categories called executive, department head or line manager, or functional. It is important to explore their characteristics. In order that we better understand each category, I have always asked the following question: *what would be their interest in the success of the project, that is, what would make them happy with the new system?* Let's apply this question for each user category.

1. *Executive users*: Individuals at this layer are most interested in the concept of return-on-investment (ROI). ROI basically focuses on whether an investment will provide a financial return that makes the effort worthwhile to the organization. While there are many comprehensive formulas that are often applied to the study of ROI, our context pertains to the short-term and long-term benefits of investing in building new software. There are generally five reasons why executives agree to fund software development. They are listed in order of significance to the investor.

    a. *Monetary return*: Simply put, this means that the software will generate dollar revenue. An example might be the Internet software that supports on-line ordering systems such as Amazon has for book shipments. Their system not only provides the functionality to handle shipments, but also provides a web interface that can be directly associated with revenues provided by book orders through the Internet.

    b. *Increased productivity:* Many software systems are unable to demonstrate direct monetary benefits; however, many of them are developed to increase productivity. This means that the system will allow organizations to actually produce and deliver more. Thus, the system allows the organization to derive higher revenues through increased productivity of its resources.

c. *Reducing costs*: Software projects are approved so that organizations can reduce their existing overhead costs. This typically relates to the replacement of manual activities with computer ones. While reducing costs appears to be similar in nature to increasing productivity, they are often implemented for different reasons. Increased productivity usually relates to organizations that are growing and are looking for ways to improve output because of very high demand. Reducing costs, on the other hand, can represent a defensive measure, where an organization is seeking to find ways to cut costs because of a shrinking market.

d. *Competition*: Software systems are created because the competition has done so. Therefore, competitive reasons for producing software are a defensive measure against someone else who has demonstrated its value. An example of this is in the banking sector. Citibank was one of the first banks to introduce automated teller machines (ATMs). Other banks soon followed because of the success that Citibank had with proliferating ATMs throughout New York State. This does not imply, however, that competitive systems are always defense mechanisms; indeed, many commercial web sites are being introduced based simply on market forecasts for their potential to increase business.

e. *For the sake of technology*: While not the most popular, some organizations will invest in new systems because they think its time to do so or they are concerned that their technology is getting old. This way of supporting new systems development is rare, as it suggests the spending of money without a clear understanding of its benefits.

Therefore, the executive category of users is one who is interested in the value of the investment. These users have a global view of needs as opposed to the details. In fact, they may know little of how things are really done. The value of the executive interface is to provide the scope and objectives of the project against their perceived value they intend to get from the software. Another popular phrase for this is called the *domain* of the system. Domain often refers to *boundaries*. Ultimately, what makes them happy is a system that delivers what was promised or the expected ROI.

2. *Department head or line manager users*: These users represent two main areas of user input. First they are responsible for the day-to-day productivity of their respective departments. Thus, they understand the importance of meeting the objectives of the organization as set forth by the executives. Indeed, they often report the executives. On the other hand, department heads and line managers are responsible to their staff. They must deal with the functional users and prescribe ways to improve both their output and their job satisfaction. These users perhaps provide what I call *the best bang for the buck,* a phrase that usually means that for the time, you get the most. One can see that the department heads and line

managers are responsible for most of what happens every day in an organization. Another phrase that can be used to describe them is your *most valuable players (MVPs)*. However, beware, MVPs are the hardest to find and get for the interviews. What makes department heads and line managers happy is the most complex. They want a system that produces the output that they are expected to provide and they need a system that makes and keeps their staff happy and productive.

3. *Functional users*: Also known as the users in the trenches, these people essentially do the operational activities. While they know a lot about their processes, they usually care little about the productivity and expected ROI. I often see these users as people who want little pain and just want to work the hours they need to. Thus, fancy systems are of little interest to them unless they provide no pain—and no pain derives to a system that makes their job easier.

The next area to understand about users is their level. By level, I mean their understanding of computers. There are three levels of users:

1. *Knowledgeable*: The determination of knowledge can be tricky and certainly based on someone's opinion. I define knowledge in reference to experience. An experienced user can be defined as a person who "has been through it before." A user who has been through the development of a new system can therefore be defined as "knowledgeable" within this context.

2. *Amateur*: The definition of an amateur is based not so much on experience, but rather to the type of experience the user has. Amateurs can be thought of as hobbyists who enjoy working with computers at home, but have no professional experience in developing software in an organization. In this perspective, I believe the meaning of an amateur is globally defined as one who does not get paid for the work.

3. *Novice*: These users have no experience with computers. While there are fewer of such users than 10 years ago, they still exist. A better way of perceiving a novice user is to relate to my definition of knowledgeable. In this context, a novice user is one who has never been part of the implementation of a new system in a professional environment.

Perhaps the most problematic of the above levels is the amateur. I have found that users who are knowledgeable provide benefit to projects. They, in many ways, act as a checkpoint for the analyst, in that they can ask good questions and particularly remember historical problems that actually can help the development process. Novice users add little value and also add few problems. They tend to do what you ask of them. Amateurs, on the other hand, tend to know enough to be dangerous. They also tend to have a profound interest in the topic that they often get-off on tangents about the technology as opposed to concentrating on the particulars of the project.

What is most important is the mapping of these categories and levels. An analyst might interview a knowledgeable executive or a novice functional user. Each permutation can affect the way interviews are conducted. For example, an interview with a group of amateurs would focus the analyst on ensuring that the agenda is very specific, otherwise, discussions could easily get-off track. Therefore, the understanding about user levels and categories can only assist in the development of effective interview approaches.

Joint Application Development (JAD)

JAD is a process that was originally developed for designing computer-based systems. JAD centers on a three-day to five-day workshop that brings together business area people (users) and IS (information systems) professionals. Under the direction of a facilitator, these people define anything from high-level strategic plans to detailed system specifications. The products of the workshop can include definitions of business processes, prototypes, and data models.

Simply put, JAD is a method for holding group sessions with users, instead of individually. You may have no choice but to use JAD when there are simply too many users to interview. JAD is also an excellent tool for use in highly political situations where obtaining consensus among users is difficult. JAD significantly differs from standard analysis in that it requires an up-front commitment from the user community. Specifically, the users must ultimately run the sessions themselves and make commitments to provide the requirements of the system. Finally, if prototypes are used, JAD is an excellent means of applying rapid application development (RAD). Both prototyping and RAD will be discussed in greater detail later.

The most important part of implementing JAD is the management of the process and the determination of the appropriate individuals to be involved. The standard roles used in JAD are as follows:

- *Executive sponsor*: This is an individual who plays effectively the same role as the executive supporter introduced earlier in this chapter. This person is typically at the Vice President level and ultimately has the responsibility for the business area. The ideal person for this role is someone to whom a user will have to report if they plan to miss a session and who can reprimand them if they do. This thinking may seem harsh or cynical, but the risk is high that users may find more important things to do when the sessions begin. Such absenteeism can entirely undermine the process, and IS should not be called upon to police users.
- *Facilitator*: In the best situations, the facilitator should not come from either the user community or IS, but rather an independent area or consulting firm. This arrangement allows the session to be independent. That is, the facilitator of the JAD must be impartial and have overall responsibility for controlling the flow of the sessions. In the ideal scenario, the facilitator should report to the executive sponsor.
- *Scribe*: A person who is designated to record minutes and decisions and who in many cases actually produces the models using a computer-aided software engineering (CASE) tool. A good scribe has knowledge of the business area, good analytical skills, and knowledge of CASE software. For these reasons, scribes often come from IS.
- *IS representatives*: IS should not be in the meetings to provide requirements, but should rather be available to answer questions about the existing hardware and

software. This information can be critical when discussing physical constraints of the existing systems and what data are currently available.

Below is an example of an 11-phase implementation outline for a JAD session with approximately 60 users in 10 different business areas:

Phase I: Define JAD project goals

The purpose of these sessions will be to meet with senior management and other key organization people in order to:

- get a clear understanding of the history of the project;
- finalize the scope and time frame requirements of the existing plan;
- understand the current organization and whether political or other constraints exist;
- jointly determine the number and size of JAD sessions to be held;
- determine the best role of information systems in the JAD; and
- define which key users and other managers should be interviewed individually prior to the JAD.

Produce a management guide after Phase I. Its purpose will be to define management's purpose, scope, and objectives of the project. That is, it communicates management's direction and commitment. The management guide will be approved and issued by upper management to the participating users and information system personnel.

Phase II: Meet with key users and managers

Estimate that you may need to interview about 20 people from key organizations prior to the JAD. These key users and managers should typically represent three levels of the organization. The purpose of these meetings will be to

- get familiar with the existing systems;
- validate the number of sessions and specific participants needed;
- assess the technical expertise of the participating users;
- determine what specific information can be gathered by the users prior to the JAD sessions;
- gather previous analysis and design materials and documents that may exist and explain user requirements;
- discuss types of agendas and length of sessions; and
- focus on specific requirements of certain users.

Schedule interviews to last about 60–90 min and prepare an agenda that will put the purpose and scope of the interview into perspective.

Phase III: Meet with information systems

Get a technical overview of the existing analysis performed and state of all working documents. Gather information on

- project history;
- potential problems envisioned in implementing the new system;
- proposed hardware to support the new system (if relevant);
- IS representatives to participate in the JAD sessions; and
- models and information that can be used in the JAD sessions.

Phase IV: Prepare JAD approach

Prepare a complete JAD program that will outline recommendations for the number and types of sessions to be held. The JAD approach will also consider the modeling tools to be used and the methods for getting user sign-off. You should focus on the following specific issues:

- the number and type of preparation sessions necessary to get users familiar with the modeling terminology;
- what business processes have already been previously modeled and can be reviewed during the sessions. This is done to avoid discussing processes that users feel have already been defined from previous analysis sessions;
- the number and types of sessions along with specific users in attendance at each session;
- a work document of the proposed agendas for each type of session;
- overview of materials to be used such as overheads, flip charts, and room requirements; and
- proposed format of the user sign-off documents.

You should meet with upper management to review the proposed approach for implementation.

Phase V: Finalize JAD organization structure

Assign JAD facilitators to specific sessions along with information systems support personnel (scribes, etc.). Determine the number of JAD facilitators required. You may need one JAD project leader to take overall responsibility for the entire engagement. A detailed timeline of specific deliverables and reviews should be produced for the entire project, including reports to upper management on the JAD session progress.

Phase VI: Hold overview training sessions

Depending on the results of Phase IV, hold any necessary sessions to get users familiar with the methods that will be used during the JAD. This is typically a one-day course on analysis and includes an overview of modeling lingo and tools such as

- Business area analysis
- Process flow diagrams (data flows)
- Entity relational diagrams and normalized data modeling
- Process specifications
- Activity matrices
- State transition diagrams
- Decomposition models
- Object-oriented techniques
- Prototyping

Phase VII: Hold JAD workshop sessions

Prior to these sessions, participants will be asked to come prepared with certain information that they will need to assist in the process. This information may typically include sample forms and reports that they use or need. The workshop sessions will be held with a set time frame and an agenda of items typically including

- *Assumptions*: These will be reviewed with the users and opened for discussion. An assumption will either:
  - stay as it is;
  - be revised; or
  - become an open issue (if consensus cannot be reached).
- *Design business processes*: Review the collection of activities relating to the business and the system.
- *Data requirements*: Data are defined to support the business process. Data models are used, developed, and reviewed as necessary.
- *Design screens*: The screens will typically use a series of menus or other branching techniques to define how users need to access the various functions. This is usually accomplished by identifying main menu and submenu selections.
- *Design reports*: Report names are collected and completed with detailed report descriptions. This normally includes
  - Report name
  - Description
  - Frequency
  - Number of copies
  - Distribution list
  - Selection criteria
  - Sort criteria
  - Data elements
- *Open issues*: These issues are added throughout the sessions. Open issues are those that are not resolved after a period of discussion. These are kept on a separate chart.

Throughout the above processes, the scribe will be tracking minutes of the meeting as well as the open issues and new diagramming requirements.

Phase VIII: Resolve open issues

Prior to subsequent sessions, all open issues must be resolved, either by smaller work groups or if necessary by upper management. In any event, it is critical that this is managed by both the facilitator and upper management prior to moving to the next level sessions.

Phase IX: Prepare materials for workshop review sessions

The facilitator should produce a sign-off level document for review. Process and data models and process specifications will be reviewed and finalized. These sessions can also include prototype screens and reports.

Phase X: Hold sign-off workshops

These workshops will be designed to review the results of the initial JAD sessions. The process and data models will be reviewed. If prototypes are used, the sessions will utilize screen walkthroughs as a method of gaining user acceptance. The exact number of review sessions will depend on the complexity of the system as well as the number of screens and reports to be prototyped.

During these sessions, user acceptance test plan may also be discussed and outlined for eventual submission to the responsible QA organization. This will typically involve a discussion of the minimum acceptance testing to be validated against the product and the mechanism for testing in the field.

Phase XI: Finalize specification document

After review sessions are completed, the facilitator will prepare the final document to be submitted for approval and eventual implementation. If prototypes are used, the screens and reports can be moved into the software development (construction) phase. There should also be post-JAD reviews with the development teams to clarify information supplied in the final system specification document.

JAD is introduced and discussed in this chapter because of its generic inclusion in the user interface phase of analysis. However, it should be noted that the above outline can be integrated with many of the subjects contained in later chapters of this text. The analyst may, therefore, wish to review this outline again after completing the book in order to determine how the other concepts of analysis can be used in a JAD session.

Problems and Exercises

1. Why is it so critical for the analyst to understand the "culture" of the organization?
2. What is a Gantt Chart? How are Gantt Charts used and why is it important that they be realistic estimates of how the project will occur?
3. Management support is a key component of the success of any project. Sometimes management may unfairly dictate the terms and deadlines of projects. Provide examples of different possible management opinions and how analysts can prepare effective responses to them.
4. What are the benefits of obtaining an organization chart prior to conducting interviews with users?
5. How does politics affect the role of the analyst and his/her approach to the information-gathering function of the interviews?
6. Why does understanding user skills provides the analyst with an advantage during interviews?
7. Explain how meeting a user in their office or place of work can assist the analyst in developing a better approach prior to the interview.
8. What is the purpose of JAD sessions? How do they compare to individual interviewing? Discuss the advantages and disadvantages of JAD.
9. Define each of the roles necessary for effective JAD sessions.
10. What is the purpose of a management guide?
11. Develop a proforma JAD outline for a project of 20 users in 3 business locations.

Build vs. Buy

3

This chapter addresses a difficult and controversial decision that is made every time an organization seeks a software solution to meet its needs: do we make it to our specific needs or do we buy something that is made to order but may not do everything we want? Often the build decision is called the "make" alternative and suggests that the product will be made in-house vs. the buy concept that can be referred to as outsourcing. I do not believe these simple labels are accurate or appropriate. Whether something is build or bought has little to do with whether the process is outsourced, so we need to be careful in the way we label these two alternatives.

Inman, Sale, Green, and Whitten (2011) suggest that build and buy decisions need to be made at both the strategic and operational levels. Burt, Dobler, and Starling (2003) provided some direction on the strategic reasons for buying and tied it into a definition of outsourcing, providing three concrete categories of reasons NOT to outsource:

1. The item is critical to the success of the overall product and is perceived so by the company's clientele.
2. The item requires specialized design and skills and such skills are limited in the organization.
3. The item fits into the firm's core competencies but needs to be developed in the future.

Historically, most organizations selected the buy option because their assumption was that it lowered costs. Indeed, over 70% of product ownership usually occurs after implementation. So where is this cost? It occurs in maintenance, where in-house teams must continually alter and develop. The off-the-shelf concept tends to keep costs lower because in theory the sum of all the clients will create better software for all. Others suggest that a company should always first seek a package because of common business challenges including

- Cost
- Time to market
- Political situation in the environment
- Architectural differences
- Skill sets of existing staff

A.M. Langer, *Guide to Software Development*,
DOI 10.1007/978-1-4471-2300-2_3, © Springer-Verlag London Limited 2012

However, The Gartner Group in 2003 published a report that suggested this trend was changing and that there were a growing number of firms that were returning to building applications internally. Gartner cited the following reasons for the change of heart:

- Rising competitive advantages of using emerging technologies
- Increased availability of talented software developers
- Poor reputation of prior uses of package software—that it is not agile enough and difficult for departments to use
- Increased needs to adapt to unique and changing business needs

Ledeen's (2011) and Moore's (2002) analysis of how to approach make vs. buy is quite useful. He established a step-by-step criterion to help organizations to make the best decision. This criterion included the following:

- Core vs. context
- Coverage
- Direction
- TCO
- Scale
- Timing
- Standards

Core vs. Context

This decision point relates to the strategic importance of the application. The more strategic the application, the more likely that the organization develop software internally (also see Langer, 2011, below). The concept is simple: if the application relates to basic functions in accounting, HR, or payroll, then it is not core. However, software used by Walmart, although accounting related is used as a supply chain management tool that drives every aspect of their competitive advantage as a company. The result of course is that Walmart developed their supply chain as a core and unique application. Moore's chart (Fig. 3.1) provides an interesting matrix of how core can be determined.

Figure 3.1 reflects that mission critical application should be developed in-house with context-oriented applications may be modified to meet package requirements.

	Core Engage	Context Disengage
Mission Critical (Control)	MAKE	OUTSOURCE
Supporting (Entrust)	PARTNER	CONTRACT

Fig. 3.1 Build vs. buy chart

Coverage

The coverage assesses the extent of the match of the packaged product with the business requirements. The general rule is that a package should have at least 80% of the features and functions needed by the organization. However, Ledeen states that this could be a trap, suggesting that package's capabilities outside of the immediate needs of the business are equally as important. This is relevant, given that business needs are continually evolving, organizations must be cognizant of having applications that can not only handle what is, but what may be future needs of the business. In addition, a certain feature in a packaged solution may actually offer a better business alternative than currently used by the business—so it's a complex issue as they say.

Direction

The keywords relating to direction is flexibility, maintainability, and extendibility of the software throughout its life. Ultimately, direction relates to how much control the organization has over the product, especially those products that may need to change, that is, the volatility of what the software does. For example, if the product is a basic accounting system, it is likely not to change substantially over its life. However, if it is a healthcare product that is regulated by government requirements in a highly fragile market, then direction is a key decision factor. Much of this relates to the design and architecture of the product itself. Can it be easily modified? What is the extent of changes that can be controlled via user input? All of these factors are significant to whether a package is the wise choice.

Total Cost of Ownership (TCO)

The TCO represents entire cost. Components of this cost include license fees for the product, maintenance, product customizations, and support. The major variable in TCO is custom modifications. Vendors will often provide an estimate but managers need to be careful of "scope creep" where original requirements for customizations become greatly expanded during the design phase of the project. A good approach that can help this decision is to determine the number of features and functions in the package that the organization does *not* need. A packaged solution that has many features and functions that are not needed might suggest that the application is not a great match and is likely designed for a different audience. It is important to note that many application packages were developed first as a custom application for a specific client and then tailored for others. This process was a typical evolution of how many software packages evolved in the market. Therefore, understanding the history of how the application package was developed might provide a hint as to the TCO and the fit in general—the two tend to go together.

Scale

The size of the package is a factor, especially when it has many modules. This is very relevant in large enterprise resource planning (ERP) products where a high degree of scaled interoperability is important. These modular products also allow clients to purchase business components at later periods and easily retrofit them. However, if it is *not* the intention of the organization to scale, then a large integrated package may be overkill.

Timing

There are many who would believe that a packaged solution will be faster to implement—but be careful—often this is not the case. Packaged solutions may add steps to the SDLC and as a result could actually prolong the timing of going live of the product. Ledeen suggests that while COTS provides greater predictability it could be a reflection of the limits of flexibility and imposed restrictions. Either case, I would strongly recommend that the decision whether to have a make vs. buy not be contended solely based on speed to completion—the organization may be in for a big surprise. The more an organization can accept the base package, the faster the implementation will be, for sure. However, accepting the package as is does not necessarily mean that it is the best thing for the business.

Standards

Ledeen defines standards as the consistency across systems of the way things get done. I see this issue more in terms of consistency of architecture of the organization. This means that the hardware platforms and software architecture (middleware, office products, etc.) should be consistent for package software to maximize its benefits. If this is not the case, that is, where you have multiple architectures across the organization, then the value of a package becomes less evident. This is especially true if the package requires a specific architecture for all of the systems. This is why open systems are so attractive to organizations Unfortunately, in multinational firms having many architectures is not unusual. Much of this may have occurred due to corporate acquisitions of other firms—when you acquire a new business you often acquire a new systems architecture—both hardware and software!

Other Evaluation Criteria

The above issues are important but there are other contextual things to consider when making the decision:
* *Complexity of product:* The more intricate the software application, the harder for COTS to work. Complex products also tend to shorten the life cycle and have more evolving needs.

- *State of the art:* Users who seek packaged solutions often require the latest and greatest up-to-date product. They may be disappointed to learn that package software has some unique limitations in this area. First, vendors of packages have user bases to take care of—who ultimately have older versions and hardware that they must support. This results in difficulties with downward compatibilities of their user base. Just look at Microsoft's problems when they upgrade operating systems and software. IBM used to issue "no support" edicts to its customers who failed to upgrade their products over time. The better vendors force their users to upgrade but it is always messy.
- *Maintenance*: COTS often involves product upgrades and new maintenance releases. Sometimes maintenance releases include bug fixes and workarounds for packaged discovered problems. Maintenance can also be very tricky—how do organizations load new versions from the vendors when there are customizations, for example? It gets to be a challenge especially when the updates are regulatory in nature. COTS that have customizations inevitably need to go through a retrofit, where the customized portions have to be "re-customized" to deal with package software upgrades. This certainly adds to the cost equation over the life of the package.

While the above suggestions offer guides on what to think about and measure, the process is still complex without a real scientific methodology to determine ultimately whether to make or buy or both. However, Langer (2011) provides yet another concept called driver/supporter theory in which "buy" decisions would only be made for applications that were considered "supporters." Figure 3.2 depicts a

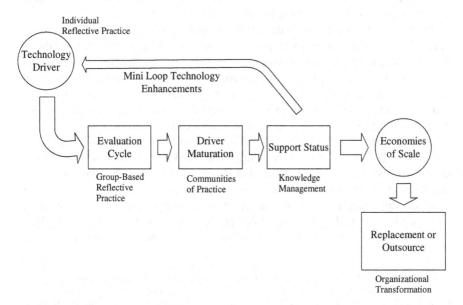

Fig. 3.2 Langer's driver/supporter life cycle

supporter item as something that has reached the stage of commodity notated in the circle labeled as "Economies of Scale."

Figure 3.2 shows that all technology needs start out as drivers but eventually become supporters, thus lose their uniqueness in the marketplace. It is as if you were creating a strategic advantage by implementing a new e-mail system—this would not really provide the organization with a competitive advantage—rather as an enabler to compete—a very different concept. The point I am making here is that a new e-mail system would likely be "bought" and possibly implemented using an outsource vendor. In accordance with Burt et al. this would be a case for buying as opposed to making.

Drivers and Supporters

I think this concept of driver/supporter is essential to understand make/buy decisions. This section provides further details on this theory and practice as a vehicle for better determination of make vs. buy.

To summarize driver/supporter, there are essentially two types of generic functions performed by departments in organizations: driver functions and supporter functions. These functions relate to the essential behavior and nature of what a department contributes to the goals of the organization. I first encountered the concept of drivers and supporters at Coopers & Lybrand, which was at that time a Big 8[1] accounting firm. I studied the formulation of driver vs. supporter as it related to the role of our EDP (electronic data processing) department. The firm was attempting to categorize the EDP department as either a driver or a supporter.

Drivers are defined as those units that engaged in front-line or direct revenue-generating activities. Supporters are units that did not generate obvious direct revenues but, rather, were designed to support front-line activities. For example, operations such as internal accounting, purchasing, or office management were all classified as supporter departments. Supporter departments, due to their very nature, were evaluated on their effectiveness and efficiency or economies of scale. In contrast, driver organizations are expected to generate direct revenues and other ROI value for the firm. What was also interesting to me at the time was that drivers were expected to be more daring—since they must inevitably generate returns for the business. As such, drivers engage in what Bradley and Nolan (1998) coined "sense and respond" behaviors and activities. Let me explain.

Marketing departments often generate new business by investing or "sensing" an opportunity, quickly—because of competitive forces in the marketplace. Thus, they must sense an opportunity and be allowed to respond to it in timely fashion.

---

[1] The original "Big 8" consisted of the eight large accounting and management consulting firms: Coopers & Lybrand, Arthur Anderson, Touche Ross, Delloite. Haskins & Sells, Arthur Young, Price Waterhouse, Pete Marwick Mitchell and Ernst and Whinney, up until the late 1980s, when these firms began to merge. Today there are four: Price Waterhouse Coopers, Delloit & Touche, Ernst and Young, and KPMG (Pete Marwick and others).

The process of sensing opportunity and responding with competitive products or services is a stage in the cycle that organizations need to support. Failures in the cycles of sense and respond are expected. Take, for example, the launching of new fall television shows. Each of the major stations goes through a process of "sensing" what shows might be interesting to the viewing audience. They "respond" after research and review with a number of new shows. Inevitably, only a few of these selected shows are actually successful; some fail almost immediately. While relatively few shows succeed, the process is acceptable and is seen by management as the consequence of an appropriate set of steps for competing effectively—even though the percentage of successful new shows is very low. Therefore, it is safe to say that driver organizations are expected to engage in high-risk-oriented operations, of which many will fail for the sake of creating ultimately successful products or services.

The preceding example raises two questions: (1) how does "sense and respond" relate to the world of information technology and (2) why is it important? Information technology is unique in that it is both a driver and a supporter. The latter being the generally accepted norm in most firms. Indeed, most IT functions are established to support a myriad of internal functions such as

Accounting and finance

Data-center infrastructure (e-mail, desktop, etc.)

Enterprise level application (ERP)

Customer support (CRM)

Web and e-commerce activities

As one would expect, these IT functions are viewed as overhead related, as somewhat of a commodity, and, thus, constantly managed on an economy-of-scale basis, that is, how can we make this operation more efficient, with a particular focus on cost containment?

So what are IT driver functions? By definition, they are those that engage in direct revenues and identifiable return-on-investment (ROI). How do we define such functions in IT, as most activities are sheltered under the umbrella of marketing organization domains? (Excluding, of course, software application development firms that engage in marketing for their actual application products.) I define IT driver functions as those projects that, if delivered, would change the relationship between the organization and its customers, that is, those activities that directly affect the classic definition of a market: forces of supply and demand, which are governed by the customer (demand) and the vendor (supplier) relationship.

The conclusion of this section, therefore, is that no driver application product should be implemented using complete outsourcing, rather be made in-house and owned by the firm. This does not, however, suggest that certain services and components be subcontracted out as long as the ownership remains within the company.

The Supporter Side of Buying

Based on the definition of a driver, the supporter side may indeed represent the need to buy a packaged solution. Since supporter functions are "operational" by definition, they are considered to be a commodity and thus able to be implemented using more standardized application software. Thus, all of the advantages of using package software apply. In addition there should be less need for customization. For example, think of the choice to build an e-mail system—you would only build it in-house if you required unique capabilities that provided a competitive advantage. That is, the e-mail system would be a driver application because it would change the relationship between the buyer and the seller. This is exactly the situation that occurred with Walmart, where what would ordinarily have been considered a commodity accounting system became an application of great strategic advantage. On the other hand, an e-mail system that could provide such advantage would be unlikely for most organizations, and therefore they would seek a product that does what most organizations need in any e-mail system—as a supporter solution.

Open Source Paradigm

Open source software can be defined as free source code developed among a community that believes strongly in a free software movement. Initial examples of successful open source products are Linux and Netscape Communicator. The open source movement is supported under the auspices of the open source initiative (OSI) that was formed in 1998 to provide guidance and standards of application.

As I previously mentioned, the evolution of open source as an alternative to developing software has grown enormously in the software industry. Open source can also represent an option with make vs. buy. Choices of whether to make or buy do not necessarily need to be binary, that is, one or the other, but rather could end up as a hybrid decision. For example, an organization can develop its own application using open source within its application development strategy or it can license a third-party product that also contains open source. Finally, packages may be licensed that can be bridged or integrated with various open source modules. In any case, open source broadens the range of choices when determining the best application solution.

Open source users must, however, agree to the following conditions of use as well as providing conditions of use to others:
- Free distribution
- Inclusion of source code
- License must allow modifications and derived works
- Allowed redistribution of modifications under the same license of the original software. License may require the derived work to carry a different name or version to protect the integrity of the original author
- No discriminations against any specific groups or fields of endeavors
- License cannot be restrictive to any software and be technology platform neutral

To a certain extent open source provides organizations with the option to use package software that is free to modify and then offer their changes back to those that need it in the user base—so it can be a forum where organizations can share needs. The negative aspect to sharing is if the modification contains proprietary algorithms that represent a competitive advantage for the firm. The software must also be hardware neutral which presents challenges for those applications that run on proprietary systems. Still, open source applications are growing in popularity especially as a cloud computing option.

Furthermore, open source might present some unexpected legal issues particularly as it relates to ownership of the software. Suppose you use an open source routine or module in your proprietary application and then the company is acquired by another entity. The question then is who owns the product? Legally the portion that is open source cannot be owned, which creates a dilemma that was likely not foreseen by the organization's IT management. This dilemma is particularly relevant to vendor software products.

Cloud Computing Options

Cloud computing is the ultimate server-based paradigm. Simply put, the host (cloud) has all of the hardware, software, services, and databases to support your business or enterprise. The organization essentially has the terminals and printers to do the work. Figure 3.3 depicts a cloud configuration.

Fig. 3.3 Cloud configuration

Cloud is about reduction of cost and perhaps using products that are shared by others. This does not mean that clouds cannot have proprietary products, rather that they have the ability to mix and match what is available in the cloud to meet specific needs of the organization. Because many of these applications can be shared in the cloud, the cost of ownership is very much lowered. Perhaps the largest benefit for using a cloud is in the savings for infrastructure and operations staff who would otherwise need to support the operation internally.

Deployment Models

There are essentially five different deployable models for cloud computing:
1. *Public/external*: this is the basic model that allows users to access a network via the Internet and typically pay on a usage or application access basis. It resembles the 1970 concept of timesharing.
2. *Private/internal*: a private cloud in many ways resembles an Intranet concept in that it is an internally developed shared service for the organization. As in an Intranet, a private cloud requires organizations to design the network and support it as if it were public—of course with less complexity.
3. *Community*: this configuration represents a group of organizations that share resources. In effect it is a restricted public cloud—only certain organizations can use it. Community clouds are attractive for specific industries that have similar needs or associations.
4. *Hybrid*: a hybrid cloud really relates to providing specific administrative IT functions like backup, performance, and security for both public and private cloud deployments. So it is more a utility type of cloud service often provided by internal IT services or vendors like Oracle, etc.
5. *Combined:* this is the application of multiple types of clouds that allow organizations to enjoy the best provisions that it provides to each business.

Figure 3.4 depicts the graphical representations of these cloud-type deployments.

Obviously cloud computing has its drawbacks—it is essentially outsourcing major parts of your operation to a third party—for which is always a risk, so these should be measured as follows:
- *Security:* while all third parties promise security, history has shown that they can be pierced from the outside. So security remains a concern for private and important data. For example, having healthcare information and other personal information in a cloud could be very dangerous.
- *Governmental and political issues*: if stored data are kept in other locations under the auspices and control of other countries, it could be restricted, taken, or kept from those that need it. The data could also be compromised because of different legal systems and changes in government policies. We see such problems in multinational firms quite often.
- *Downtime*: how much can any vendor guarantee ongoing service without outage and to what extent can clouds have failover abilities and at what cost?

Fig. 3.4 Cloud deployment types
Source: Wikipedia.

- *Conversions*: if you should need to move from one cloud provider to another, what are the risks and problems with moving applications and what compatibility problems will occur especially with data conversion?

Summary

This chapter examined the complexities of whether to make or buy an application solution. Hybrid solutions, which involve both a third-party package and internally developed applications, are very realistic alternatives. The evolution of open source and cloud computing offer new opportunities to design and create hybrid systems that provide broader alternatives than historically were available. Furthermore, the concept of driver/supporter provides a more scientific way of determining whether to make or buy software solutions.

Problems and Exercises

1. Explain what is meant by core vs. content.
2. Why is TCO so important?
3. Describe Langer's theory of driver/supporter.
4. Define open source. How can open source change the decision process on make vs. buy?
5. What is cloud computer? Explain the different types of clouds.

References

Bradley, S. P., & Nolan, R. L. (1998). *Sense and respond: Capturing value in the network era.* Boston: Harvard Business School Press.

Burt, D. N., Dobler, D. W., & Starling, S. L. (2003). *World class supply management: The key to supply chain management* (7th ed.). Boston: McGraw-Hill/Irwin.

Inman, R. A., Sale, R. S., Green, K. W., & Whitten, D. (2011). Agile manufacturing: Relation to JIT, operational performance and firm performance. *Journal of Operations Management, 4(29),* 343–355.

Langer, A. M. (2011). *Information technology and organizational learning: Managing behavioral change through technology and education* (2nd ed.). New York: CRC Press.

Ledeen, K. S. (2011). *Make v. buy: A decision paradigm for information technology applications.* Cambridge: Nevo Press.

Moore, G. (2002). *Living on the fault line: Managing for shareholder value in any economy.* New York: HarperCollins.

Establishing Requirements Using RFP and RFI

4

Organizations may need to create formal documents that articulate the needs they have for a software solution. These formal documents or requirements could be either for a package solution or for customized development or both. There are of course intricacies to creating these documents which also need to address related needs such as project management, ownership, quality assurance, indemnifications, and delivery schedules. There are two common methods of communicating these formal requirements: a request for information (RFI) or a request for proposal (RFP). An RFI is usually seen as a subset for an RFP, so an RFI might precede a more detailed RFP. Therefore, the purpose of this chapter is to provide the details of what should be included in each document, when one might be more advantageous than the other, and the process for obtaining responses from vendors.

RFI

An RFI is a document that can obtain feedback from prospective vendors who can provide a solution to the request. An RFI (as well as an RFP) should always state the problem—which is typically the need to address a business issue that needs an application software solution. However, the major focus of the RFI is to collect information about potential vendors so that the organization can do comparative analysis on what is available in the market and to some extent the costs associated with various application solutions. Another way of looking at an RFI is a way of surveying the marketplace before presenting a full-blown RFP, which typically requires a cost proposal from a vendor. Another advantage of an RFI is that it is relatively quick to put together. Of course this is relative to the complexity of the project. A typical RFI consists of the following sections and content:

- Introduction
- Background of the company
- Information about the project
- Reasons for the RFI—purpose and scope
- Specific requests—what is the requestor asking vendors to provide

A.M. Langer, *Guide to Software Development*,
DOI 10.1007/978-1-4471-2300-2_4, © Springer-Verlag London Limited 2012

- Due date for the response
- Confidentiality requirements
- Vendor qualifications
- Appendices of detailed information pertinent for the responding vendor
  A sample RFI (source: sourcing4oem.com) is presented in Fig. 4.1.

Request for Information

[Sample]

Company name
Date:

Contents

Fig. 4.1 Sample RFI

Confidentiality & Non Disclosure
All information included in this RFI is confidential and only for the recipient knowledge. No information included in this document or in discussions connected to it may be disclosed to any other party.

Introduction
This RFI is a request for information regarding your company and your products/services. The same information will be gathered from different companies and will be used to evaluate what vendors we will follow up the sourcing process with a RFP.

Scope
Specific information is requested according to the form below.

Abbreviation and terminology
[Special Terms specific to the industry]

RFI Process
Please fill in all information on the attached form.

Response
Vendor responses must be forwarded hardcopy and via email [company email account]

Contacts
For questions regarding this RFI, you are welcome to contact:
[Name of Individual Responsible]
[your title]
[Company Name]
[your phone number]
[your email address]

Timeframe
This is the timeframe for the RFI responses
9/28/2011 – The RFI is sent out
[MM]/[DD]/[YY] – Last date for questions by Vendors
[MM]/[DD]/[YY] – Last date for submission of RFI response
[MM]/[DD]/[YY] – Results from the evaluation
[MM]/[DD]/[YY] – RFP sent to select vendors who are deemed appropriate by requestor

Fig. 4.1 (continued)

Background description of what is requested

Of [your company]

[Your company] was established [XXXX] is a company listed on [XX], and produces [XX]. Our production is located at [XX] and [XX]. Our main products are [XX]. Our annual turnover is about [XX]. Our mission is [XX].

More information can be found on [www.xxxxxx.zzz].

Context of the product or service

[Describe what kind of information is being requested regarding the vendor's product and/or service.]

Statement of Need

[Describe the solution being requested.]

Requirements

[Describe the requirements, such as technical needs that the product or service must address and fulfill.]

Qualifications

[Description of what qualifies a vendor for delivering the products and/or services.]

Other Important Information

Payment term: XX days

Delivery term: EXW/FCA/etc

Delivery address(es):

Quality requirements (such as PPM):

Other requirements:

Fig. 4.1 (continued)

Form to fill in as answer to the RFI

Question	Answer
Company name	
Company address	
Company web page	
Main products/services	
Main market/customers	
Ownership structure	
Structure of parent corporation, joint ventures, subsidiaries, partnerships or other relevant relations	
Number of years in business	
Company location(s)	
Employees	
Production	
R&D	
Marketing and sales	
Quality department	
Most Recent Financial information (FYE MM/YY)	
Gross Sales	
Gross margin	
Profit/Loss	
Stock markets where your company is listed	
Contact person responsible for answering this RFI	
Telephone	
Email	
Products/Services listed in RFI not available	
Reference customers using comparable products or services (including contact information)	
Reference customers using your products or services today, although they are not comparable with what is requested in this RFI (including contact information)	
Locations available for implementation, if not worldwide.	
Availability of support worldwide	

Fig. 4.1 (continued)

Figure 4.1 reflects a relatively simple request for vendor information. The RFI should be used to obtain information about the number of potential vendors who can offer a solution and who are interested in bidding. Another alternative for producing an RFI is to hire an outside consulting firm that can manage the process for the organization. Such firms typically have a list of preferred vendors, so that the RFI step can be eliminated and the consulting firm can just send the RFP out to their list of potential solutions. Such consulting firms can also produce the RFP so that the entire step is somewhat outsourced. There are obvious benefits to outsourcing this task to a third party:

1. Existing IT staff does not have the expertise or time
2. An outside view can be very advantageous
3. Existing list of preferred solution providers
4. Overall savings
5. Faster solution
6. Less politics

RFP

As discussed the RFP represents the more detailed requirements document that allows prospective bidders (vendors) to provide a cost proposal and solution for the reported needs of the organization. RFPs must be specific to the needs of the application to ensure that a vendor has enough information to provide an accurate quote. Figure 4.2 provides a sample RFP for a Web solution.

PREFACE

This RFP has been prepared to meet the unique requirements of XYZ. This investment banking corporation is headquartered in New York City and provides financial services in the US well as interfacing with its Global counterparts globally.

XYZ requires services to support a number of initiatives relating to the development of internal and external websites:

1. Integrated Intranet to support various components of each business segment
2. Internet applications to support outside markets and recruitment
3. Integration and consistency of database applications
4. Support systems such as maintainable content-based management systems that are developed specifically to support XYZ applications.
5. Branding and creative design

XYZ Commitment

XYZ is committed to:

- providing user requirements specifications and supporting documentation (see Appendix I).
- purchasing necessary hardware and software for the websites.
- providing analysis of data.
- providing internal project management and interfaces with vendors.

I-COMPANY INFORMATION

XYZ is a major force in global investment banking. Its clients around the world include major corporations and governments. As the investment banking division of the XYZ Group it adds value by combining the global resources of one of the USs largest banks with market-leading international expertise.

Fig. 4.2 Sample RFP

XYZ has over 1800 employees in North America, and will shortly merge with other firms to form a larger and more diverse entity. The major components of its operation today include:

1. Equity business
2. Corporate Finance
3. Global Finance/Private Equity
4. Loans and Structured Finance
5. Consulting services

While XYZ North America is a self-sustaining member of XYZ global, there are a number of joint interfaces that require the coordination of resources particularly with the London office. These interfaces typically relate to branding, image, logo, and integrated global services that affect multiple entities. There are also cases where economies of scale and common clientele dictate a level of partnering within groups.

Each business area's activities are more often treated and operated as separate businesses within the bank. As such, there are multiple liaisons that are necessary to ensure that each unit specific needs are met, particularly in the information services area. Many of the internal departments are seeking to enhance their image at XYZ, and therefore are seeking to establish or enhance their presence by providing more access to information through a corporate Intranet. Furthermore, there are certain departments that need to provide external initiatives through the firm's Internet site. Specifically this includes college recruitment as well as constant new initiatives in a dynamic business. While XYZ has a large IT infrastructure, there was no formal organization to provide e-business solutions to these units. An e-consulting organization was formed to address these needs. This group, called e-Solutions reports to the Corporate Affairs department (CA). Part of the mission of CEA is to ensure a consistent corporate brand image, thus providing this Intranet and marketing web services through CEA was the appropriate department to provide the service.

II-e-COMMUNICATIONS Department

The purpose of the e-Communications Lab is to establish and launch e-business service for XYZ in North America. This service unit will implement Intranet and Internet solutions to provide added value to various entities at XYZ. Its initial business plan is to establish credibility within the company by providing a central service organization that can understand the needs of business units and create quality, cost effective, and state-of-the-art e-commerce systems. Specifically e-Communications Lab will:

2. Develop an Internet mini-site highlighting specific products and services.
3. Develop intranet sites for business lines and service companies enabling them to raise their profiles within the company.
4. Maintain Internet/Intranet content ensuring the company's presence as being on the cutting-edge of contemporary e-commerce technology.

Fig. 4.2 (continued)

The diagram below provides a pictorial of the e-Communications Lab business functions and interfaces to provide these services:

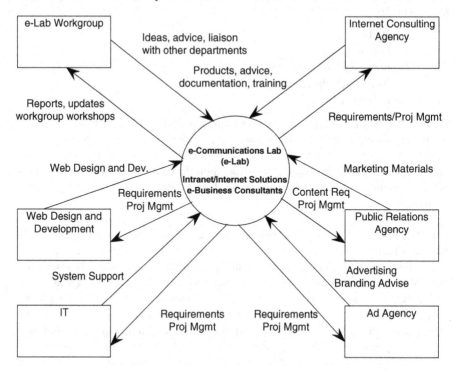

III Web Design and Development Projects

The focus of these projects is to implement more centralized Intranet applications that can provide consistency, credibility, and quality within the company, yet at the same time provide a consistent vision of the companies resources. The Internet projects are limited to North American products and services at this time, but certain projects may span into the global international community, as well as focus on external Internet products and services. Most of the projects in the short term, however, will relate to the development of Intranet sites for business lines that need to raise their profiles within the company. Projects will vary in size and cost—some requiring the storing of data and content in databases; others simply requiring the movement of content among well-designed and thought-out screens. XYZ seeks a business partner that can provide the following services:

Identity and Branding: this involves helping XYZ form a vision of their business units over the Web. XYZ seeks firms that have established a number of methods to assist clients in re-defining themselves in the Internet network era, particularly in the financial community. It is expected that this will involve the translation of XYZ's existing and forthcoming brand to the on-line world via the Web.

Fig. 4.2 (continued)

Creative Design: this requires vendors to provide creative and artistic web designs that are consistent with the firm's business themes, yet provide attractive and intuitively useable systems. We seek to find partners that can integrate the creative process and at the same time provide the technical vision and implementation as well.

e-Commerce: it is our expectation, as stated above, to have one vendor provide the entire life-cycle of web and e-commerce systems. The selected partner must provide the internal technical development team that is necessary to integrate legacy applications, provide complete database design and support for Microsoft SQL_Server and possibly Oracle. Furthermore, we expect our partner to have a systems-development cycle that reflects a well thought out analysis-to-design-to development foresight, that in effect convinces the XYZ of the vendor's ability to bring projects to fruition. Vendors are also expected to have development teams that can implement user tracking, reporting, traffic analysis, and security.

System Integration: this involves the need to interface new applications with existing XYZ systems. As such our vendor must be capable of providing systems architecture support, conversion expertise, and security experts to help formulate Web interfaces.

Intranet Tools Development: this area focuses on the ability of the Intranet to improve internal communication and workflow using flexible and tailored content management and publishing tools that foster the specific needs of the XYZ community.

Maintenance and Support: vendors need to provide maintenance and support services to assist in the ongoing relationship with XYZ. This can involve the need to get timely changes or enhancements made to a particular site, or providing documentation and training to a complimentary internal staff of XYZ Web developers. Help-line support should also be provided at both peak and off-peak times.

Existing System Issues

There have been a few year-end projects that have been completed to establish the presence of e-Lab. This consists of a new central Intranet home site, a Risk Management Reporting site, a Loans organization site, and a Human Resources central forms and handbook site. It is important that the image of the these sites be consistent with the new firm.

IV SPECIFICATION REQUIREMENTS

Vendors will be provided with technical specifications that are prepared by XYZ. Specifications will consist of an overview business specification, followed by detailed specifications that outline each site's functions, data needs, and reporting requirements. Flow diagrams showing the options of page selections are also included. A sample specification is shown on the following pages.

Fig. 4.2 (continued)

(Note: Attach Sample Specification)

V SERVICE PROPOSAL REQUIREMENTS

The submitted proposals should be organized according to the basic outline set forth below:

GENERAL COMMENTS

Provide a brief description and history of your firm and its current size. This should be in the format of a statement of qualifications and should include a brief financial history. If your proposal represents a joint effort between your company and another vendor, detail the relationship between your firm and the other involved. In addition, the specific responsibilities of each participating vendor in the joint effort should be described.

Vendors should also include a summary of the major benefits of working with their company.

Database And Application Software

Provide a list and explanation of the types of development environments supported. This should include program languages, databases supported, and third-party tools used, including content management products supported or developed.

Vendors are required to include as part of their bids costs for project management, testing and post implementation activities. Additional requirements include:

1. Methodology of creative design to development process (Life-cycle).
2. Delivery Schedule - provide the lead-time required for each application to be delivered and installed.
3. Software Support - indicate the manner in which database application software support will be provided and the pricing arrangement for each support.
4. Maintenance - describe maintenance provided, including warranty period, the availability and location of service and expected delivery time.
5. Security - describe the types and levels of system and software security. Specify how security is set-up and maintained and whether security can be controlled at the screen level.

Vendor Assistance And Training

Any assistance to be provided by the vendor should be described. Vendor assistance should be clearly defined, including whether the assistance is chargeable or supplied at no additional charge. Areas to be addressed should include, but not limited to:

1. Training - include description, location, and frequency of available training.
2. Installation Support - describe the recommended approach for installing your proposed system including a sample time-phased schedule of vendor and company manpower requirements, in detail and summarized form.

Fig. 4.2 (continued)

3. On-Going Support - describe the support provided such as "help lines", etc. In addition, explain your software upgrade procedures including frequency of new releases/upgrades.

Cost Summary

All cost considerations should be included in this section of the proposal.

1. Web Application software (including source and object code) by application:

   - *Hourly/daily rates*
   - *One time charges to develop and quality assure*
   - *Warranty and Maintenance fees*
   - *Tiered pricing structure alternatives and fixed fee basis*

2. Project Management
3. Maintenance and Support

Other Requirements

Please provide the following information:

1. List of users with installations similar to the proposed number of database applications and scope of the CG requirements, including company name, address, telephone number, contact person, and length of time the system has been installed. Vendors must also complete the Client Reference questionnaire.
2. Financial Statements Last two fiscal years.
3. Sample contract.

Examples of summary and detailed implementation

Responding To The Questionnaires

A comprehensive listing of company and web system requirements stated in the form of questionnaires can be found in subsequent sections. Some questions require a written response while others may be answered using codes listed below. To the right of each desired requirement a space provided for code responses. The following codes may be used:

Y   Capability can be provided

N   Capability cannot be provided

N/A   Not Applicable (state reason)

Many of the questions will require an in-depth response typically needing an attachment. In these situations, Vendors should provide the appropriate attachment identification in the response area.

Confidentiality

This request contains information about XYZ that is confidential. We ask that you respect this confidence and not disclose this information to any third parties. XYZ, in turn, will treat the information you submit as confidential.

Fig. 4.2 (continued)

VENDOR REQUIREMENTS

01	General Information	Response
1	How many years have you been in the software business?	
2	When did your business start ?	
3	Have you developed software in a similar industry ?	
4	How long is the Warranty Period ?	
5	What are your typical terms and conditions of doing business?	
6	Are references available ?	
7	Do you have assigned Account Representatives ?	
8	Are user sites available for visitations ?	

02	Financial Evaluation	Response
1	Does the Firm have annual audited financial statements?	
2	Will prior fiscal year statements be available ?	
3	What is the Firm's fiscal year end ?	
4	List statistics for prior fiscal year end: ?	
4a	Total Gross Revenues	
4b	Total Net Revenues	
4c	Total Net Income	
4d	Total Assets	
4e	Percent of Gross Sales related to Software Development	
4f	R&D Budget	
4g	Number of Customers	
5	How many consecutive years have been profitable ?	
6	Are Revenues by Product Division Available ?	

03	Employee Analysis	Response
1	Number of full-time Employees	
1a	Sales	
1b	Advertising/Creative Design	
1c	Web Design	
1d	Project Management/Consulting	
1e	Development/Programming	
1f	Middleware and XML	
1g	Database/Backend	
1h	Customer Support/Training	

Fig. 4.2 (continued)

1i	Maintenance	
1j	**R&D**	
1k	Administration	
2	**Number of full-time Employees last year**	
3	**Percent of turnover in last three (3) years**	

04	Development and Flexibility Evaluation	Response
1	What is your internal procedure for Revision Control ?	
2	What is your procedure for informing clients of new versions?	
3	Is Custom Programming always available ?	
3a	What is the hourly rate ?	
4	Do you supply your own:	
4a	Content Management Software ?	
4b	Value Added Resseller (VAR) relationships ?	
5	Does your contract assure clients the receipt of:	
5a	New Release information and Documentation ?	
5b	Source and Object code and all development routines ?	
6	Do you provide on-site support ?	
6a	Toll-Free Help-line available ?	
6b	24-hour Hot-line available ?	
7	When is support available (M, T, W, Th,..F,..Sa,..Su.)	
8	Is Support available 5 pm to 8 am ?	
8a	weekdays ?	
04	**Development and Flexibility Evaluation (cont'd)**	**Response**
8b	weekends	
9	Where are your software support offices ?	
9a	Which location(s) will support Dresdner ?	
9b	How many employees will be available to support Dresdner's software ?	
10	Enclose a copy of policies regarding application software support	
11	Enclose a copy of programming standards	
12	How are web enhancements distributed ?	
13	Are new manuals/documentation provided with each version released ?	
14	Do you support old releases of any proprietary package software ?	

Fig. 4.2 (continued)

15	Are you involved with any Web Industry Groups ?	
15a	How often does the Group meet (per year)	
15b	Who conducts the meetings (Users or Vendor)	
15c	Where do they meet ?	
15d	Is there a membership fee ?	
15e	Is there a Newsletter ?	
15f	Are user recommendations implemented ?	

06	Project Management/Implementation	Response
1	Do you provide project management services ?	
2	Do you assist in determining personnel resources required on the project?	
3	Do you define the roles and responsibilities for:	
3a	vendor ?	
3b	user ?	
3c	IT department ?	
4	Do you conduct kick-off meeting to introduce project ?	
5	Do you prepare weekly and monthly status reports ?	
6	Do you provide requirements documentation for:	
6a	hardware ?	
6b	software ?	
6c	necessary network configurations ?	
7	Do you prepare a Server capacity plan ?	
8	Do you prepare a site planning document ?	
9	Do you implement a methodology for migrationg from test to production ?	
10	Do you provide user security ?	

06	Branding/Design (cont'd)	Response
11	Do you provide branding services?	
12	Do you integrate branding and web site design to do:	
12a	logos ?	
12b	Interactive video?	
12c	Content design?	

Fig. 4.2 (continued)

13	Relating to design:	
13a	Provide content design images ?	
13b	define data requirements ?	
13c	identify update strategies ?	
13d	develop the interface methodology ?	
13e	design all required interfaces ?	
13f	document interface designs ?	
13g	test all developed interfaces ?	
13h	install all interface programs ?	

06	Testing and Quality Assurance	Response
14	Relating to testing, do you:	
14a	provide a test plan ?	
14b	identify additions to the production system ?	
14c	identify deletions to the production system ?	
14d	create test input data ?	
14e	list steps and procedures to create or extract test data ?	
14f	identify valid test results prior to testing ?	
14g	run tests with valid data ?	
14h	run tests with invalid data ?	
14i	be responsible for unit test plans ?	
14j	be responsible for system and volume testing ?	
14k	base acceptance for payment on client supplied test results ?	
15	Relating to conversion of existing data, will you:	
15a	identify data to be converted ?	
15b	develop conversion methodology ?	
15c	prepare conversion specifications ?	

Fig. 4.2 (continued)

06		Testing and Quality Assurance	Response
	15d	design necessary file formats ?	
	15e	test file conversion programs ?	
	15f	install conversion programs in production ?	
16		Relating to implementation, will you:	
	16a	prepare a complete workplan to get into production ?	
	16b	develop alternative procedures should implementation plan fail ?	
	16c	be responsible for problems encountered with software ?	
	16d	be responsible for problems encountered with hardware ?	
	16e	provide operations procedures for application software ?	
	16f	provide operations procedures for recommended operating system ?	
	16g	provide operations procedures for recommended hardware ?	
17		Supply an implementation workplan with activities and time frames.	

07		Documentation	Response
1		Will the system come with the following Documentation:	
	1a	Operator Manuals ?	
	1b	Technical Manuals ?	
	1c	Programmer Manuals ?	
	1d	User Manuals ?	
	1e	System Flowcharts and/or Data Flow Diagrams ?	
	1f	System Narratives ?	
	1g	Table and File Layouts ?	
	1h	Data Element Descriptions ?	
	1i	Screen Formats ?	
	1j	Data Validation Routines ?	
	1k	Utility Programs ?	
	1l	Backup and Recovery Programs ?	
	1m	Security Routines ?	
	1n	Logic Design (Data Flow Diagrams, Entity Relations, etc.) ?	
	1o	Program Flowcharts ?	

Fig. 4.2 (continued)

07		Documentation (cont'd)	Response
	1p	Program Narratives ?	
	1q	Audit and Control descriptions ?	
	1r	Quality Assurance Testing Scripts ?	
2		Will the system contain documentation for configuring the software:	
	2a	Required Library Names ?	
	2b	Required file or database names ?	
	2c	File allocation and initialization ?	
	2d	File distribution and directory placement ?	
3		Will the system contain documentation for product administration:	
	3a	Database file system ?	
	3b	End-User Security/Function Security Access ?	
	3c	Master File Maintenance ?	
	3d	Updating Applications Software ?	
4		Will the system contain the documentation for operations procedures:	
	4a	User procedures at the screen level ?	
	4b	Daily Operations ?	
	4c	Evening/End of day operations ?	
07		Documentation (cont'd)	Response
	4d	Recovery/Restart ?	
	4e	Error handling and exceptions processing ?	
	4f	Requesting Vendor Support ?	
5		Will the system contain documentation for data input and output control:	
	5a	Input forms and how to use ?	
	5b	Data Entry procedures ?	
	5c	Balancing and reconciliation ?	
	5d	Report verification ?	
6		Will the following documentation be provided periodically:	
	6a	Features contained in new releases ?	
	6b	Software bug fixes and operating system patches/new versions ?	

Fig. 4.2 (continued)

08	Training	Response
1	Is implementation training provided ?	
2	Is User Training provided ?	
2a	On-Site training ?	
2b	Off-site training ?	

09	Security	Response
1	Can you provide applications that have:	
1a	Field level security ?	
1b	Program security ?	
1c	Screen security ?	
1d	Menu level security ?	
1e	Application level security ?	
1f	Logged transactions (change, delete, etc.) ?	
2	Is security defined in a:	
2a	Master table ?	
2b	Data dictionary format ?	
3	On-line security is maintained by:	
3a	Batch update ?	
3b	On-line entry-batch update ?	
3c	On-line real-time ?	
4	Will there be the ability to create access profiles:	
4a	Attach and relate user to profile real-time ?	

10	Editing and Error Handling	Response
1	Will the Screen be capable of:	
1a	Providing on-line editing after individual fields are entered ?	
1b	Providing a means of changing field edits ?	
1c	Displaying standard error message and codes ?	
1d	Providing on-line help feature ?	
2	Provide an overriding key/command to cancel a transactions ?	
3	Database capabilities:	
3a	Logging of errors and dumps ?	
3b	To provide system failure recovery programs ?	

Fig. 4.2 (continued)

VII CLIENT REFERENCE QUESTIONS

Complete a separate questionnaire for at least three users who can be contacted for reference. References used should be able to demonstrate a similar implementation requirement and in particular, any companies involved in financial operations.

Reference

1. Company Information

        Company Name: _____

        Street Address: _____

        City: _____ State: _____ Zip: _____

        Phone: _____

        Website: _____

        e-mail Address: _____

        Contact's Name: _____ Position: _____

2. Website Design

        Number of Site Pages   _____

        Number of Database Interface   _____

        Hits per Month   _____

        Number of Users   _____

        Highest number of simultaneous access   _____

3. Hardware/Software Installed

        System Platform (model)   _____

        Browsers   _____

        Middleware   _____

        Database   _____

        Operating System   _____

4. Application Software Installed

        Security Access   _____

        Encryption/Decryption   _____

        Application Development Language   _____

        Screen Software   _____

        Report/Writer   _____

        Communications Package   _____

        3GL Software Interfaces   _____

        Others: List   _____

Fig. 4.2 (continued)

Figure 4.2 serves as a template for creating an RFP. While this template provides information about the company and some high-level requirements, an RFP process also requires a detailed requirements document that vendors can review in order to determine a best price for the requested services.

Requirements Document

The requirements document is an adjunct specification often called a business specification. The purpose of the business specification is to provide a document that provides readers with a functional understanding of the needs of a software application. The specification should be written in prose format so that vendors can easily understand its meaning and intent. The business specification

Client: XYZ Corporation	Date: 9/5/11
Application: Operations Database	Supersedes:
Subject: Contact Management	Author: A. Langer
Process: Overview - Business Spec	Page: 1 of 2

Overview

The Contact Management Process will allow users to add, modify or delete specific contacts. Contacts will be linked to various tables including Company. A Contact refers to a person who is related to XYZ for business reasons. It can be a Client, a Vendor, a consultant, a person involved in a negotiation, etc.

Contact General Information:

The Database must allow for the centralization of all the contacts handled by all the departments in XYZ.
The database and screens will be focused on the following information component groupings:

Basic Information
This is the minimum data requirement and includes such elements as Name, Title, Organization, Phone, Fax, Address, Country, etc.

Contact Profile Information
Further qualification and related elements. Relations include:

- department
- type of client
- nature of client (primary, technical)
- interest of prospect
- importance of client
- memberships (FTUG)
- FT employee

> *This is a Business Specification which reflects the overall requirements in prose format. Its focus is to provide the user who is not technical with a document that they can authorize.*

Fig. 4.3 Sample business specification

is not technically complete, rather enough that lets vendors to determine the architectural needs and inputs and outputs required by the applications. Good business specifications include forms that articulate the logical requirements as shown in Figs. 4.3 and 4.4.

Chapters 7, 8, and 9 provide more details on how to create formal requirements documents with both business and technical specifications.

Client: XYZ Company	Date: 9/15/11
Application: Contact Management	Supersedes: 9/5/11
Subject: Program Specification Detail	Author: A. Langer
Spec-ID FTCM01 - Add/Modify Screen Processing	Page: 1 of 1

Process Flow Description:
The user will input information in the top form. At a minimum, at least the Last Name or Contact ID will be entered. The system must check a Security indicator prior to allowing a user to modify a Contact. The Security will be by Department or Everyone. Therefore, if the Modify button is selected and the user is restricted by a different department, Display:
    " Access Denied, not eligible to modify, Department Restriction"

If Security authorized, the Add/Modify Button will activate the following business rules:

    If Contact-ID (cntid) not blank
        Find match and replace entered data into record
        If no match display "Invalid Contact-ID" and refresh cursor

    If Contact-ID (cntid) Blank and Last-Name (cntlname) Blank then
        Display "Contact-ID or Last-Name must be entered"
        Place Cursor at Contact-ID (cntid) entry.

    If Contact-ID (cntid) Blank and Last-Name (cntlname) + First-Name (cntfname) is Duplicate
        Display Window to show matches so that user can determine if contact already in
        system
        If user selects the Add Anyway button
            assume new contact with same name and assign new Contact-ID (cntid)
        Else
            upon selection bring in existing data and close window.
    Else
        Create new record with all new information fields and assign Contact-ID (cntid)

    If Company button activated
        Prompt user for Company-ID (cmpcd) and/or Company-Name (cmpna)
        If duplicate
            link foreign-key pointer to matched company
        Else
            Add Company-Name (cntcmpna) to Contact Table only
            Display "You must use Company Screen to Link, Company Master File Not
            Updated"

Fig. 4.4 Business specifications

Problems and Exercises

1. What is an RFI?
2. What is an RFP?
3. Compare the differences between an RFI and an RFP.
4. What is the purpose of having a confidentiality and non-disclosure clause?
5. Explain why an RFP needs to be associated with a requirements document.
6. What is meant by logical requirements?

Searching for Solutions

5

The purpose of this chapter is to provide guidelines on the process of finding possible solutions for application needs. Thus far the preceding chapters have provided the structure and build vs. buy alternatives. It is now important to define the steps necessary to find the solution and prospective partners that meet the RFP needs.

The Team Selection

Searching for the right solutions starts with forming an internal team responsible for managing the process through selection decision. The following roles and responsibilities should be considered:

- *Selection team director/lead:* this individual should be at a senior level, perhaps director or above and have responsibility over the project selection team process and any other members who are needed. This individual could either be from IT or from a business unit. I suggest that this individual come from the business with assistance from IT management; in this way it allows the business to feel that they "own" the project.
- *Business/functional members:* these individuals should provide representation from all of the affected parties, including business unit personnel and administrative organizations such as accounting and human resources. These representatives should be at a line manager level, that is, knowledgeable about day-to-day needs and familiar with current systems in place.
- *Experts:* these are individuals who have specific knowledge in areas as opposed to specific business lines—they usually are technical experts in their fields and are needed at certain times during the evaluation process.
- *IT manager:* this individual should be a senior representative from the IT department who essentially provides facilitation and direction from an architectural perspective. That is, providing information about the technical capabilities of possible solutions as well as upholding certain architectural standards necessary to maintain capabilities among other systems.

- *Outside consultants*: depending on the size of the project, some firms get outsiders involved to provide objective input that is free of the cultural and political constraints of the company. Outsiders can be from two areas: (1) from industry and are familiar with the applications or (2) have technical and project experience.

The question is who makes these individual choices? Smart firms select an executive to make some of these decisions. Often this will likely be the chief information officer (CIO) along with an operations executive. Sometimes it falls under the auspices of the chief financial officer (CFO) or chief operating officer (COO).

In terms of the actual participant choices, Tayntor (2006) suggests focusing on diversity of composition. She breaks composition into two major components:

1. *Functionality*: these individuals are focused on the operational aspects of the solution—that is—does it get the functions done so that the day-to-day business can run. To this extent, Tayntor recommends that there be multiple levels of operational personnel involved, so that varying perspectives on needs of the business are considered. Remember, levels of user views, as previously discussed, vary by responsibility because it affects what is valued.
2. *Technical*: the necessary expertise that can determine the automation considerations of any possible solution. Again, this includes architecture and product software issues. Product software issues can include system software, applications software, and productivity software (databases, spreadsheets, etc.).

There are, of course, generic factors that should be considered when forming the evaluation team. This includes selecting people who are group thinkers, can cooperate with others, are respected by employees, and are politically astute. Further, the evaluation team could become too large, resulting in a team that is difficult to manage and may not be able to reach consensus.

Due Diligence

Whether or not an RFP is used or not or whether an organization uses a consulting firm to assist them, it is important that the company engage in due diligence practices before selecting any vendor—for package development of specific application development. Due diligence is defined as a process of investigation before making a contractual decision. Effectively, it ensures that you know as much as possible about the vendor you are selecting. There are a number of components to the due diligence process:

- Reference checks
- Review vendor financial statements
- Bank references
- On-site and client site reviews
- Training
- Upgrade process
- General questions to ask
- Understand the company ownership

Reference Checks

Vendors need to provide a list of clients that can be used as a positive reference. Most vendors will provide the names and contact information of their selection. Obviously, these clients represent a positive experience. Organizations are better off asking vendors for a list of all their clients and then select from that list. This process will provide a more accurate depiction of satisfaction. Furthermore, I would suggest knowing about how a vendor deals with crisis—you want to know more about how a vendor will support you during problems than when things are going smoothly. Almost all vendors have problem accounts.

Review Financial Statements

This is a very important process. I suggest that the vendor provides 3 years of historical financial statements. Public companies must have a certified audit, but if the vendors are privately held, they are not required to do so, which means that the statements may be prepared by someone internally—so they may not be accurate. In any case they must be able to provide them. The next question is what to look for? I would get your CFO or controller involved with the review because financial statements can be very tricky to read. However, here are some critical things to look for in the vendor's financial statements:

- *Cash on hand:* this simply tells you how much actual cash the company has.
- *Accounts receivable:* how much is outstanding from their clients and to be collected.
- *Accounts payable:* this represents the size of the company's debt—that is money they owe.
- *Accrued expenses:* this usually represents the amount of accrued payroll due to the vendor's employees—it is another form of cash debt.
- *Retained earnings:* provides a perspective of previous earnings from profits. This should be matched against the company's profit/loss statements.

So what do you look for in the above data, Here are some "red flags!":

1. If the cash on hand is less than accounts payable it may mean that the company has exposure if they do not collect their accounts receivable. I would also require an aged accounts receivable so that your organization can determine how much of the accounts receivable are within 30 or 60 days—meaning that it will likely be collected. If the accounts receivable shows a lot of cash due over 60 days it might mean that the vendor is having problems collecting, or cannot finish the work to get paid, or they have unhappy clients who do not want to pay them!
2. Ask for an aged accounts payable schedule as this will show how soon the debt is to be paid. If most of the debt is due within 60 days it further allows you to determine the solvency of the vendor.
3. Ask for a detailed schedule of the accrued expenses as this will let you know how much is due for payroll and payroll taxes. Payroll must be paid timely.

4. If the accounts payable and accrued expenses are larger than the combined cash on hand and the accounts receivable, then the vendor may not be very solvent.
5. If retained earning is negative it means that the vendor has not yet reached a profit stage in the company, that is, the vendor has not yet reached a profit cumulatively since its inception.

The financial statements do not always paint the complete picture financially. The organization or its attorney should do a search to ensure that there are no outstanding law suits against the vendor, or past ones, as well as liens from third parties. Further, a Dun & Bradstreet (D&B) search should be done which will provide a rating on payment ability of the vendor—specifically if they pay their bills late.

Bank References

The organization should obtain authorization to contact the vendor's banks to verify cash on hand and to verify that the vendor has a good standing with the bank. This is a simple process and one that every vendor will likely agree to do. Unfortunately, it is often overlooked or considered unnecessary. The organization should request a complete list of financial institutions and types of accounts maintained by the vendor.

On-site Demonstrations

Organizations should arrange for prospective vendor solutions to come on-site and demonstrate the capabilities of their product. This demonstration should be accomplished by first having meetings with the vendor and providing them with test data. In this way the demonstrations actually show company information and how it can be accessed by the users of the product. This can be very effective, especially for the general business user who may be challenged to imagine how the software will actually operate on the data of his/her business unit. Having on-site demonstrations also allows the vendor to get a better grasp of the politics of the company and how they can compliment the operating team.

Vendor On-site Review

Organizations should visit the vendor's corporate or local office. You want to see the organization at work and meet the administrative people who you might be dealing with in the future. Doing a vendor site visit is extremely important for non-public companies and for very small vendors. Today, websites make companies that are very small look very big, although size is not always an indicator of corporate solvency. Doing actual client site reviews is also very constructive. While calling a vendor client is productive, actually seeing the implementation and meeting more than one person can tell a lot about how the vendor operates.

Training

A number of packaged products require significant training of staff to be successful. The vendor may have an excellent product but lousy support and training.
Organizations should review the training philosophy of the vendor, review the materials, and cover how their clients rate training. Initial training, however, is only one
aspect of training. As organization lose and add employees there may be needs
for continual support or sporadic training based on new versions of the product.
Interviewing some of the vendor trainers is another effective way of determining the
strength of their staff. Some large vendors can also make training available through
third-party firms that specialize in supporting them. This may or may not be an
effective solution. Problems occur when a training company is out of sink with the
software company especially when there are product bugs for which the training
company cannot fix or offer a temporary "work around."

Upgrade Process

Software enhancements are realities. It is important to understand the vendor's
approach to handling this process. Due diligence should cover the number of
upgrades historically provided to clients, how the process works, and how upgrades
are retrofitted to software that has been customized (this process addresses the
problem of software enhancements that overlay customized code from an earlier
version). Organizations should also understand the costs associated with receiving
upgrades. This often is included as part of the annual maintenance fee but sometimes such costs are not included and must be paid each time there are maintenance
releases. If customizations are involved, organizations should understand the costs
for retrofitting upgrades with the customized changes. Maintenance fees usually
are 15% of the then-going software license fees. Maintenance and upgrade costs
become more complex when the applications are developed specifically for the
client. In these cases the method of upgrade and associated costs must be carefully
reviewed during due diligence.

General Questions to Ask

Perhaps the most important part of the due diligence process is knowing what questions to ask and how to ask them. For example, when checking client satisfaction,
do not ask the vendor's client if they are happy. Ask them how the vendor supported
them when they had difficulties. This type of phrasing gets the right answers—you
want to know how the vendor will treat you when you disagree, not when you agree.
This is also true when asking about implementation schedules—do not ask how they
keep on schedule, ask them what they do when they are behind!

Understand the Company Ownership

One can never be sure what represents a comfort zone when dealing with a vendor's ownership. If it is a private firm, ask whether a venture firm owns the controlling shares. Venture and private equity firms invest in companies for one reason—to flip them and make money. This means they will either sell the company at some point or help the entity to go public. The latter is a good thing in most cases, but the former— selling the company—could mean lots of changes, both in the firm's philosophy and in its personnel. So the only answer, to a large degree, is to understand the vendor's timetable—are they in a growth period when the investors might want to get out. Also, who are the original founders? Do they want to sell or expand the company? You might not get an honest answer, but why not ask!!

Architecture Review

The type of software and systems required by the vendor and the overall architecture of the solution are extremely important issues not to be overlooked. Therefore, organizations should do a complete "platform" review to ensure that the product will operate properly across all of their systems. Organizations should be particularly sensitive when considering software that has not demonstrated that it can successfully execute on a new or different architecture. Although we believe that we live in a world of open systems, there are still products that are very dependent on specific versions of operating systems and specific systems environments. An example of this problem can be related to the Cone Mills case against System Software Associates (SSA)–Enterprise Resource Planning (ERP) product called BPCS (Business Processing and Control System). The product was originally designed to operate under the IBM mid-range product lines (Systems 36, 38, and AS400), which are very proprietary platforms. When the software industry began to transition to open systems particularly Windows and UNIX, SSA attempted to convert its product and advertise that its product could run under the HP-UX architecture. Cone Mills selected the HP-UX environment and although SSA stated that it would operate, there were problems. Apparently, BPCS could only operate on HP-UX if the entire system was installed. Unfortunately, Cone Mills only selected certain modules. The product was significantly delayed by over a year. Eventually, SSA declared bankruptcy in 2002. These types of results do not favor anyone—all sides tend to lose. So the message is that organization should be very wary of being the first to implement any package on a platform that the vendor cannot physically show success.

Another complication discussed earlier in this book is the use of open source. While this might be very attractive, organizations need to be sure that the open source containing any vendor license does not restrict or prohibit certain uses, and if there are any proprietary modifications made to a portion of the package using open source, what are the restrictions in use that affect the organization. Certainly, open source in this situation might preclude the organization from selecting the vendor's product.

Another factor in selection is product scalability. Should the organization grow and need to expand its use of the package or customized solution, will the software be able to run across multiple platforms or on a larger system? This again becomes a question of architecture, so at some point the IT organization must review this information with the vendor carefully. It might also be a good idea to consider engaging a third-party reviewer, similar to an independent engineer's report before one buys a house.

Finding Vendors

This section provides input on alternatives for finding available vendors that meet the needs of the RFP. We have already discussed the use of an outside consulting firm. There are significant advantages to bringing in a large firm to help:

1. Already have a list of acceptable vendors
2. Prior relationships with many of the vendors
3. Leverage with vendors because they represent future opportunities if the vendor does a good job
4. Leverage against the large consulting firm. A third-party consulting firm that has liability insurance that can support any type of malpractice activities. Simply put, because of their size, they can be sued
5. Experience of the consulting firm with RFPs and selections of vendors

If the organization elects to not use an outside consultant then the following are alternative methods to find prospective vendors to bid:

- *Use the Internet*: searching for vendors can be very effective using the modern search engines available to the general user. Furthermore, the Internet allows the organization to easily find out information about the company, its clients, and in some cases its financial performance (if they are a public company they have their financials posted on the Internet). In addition, the Internet allows the organization to uncover any issues with the vendor's clients, e.g., articles written about problems or legal suites that are posted.
- *Facebook and chat rooms:* using today's social medias, most vendors have active "facebooks" and chat rooms. Many also have user groups that can be contacted to receive information about the satisfaction with the vendor's clients and products overall.
- *Industry groups:* there are a number of groups that provide information about suggested solutions across different product lines. Subscribing or becoming a member of such groups can be very beneficial. Industry contacts can also be used as networks, and such networks can provide informal information that can be very valuable.
- *Conferences:* many professional IT organizations exist as well as industry groups that hold regular conferences. This is another network that can provide important information from those organizations that have implemented similar solutions.

- *Research organizations:* companies, like Gartner Group, provide certain research services for a fee. A number of such firms also allow subscriptions to their databases that have information about solutions, vendors, and current clients. Another research partner can be universities, which typically have faculty who will provide research services for lower costs and for the general education of their students. Using research universities is one of the most underutilized assets available to organizations.

Paying for a Plan

Another clever approach to finding the right vendor is to ask prospective vendors to provide a project management plan showing how they would actually implement their solution for your company. This may seem like a typical project plan, but these efforts should be set up as a prelude to evaluating the effectiveness of the vendor and their ability to deliver requested tasks. The downside of this approach is that it will likely cost the organization money: you may need to pay the vendor to do this extra work. However, it may be well worth the expense to become familiar with how the vendor supports you. In many cases you can negotiate an option with the vendor which credits the payment should they win the bid, that is, the steps being taken would need to be done by the selected vendor anyway. Another downside could be that the cost and effort does not necessarily allow the organization to determine the quality of the software and the ultimate value of the solution, but it is yet another option to consider.

Summary

It is important to note that the search for a vendor is a complex step that depends heavily on whether you wish to make or buy the solution or as previously discussed both. We should not see the vendor selection as a binary one, that is, there may be a need for more than one vendor, who may represent one phase or area of the solution. While this may sound like an obvious alternative, it is not without danger. Anytime you have more than one vendor partnering to deliver one solution, you run the risk of one blaming the other and no one really responsible for the entire contract. Even getting a consulting firm to manage the effort does not ensure that they can really ensure that there will not be problems. That is why many organizations like to have a one-stop solution where the vendor is responsible for every aspect of the implementation. The benefits are obvious should the vendor actually be capable of doing all of the needed activities from programming to product delivery to training and implementation.

Another alternative is to have a firm that monitors the vendor's activities but is not really responsible for any deliveries. Once again the large consulting firms provide this project management service. Although this seems worth the investment, you are also taking on yet another vendor to manage. Perhaps, the best solution is to have an effective management team that helps ensure that the project remains on time and on budget, assuming of course that the right vendor has been selected.

Problems and Exercises

1. Explain the purpose of due diligence. Discuss three components that affect the due diligence process.
2. What is the importance of the architecture review? Who in the organization should be responsible for this task?
3. What are the alternative ways to find qualified vendors? Which of them do you prefer? Support your opinion.
4. What is the role and responsibility of an outside consultant?
5. Provide three positive aspects of retaining an outside consultant and three negatives.
6. What are the advantages and disadvantages of having someone outside the organization develop and perhaps manage the plan?

Reference

Tayntor, C. B. (2006). *Successful packaged software implementation*. New York: Auerbach.

Controlling Costs and Realistic Budgeting

6

A critical step is setting budget before starting the process. Once the budget is set then overriding estimates is difficult and tends to feed the stereotype view of IT projects as being expensive and full of project overruns. The purpose of this chapter is to provide some guidelines on how to determine a viable budget and focus on controlling runaway costs because of inappropriate management as well as project scope creep.

The most important aspect of cost analysis is to prepare a budget. The first part of creating any budget is to determine the categories of cost. Costs usually belong to categories that relate to project activities. It is suggested then that you start the budget by sequentially thinking about the steps necessary to complete the project, from the selection process through implementation and go live (post-implementation):

- Kickoff and selection
- Implementation
- Post-implementation
  Within each of these processes are categories of costs as follows.

Kickoff and Selection

- *Internal staff costs*: this includes all of the internal staff resource needs throughout the project, including the selection team. The cost for these resources is usually determined based on an internal rate, that is, the company determines the internal charge for use of its staff on special projects. Essentially, internal staff costs are a form of "funny money" or an allocation, but they usually are a correct way of measuring staff costs of the project. The individuals engaged in this allocation should consist of IT personnel, user department staff, and administrative people.
- *Travel and expenses:* this includes out-of-pocket expenses incurred during the search and decisions for selecting vendors.
- *Software costs:* this relates to any special software tools that are needed for the evaluation such as a package to assist with the assessment.

A.M. Langer, *Guide to Software Development*,
DOI 10.1007/978-1-4471-2300-2_6, © Springer-Verlag London Limited 2012

- *Consultant and legal:* these are associated professional costs for special assistance during the selection period, especially outside help with the selection process and any legal costs associated with license agreements, customized development, and project management arrangements.

Implementation

- *Software costs:* these costs include software license fees, custom modifications, utility products (e.g., EDI), databases, operating systems, and security.
- *Hardware costs:* these costs consist of servers, PCs, memory, cloud computing, printers, scanners, backup devices, and disk space.
- *Network costs:* these include infrastructure costs for cabling, racks, routers, switches, modems, leased or dedicated lines, communications software, and Internet charges.
- *Project team costs:* these are labor costs for the project manager/team lead, systems analyst, programmers, testers, and outside consultants.
- *User team costs:* these include the team leads, user managers, and support personnel.
- *Support team costs*: this includes general IT utility expenses for IS support, database analysts, and networking staff.
- *Miscellaneous project team costs:* these include costs for furniture, telephone, project management software tools, administrative support, communications, video conferencing charges, user manuals, and special education.
- *Training costs*: these costs cover user training of the various user teams, the materials associated with the training, and should also cover any travel to and from training locations.
- *Data costs:* this relates to costs associated with cleaning up legacy data before conversion as well as archiving costs to protect the data from previous systems.
- *Miscellaneous or other costs:* these costs include quality assurance, internal audit, steering groups, conferences, and general networking of personnel during the implementation.
- *Allocation overhead costs:* these costs are allocations usually for using organizational resources from central services like office space and utility expenses. Since there is no direct way of calculating these expenses they are typically done through an accounting charge method. Not all organizations use this, but many have this as part of the budget process. The CFO can usually provide this information.
- *Contingency:* this represents an old method of having a cost allocated to unforeseen expenses. Some organizations allow it, others do not. Again, the CFO usually dictates the company policy.

Post-implementation

- *Maintenance costs*: these are usually annual costs for license fees and support for guaranteed upgrades, hardware coverage, and database support. These expenses can also include data disaster and recovery costs.
  A sample budget format is shown in Fig. 6.1.

Controlling Costs

While Fig. 6.1 reflects the items to be included in a budget forecast, it does not address what might be deemed appropriate spending within these categories of expenses. As such, this section aims to provide some guidelines as to what might be considered realistic amounts and pitfalls to be wary about as the project moves from selection to implementation to post-implementation. Unfortunately, IT organizations lack financial efficiencies and may not alone be able to formulate the total costs effectively (Ryan & Raducha-Grace, 2010). Thus, it is important to get all of the business management and accounting involved to ensure that the right budget amount is carefully formulated.

Hardware and Infrastructure

The most immediate issues for these expenses relate to company direction, first for infrastructure. I have already discussed the implications of whether or not to use a cloud solution. Obviously going to a cloud architecture is much cheaper and avoids the whole issue of designing, creating, and maintaining a data center. So I would recommend comparing the actual costs of owning a data center vs. an outsourced cloud. It is also important to recognize the difference in accounting, not withstanding actual cash outlay. To be specific, most data center costs, including hardware, networking, and installation, fall under the accounting of capital expenditures. Capital expenditures are recognized in accounting standards as long-term assets, for which the actual expense is depreciated over a number of years, depending on the type of asset. The number of years that can be depreciated on the books of the company is published in various standards organizations like FASB (Financial Accounting Standards Board) and are part of what is known as GAAP (Generally Accepted Accounting Principles) and GAAS (Generally Accepted Accounting Standards). To go further into accounting concepts would be beyond the scope of this book, but essentially, if you have hardware costs totaling $150,000, the company would likely depreciate that expense over 3 years, recording in the first year only $50,000 of the total expense. That is, each year for 3 years, the organization would only record $50,000 per year. The concept behind this allocation of cost is that the organization is actually prepaying for the value of the hardware, so it takes only a portion of the useful life each year, in this case 3 years. So the question becomes, what do you put in the first year budget? Likely only $50,000; however, the project cost is still

Sample Budget   Year:

Ref	Project Expenditures	Rate $ per Unit/Day	0 Quantity Units/Days	0 $	1 Quantity Units/Days	1 $	2 Quantity Units/Days	2 $	3 Quantity Units/Days	3 $	Total $
1	**Selection process**										
1.1	Internal resources / staff costs:										
1.1.1	- Information Systems (IS) department	325	10	3250							3250
1.1.2	- user departments	250	20	5000							5000
1.1.3	- procurement department	325	2	650							650
1.2	Travel and expenses	225	12	2700							2700
1.3	Specification / RFP tools and programs	550	2	1100							1100
1.4	Consultancy assistance	0	0	0							0
1.5	Legal assistance	0	0	0							0
	Total selection costs			12700		0		0		0	12700
2	**Implementation process**										
	Software costs										
2.1	Application software user licenses	1025	0	0	55	56375	35	35875	0	0	92250
2.2	Software modifications	0	0	0	0	0	0	0	0	0	0
2.3	Additional licenses e.g. Citrix, EDI software	1025	0	0	5	5125	0	0	0	0	5125
2.4	Database user licenses	5200	0	0	1	5200	0	0	0	0	5200
2.5	Operating system	0	0	0	0	0	0	0	0	0	0
2.6	Additional security applications	0	0	0	0	0	0	0	0	0	0
	Sub total			0		66700		35875		0	102575

Fig. 6.1 Sample budget

3	Hardware costs							
3.1	Servers (new or upgraded, dedicated or shared)	22000	0	2	44000	0	0	44000
3.2	PC's (new or upgrades)	1200	0	25	30000	0	0	30000
3.3	Additional memory	0	0	0	0	0	0	0
3.4	Additional CPU	0	0	0	0	0	0	0
3.5	Additional processing services (temporary or permanent) e.g. via cloud services or other internal resource	0	0	0	0	0	0	0
3.6	Printers	1100	0	5	5500	0	0	5500
3.7	Scanners	0	0	0	0	0	0	0
3.8	UPS	0	0	0	0	0	0	0
3.9	Back up devices	0	0	0	0	0	0	0
3.10	Disk storage	0	0	0	0	0	0	0
	Sub total		0		79500	0	0	79500

4	Network costs							
4.1	Cabling or wireless LAN, WAN or other network	5500	0	1	5500	0	0	5500
4.2	Racks	0	0	0	0	0	0	0
4.3	Routers	0	0	0	0	0	0	0
4.4	Switching devices	0	0	0	0	0	0	0
4.5	Modems	0	0	0	0	0	0	0
4.6	Leased or dedicated lines	5150	0	1	5150	0	0	5150
4.7	Communications software	0	0	0	0	0	0	0
4.8	Internet access broadband, satellite	0	0	0	0	0	0	0
	Sub total		0		10650	0	0	10650

Fig. 6.1 (continued)

5   Labor costs

For implementation tasks e.g.: system installation, integration, tailoring, interface development, process re-engineering, report writing, functional and user testing, data conversion and documentation

5.1   Project team

		Rate		Days	Cost	Days	Cost			Total
5.1.1	Project manager	600	0	10	6000	10	6000	0	0	12000
5.1.2	Project leader	450	0	20	9000	20	9000	0	0	18000
5.1.3	Systems analysts	350	0	10	3500	0	0	0	0	3500
5.1.4	Programmers	275	0	20	5500	20	5500	0	0	11000
5.1.5	Systems testers	250	0	20	5000	30	7500	0	0	12500
5.1.6	Vendor consultants	800	0	3	2400	3	2400	0	0	4800
5.1.7	Additional team resources e.g. contractors, temporary staff, other consultants	0	0	0	0	0	0	0	0	0
5.1.8	Travel and expenses	0	0	0	0	0	0	0	0	0
	Sub total				31400		30400			61800

5.2   User team

5.2.1	User team leader	0	0	0	0	0	0	0	0	0
5.2.2	User team members	0	0	0	0	0	0	0	0	0
5.2.3	User team managers	0	0	0	0	0	0	0	0	0
	Sub total				0		0			0

5.3   Support costs

5.3.1	Client manager	450	0	4	1800	4	1800	0	0	3600
5.3.2	IS support	325	0	6	1950	6	1950	0	0	3900

Fig. 6.1 (continued)

Item	Description	Unit cost	No.	Cost	No.	Cost	No.	Cost
5.3.3	DB analyst	250	2	500	2	500	0	1000
5.3.4	Networking support	0	0	0	0	0	0	0
	Sub total		0	4250	0	4250	0	8500
5.4	**Project team and office costs**							
5.4.1	Temporary office accommodation	0	0	0	0	0	0	0
5.4.2	Furniture, stationery and supplies	0	0	0	0	0	0	0
5.4.3	Additional telephones and lines	0	0	0	0	0	0	0
5.4.4	Project tools e.g. project management software, testing programs	0	0	0	0	0	0	0
5.4.5	Project website set up and maintenance	0	0	0	0	0	0	0
5.4.6	Administrative support	0	0	0	0	0	0	0
5.4.7	Communications costs	0	0	0	0	0	0	0
5.4.8	Video teleconferencing	0	0	0	0	0	0	0
5.4.9	Printing e.g. user manuals	0	0	0	0	0	0	0
5.4.10	Project information / education / marketing materials	0	0	0	0	0	0	0
	Sub total		0	0	0	0	0	0
6	**Training**							
6.1	Technical training for implementation team (by vendor)	900	10	9000	0	0	0	9000
6.2	Training key users (by vendor)	900	4	3600	10	9000	0	12600
6.3	Temporary internal training facilities	0	0	0	0	0	0	0
6.4	Training remainder of users (internally or by vendor)	0	0	0	0	0	0	0
6.5	Training materials	125	10	1250	50	6250	0	7500
6.6	Travel and expenses to attend training	0	0	0	0	0	0	0
	Sub total			13850		15250	0	29100

Fig. 6.1 (continued)

7　Data costs

7.1	Data clean-up / de-duplication
7.2	Data archiving
	Sub total

8　Other costs

8.1	Quality Assurance
8.2	Internal audit review(s) of new system(s)
8.3	Project steering group
8.4	Decommissioning of legacy systems
8.5	Networking with other organizations, who are using / implementing the same system(s) - travel and expenses costs
8.6	Attending conferences, software vendor user groups, networking, meetings - fees, travel and expenses costs
	Sub total

9　Allocated Costs

9.1	Additional heat, air conditioning, light, power for project implementation and ongoing live running
9.2	Other allocated business costs
	Sub total

Fig. 6.1 (continued)

	Unit cost	Qty	Amount	Qty	Amount	Qty	Amount	Total
10 Contingency								
10.1 Estimated 10% of total implementation costs	0		20000		10000		0	30000
Total implementation costs	0		226350		95775		0	322125
Post Implementation Process								
11 Maintenance costs								
11.1 Annual vendor maintenance / service charges for:								
11.1.1 - software	12500	0	0	1	12500	1	12500	25000
11.1.2 - hardware	14600	0	0	0	0	0	0	0
11.1.3 - database	1200	0	0	1	1200	1	1200	2400
11.2 Internal IS support	0	0	0	0	0	0	0	0
11.3 Disaster recovery for systems and data (internally or outsource to remote location)	1100	5	5500	2	2200	2	2200	9900
Total ongoing costs	0		5500		15900		15900	37300
Project cost calculations								
Total project cost								372125
Number of users (software licenses)								90
Total project cost per user								4135

Fig. 6.1 (continued)

$150,000. However, allocating a cost across 3 years may have more value to the business than let's say a hardware alternative that would be $125,000 expensed in the first year for a cloud!! To say the least, this can be tricky!

Going with a cloud, on the other hand, would mean a rental expense for the use of the equipment and services, so the total cost per month is the total cost—there is no depreciation because there is no ownership of the asset. Whether the hardware cost can be allocated to other benefits is also questionable, but in reality it could be very important. So let's say the data center can be shared or leveraged for another system. It appears that the trend suggests that companies should avoid owning and operating their own data centers, so the cloud could be the answer.

Software

Software falls into two categories: package and developed. For the purposes of this section I focus on the package software price or license fee. Software is licensed because vendors typically do not sell the rights to the code, but rather the "right to use the package" under the rights and limitations granted by the license agreement. So you basically rent the right to use the software package so long as the organization abides by the terms and conditions of the license agreement.

More important is understanding the cost of the license. The license fee can be complex. Certainly, there will be an initial license fee to use the product—the price of the initial purchase. Then there are certain license costs that may relate to third-party utilities that the software package requires—like a database product (Oracle, for instance) that may have separate license requirements or what is known as "run-time" software, which can be programs owned by others or needed in a specific operating system for the product to run. Often such products also carry a "per user" cost, so the more concurrent users on the system, the higher the cost. The last component of cost is the software maintenance fee. While this is usually presented by the vendor as optional, it may very well not be—in the sense that if your organization does not have the maintenance you will not receive automatic upgrades, bug fixes, and general vendor support.

In terms of pricing, software packages like any product in the market are priced on two factors: (1) what the market will bear and (2) the competitive landscape. The market price is very vague at times, but is usually set by the "best of breed" in the industry. This tends to work in the same way that top luxury cars set the price. Certainly, what organizations are willing to pay is a factor, but the leader in a category of software typically leads the acceptable price. So the recommendation when budgeting the cost for the package is to survey the market and review the feature/functions of the software in the marketplace and what tends to be the price.

The competitive landscape also relates to the market but yet it is different. The competition can upset the leaders pricing, in the same way that a new car undersells what was perceived as the standard price within a class of car. We even see this at the top class, where Lexus and Acura invaded the luxury class car price which was previously dominated by the German manufacturers. The prices were lower and yet the quality was high. Such is sometimes true in the software industry as well. New technologies or open source can provide pressure on the industry leaders to lower prices—hardware does the same as we saw when the PCs began to take market share away from the mid-range computer industry. The technology industry has also been regulated by Moore's law, which predicts a doubling of processing capabilities—which again drives prices down as we saw in the PC chip market.

Other prices, like per user fees and maintenance, are more predictable. For example, the market price for maintenance is usually 15% of the "then going" license fees—meaning that your maintenance can increase over the years! Per user fees often hover in the $50–100 range per user. There are also more cost options here. For example, many software vendors offer multiple year maintenance plans. This means if you prepay 3 years of maintenance at the time of purchase organizations typically receive a huge discount. You can also reduce per unit costs by buying more users than you might need at the time of purchase.

So the general recommendations are to not only budget consistent with the leading market vendor's license prices, but also look for newcomers if there is a willingness in the organization to take more risk. The other components of package costs are more predictable, but decisions on multiyear maintenance or packaged deals should be discussed during budget time with the selection committee.

Consulting Fees

Consulting fees are usually very predictable and very much regulated by the marketplace. They are driven by the laws of supply and demand and also by the type of consultation needed. For example, when SAP implementations were very much in demand and talent availability was low, hourly rates for SAP consultants were high—almost $2,000 per day at the height of demand. Today they are much lower, say $800 per day or even lower. Consulting rates for training are also lower, perhaps $300 per day, depending on the type of training needed. However, consulting rates can be purchased in blocks, by committing to a number of days up front organizations can expect reasonable discounts from vendors. So the suggestion here is to check the market prices for comparison. This can be accomplished by calling vendors, searching the Internet, or simply working with Gartner or other research firms.

Customization Costs

There are two types of budgeting here. Vendors like to get an hourly or daily rate for their development staff. Prices vary by level with a senior programmer going for $125–150 per hour and QA people perhaps at $75–100 per hour. Budgeting for customizations on an hourly basis is bad business and can become an exposure to exceeding your budget. Organizations should negotiate fixed prices or "not to exceed" costs for custom modifications. Unfortunately, organizations may not know the extent of the custom modifications required until the analysis and design is completed. There are two choices then: (1) create a budget to do the analysis and design before determining the budget for package customizations or (2) budget based on a limit—perhaps an upper limit amount that the organization is willing to spend. This may not be a bad option as it sets expectations for the selection team and user community. It might also suggest that if the package exceeds this budget amount then perhaps it is not the right fit.

The Balanced Scorecard as a Budget Tool

Another method that can be used to validate budget vs. user needs is a management tool called the balanced scorecard. The balanced scorecard was introduced by Robert Kaplan and David Norton in the early 1990s as a tool to solve measurement problems. An organization's ability to develop and operationalize its intangible assets has become more and more a critical component for success. The balanced scorecard can also be used as a solution for measuring IT outcomes that do not always have obvious financial costs associated with them. Furthermore, the balanced scorecard is a "living" document that can be modified, as certain objectives or measurements require change. This is a critical advantage because as I have demonstrated, technology projects often change in scope and in objectives as a result of internal and external factions.

The ultimate value then of the balanced scorecard in this context is to provide a means for evaluating cost vs. need, not only for measuring completion against set targets, but also for defining how expected transformations map onto the strategic objectives of the organization. In effect it is the ability of the organization to execute its strategy toward implementing an application software solution. Before explaining the details of how a balanced scorecard can be applied, I offer Fig. 6.2 that shows exactly where the scorecard fits into the overall picture of implementing package software solutions into concrete costs vs. benefits.

The generic objectives of a balanced scorecard are designed to create a strategy-focused organization. Thus, all of the objectives and measurements should be derived from the organization's vision and strategy (Kaplan & Norton, 2001). These measurements are based on the fundamental principles of any strategically focused organization and on alignment and focus. Kaplan and Norton defined these principles as the core of the balanced scorecard:

1. *Translate the strategy to operational terms*: this principle includes two major components that allow an organization to define its strategy from a cause-and-effect perspective using a strategy map and scorecard. Thus the strategy map and its corresponding balanced scorecard provide the basic measurement system.
2. *Align the organization to the strategy:* Kaplan and Norton defined this principle as favoring synergies among organizational departments that allow communities of practice to have a shared view and common understanding of their roles.
3. *Make strategy everyone's everyday job:* this principle supports the notion of a learning organization that requires everyone's participation, from the CEO to

Fig. 6.2 Balanced scorecard
Source: Kaplan and Norton
(2001).

Mobilize Change
through Executive
Leadership

Balanced

Translate the
Strategy to
Operational Terms

Strategy

Make Strategy a
Continual Process

Scorecard

Align
Organizational
to the Strategy

Make Startegy
Everyone's Job

clerical levels. To accomplish this mission the members of the organization must be aware of business strategy, individuals may need "personal" scorecards and a matching reward system for accomplishing the strategy.

4. *Make strategy a continual process*: this process requires the linking of important yet fundamental components including organizational learning, budgeting, management reviews, and a process of adaptation. Much of this principle falls into the areas of learning organization theories that link learning and strategy in ongoing perpetual cycles.

5. *Mobilize change through executive leadership:* this principle stresses the need for a strategy-focused organization that incorporates the involvement of senior management and can mobilize the organization and provide sponsorship to the overall process.

Using the core balanced scorecard schematic, I have modified it to operate with package software implementations as shown in Fig. 6.3.

1. *Evaluation of technology*: the first step is to have an infrastructure that can determine how technology fits into a specific strategy. Once this is targeted, the evaluation team needs to define it in operational terms.

2. *Align technology with business strategy*: once technology is evaluated, it must be integrated into the business strategy. This involves ascertaining whether the addition of technology will change the current business strategy.

3. *Make technology projects part of communities of practice:* affected communities need to be strategically aware of the project. Organizational structures must determine how they distribute rewards and objectives across departments.

4. *Phased-in technology implementation*: short-term and long-term project objectives are based on driver and supporter life cycles. This will allow organizational transformation phases to be linked to implementation milestones.

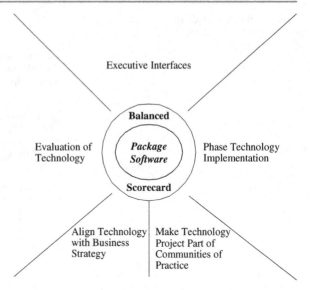

Fig. 6.3 Modified scorecard for the SDLC

5. *Executive interface:* CEO and senior managers act as executive sponsors and as project champions. This can also be related to the team leaders across the business lines.

The balanced scorecard ultimately provides a framework to view strategy from four different measures:

1. *Financial:* ROI and risk continue to be important components of strategic evaluation.
2. *Customer:* this involves the strategic part of how to create value for the organization's customers.
3. *Internal business processes*: this relates to the business processes that provide both customer satisfaction and operational efficiency.
4. *Learning and growth:* this encompasses the priorities and infrastructure to support organizational transformation through the implementation of the application software package.

The above generic balanced scorecard framework needs to be extended to address the needs of software implementations. I propose the following adjustments:

1. *Financial:* requires the inclusion of indirect benefits from technology, particularly as Lucas (1999) specified, in non-monetary methods of evaluating ROI. Risk must also be factored in based on specific issues for each technology project.
2. *Customer:* technology-based products are integrated with customer needs and provide direct customer package interfaces. Further, Web systems that use the Internet are very dependent on consumer use. As such, technology can modify organizational strategy because of its direct effect on the customer interface.
3. *Internal business processes:* technology requires business process reengineering (BPR), which is the process of reevaluating existing internal norms and behaviors

before designing a new system. This new evaluation process will addresses customers, operational efficiencies, and cost.

4. *Learning and growth*: organizational learning techniques, under the umbrella of ROD, need to be applied on an ongoing and evolutionary basis.

The major portion of the balanced scorecard strategy is in its initial design, that is, in translating the strategy or, as in the package software scorecard, the evaluation of technology. During this phase a strategy map and an actual balanced scorecards are created. This process should begin by designing a balanced scorecard that articulates the business strategy. Remember that every organization needs to build a strategy that is unique and based on its evaluation of the external and internal situations (Olve, Petri, Roy, and Roy, 2003). To clarify the definition of this strategy it is easier to consider drawing the scorecard initially in the form of a strategy map. A generic strategy map essentially defines the components of each perspective, showing specific strategies within each one, as shown in Fig. 6.4.

Balanced scorecard, particularly using a strategy map, allows practitioners to reconcile how changes will affect the entire plan.

Another important component of the balanced scorecard, and the reason why I choose to use it as the measurement model for budgeting, is its applicability to the SDLC. In particular, the learning and growth perspective shows how the balanced scorecard ensures that learning and strategy are linked in organizational development efforts and ultimately link back to costs vs. benefits.

Implementing balanced scorecards can be a critical part of the project, specifically in who does the work, what the roles are, and who has the responsibility for

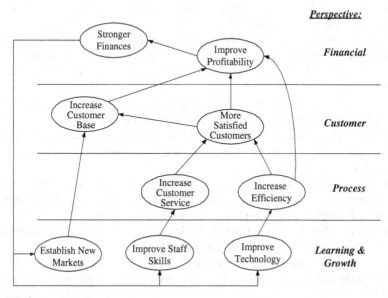

Fig. 6.4 Strategy map
Source: Olve et al. (2003).

operating the scorecards. While many companies use consultants to guide them, it is important to recognize that balanced scorecards reflect the unique features and functions of the company. As such, the rank and file need to be involved with the design and support of balanced scorecards.

Every business unit that has a scorecard needs to have someone assigned to it, someone accountable for it. A special taskforce may often be required to launch the training for staff and to agree on how the scorecard should be designed and supported. It is advisable that the scorecard be implemented using some application software and made available on an Internet network. This provides a number of benefits, namely:

- Reduces paper and/or local files that might get lost or not be secured
- Allows for easy "role-up" of multiple scorecards to a summary level
- Access via the Internet (using an external secured hookup); allows the scorecard to be maintained from multiple locations. This is particularly attractive for staff members and management who travel

According to Olve et al. (2003), there are five primary responsibilities that can support balanced scorecards:

1. *Business stakeholders*: this is typically a senior manager who is responsible for the group that is using the scorecard. This individual is an advocate of using scorecards and requires compliance where deemed necessary. Stakeholders use scorecards to help them manage the life cycle of a technology implementation.
2. *Scorecard designers*: these individuals are responsible for the look and feel of the scorecard as well as its content. To some extent the designers set standards for "look and feel," text, and terminology. In certain situations the scorecard designers have dual roles as project managers. Their use of scorecards helps them understand how the technology will operate.
3. *Information providers:* these people collect, measure, and report on the data in the balanced scorecard. This function can be implemented with personnel on the business unit level or from a central services department. Reporting information often requires support from IT staff, so it makes sense to have someone from IT handle this responsibility. Information providers use the scorecard to perform the measurement of project performance and the handling of data.
4. *Learning pilots:* these individuals link the scorecard to organizational learning. This is particularly important when measuring organizational transformation and individual development.

The size and complexity of an organization will ultimately determine the exact configuration of roles and responsibilities that are needed to implement balance scorecards. Perhaps, the most applicable variables are as follows:

- *Competence:* having individuals who are knowledgeable about the business and its processes as well as knowledgeable about IT.
- *Availability:* individuals must be made available and appropriately accommodated in the budget. Balanced scorecards that do not have sufficient staffing will fail.
- *Executive management support:* as with most technology projects, there needs to be a project advocate at the executive level.

- *Enthusiasm:* implementing balance scorecards requires a certain energy and excitement level from the staff and their management. This is one of those intangible, yet invaluable variables.

The balanced scorecard can ultimately become the tools that allow the management team to (1) better determine how much the budget will be and associate that with expected business benefits and (2) a method to measure progress and fight off scope creep.

Problems and Exercises

1. What is the purpose of a budget? Be specific.
2. What is post-implementation?
3. Explain the difference between a regular expense and a capital expense.
4. What is the balanced scorecard? How can it assist in developing a budget?
5. How does a strategy map contribute to the understanding of everyone's role in a proposed new system?
6. What is scope creep? How does the balanced scorecard address the problem?
7. What is ROI? How does it relate to a controlled budget?

References

Kaplan, R. S., & Norton, D. P. (2001). *The strategy-focused organization.* Cambridge, MA: Harvard University Press.

Lucas, H. C. (1999). *Information technology and the productivity paradox.* New York: Oxford University Press.

Olve, N., Petri, C., Roy, J., & Roy, S. (2003). *Making scorecards actionable: Balancing strategy and control.* New York: Wiley.

Ryan, R., & Raducha-Grace, T. (2010). *The business of IT: How to improve service and lower cost.* Boston: IBM Press.

Analysis Methods and Tools

The Concept of the Logical Equivalent

The primary mission of an analyst or systems designer is to extract the physical requirements of the users and convert them to software. All software can trace its roots to a physical act or a physical requirement. A physical act can be defined as something that occurs in the interaction of people, that is, people create the root requirements of most systems, especially those in business. For example, when Mary tells us that she receives invoices from vendors and pays them 30 days later, she is explaining her physical activities during the process of receiving and paying invoices. When the analyst creates a technical specification, which represents Mary's physical requirements, the specification is designed to allow for the translation of her physical needs into an automated environment. We know that software must operate within the confines of a computer, and such systems must function on the basis of logic. The logical solution does not always treat the process using the same procedures employed in the physical world. In other words, the software system implemented to provide the functions, which Mary does physically, will probably work differently and more efficiently than Mary herself. Software, therefore, can be thought of as a logical equivalent of the physical world. This abstraction, which I call the concept of the logical equivalent (LE), is a process that analysts must use to create effective requirements of the needs of a system. The LE can be compared to a schematic of a plan or a diagram of how a technical device works. At the heart of any SDLC success is the ability to understand the user's needs.

The success ratio for creating a concise and accurate schematic of the system, whether for package software or developed in-house, will be directly proportional to how well you master the concept of the logical equivalent. Very often requirements are developed by analysts using various methods that do not always contain a basis for consistency, reconciliation, and maintenance. There is usually far too much prose used as opposed to specific diagramming standards that are employed by engineers. After all, we are engineering a system through the development of software

A.M. Langer, *Guide to Software Development*,
DOI 10.1007/978-1-4471-2300-2_7, © Springer-Verlag London Limited 2012

applications. The most critical step in obtaining the LE is the understanding of the process of functional decomposition. Functional decomposition is the process of finding the most basic parts of a system, like defining all the parts of a car so that it can be built. It would be possible not from looking at a picture of the car, but rather at a schematic of all the functionally decomposed parts. Developing and engineering software are no different.

Below is an example of an analogous process using functional decomposition with its application to the LE:

In obtaining the physical information from the user, there are a number of modeling tools that can be used. Each tool provides a specific function to derive the LE. The word "derive" has special meaning here. It relates to the process of long division or the process or formula we apply when dividing one number by another. Consider the following example:

$$
\begin{array}{r}
\underline{256 \quad \text{remainder } 4} \quad \} \text{ Result or Answer} \\
5 \overline{\smash{\big)}\ 1284} \quad\quad\quad \} \text{ Problem to Solve} \\
\underline{10} \\
284 \\
\underline{25} \quad\quad\quad\quad\quad \} \text{ Formula applied to produce result or answer} \\
34 \\
\underline{30} \\
4
\end{array}
$$

The above example shows the formula that is applied to a division problem. We call this formula long division. It provides the answer, and if we change any portion of the problem, we simply reapply the formula and generate a new result. Most importantly, once we have obtained the answer, the value of the formula steps is only one of documentation. That is, if someone questioned the validity of the result, we could show them the formula to prove that the answer was correct (based on the input).

Now let us apply long division to obtain the LE via functional decomposition. The following is a result of an interview with Joe, a bookkeeper, about his physical procedure for handling bounced checks.

Joe the bookkeeper receives bounced checks from the bank. He fills out a Balance Correction Form and forwards it to the Correction Department so that the outstanding balance can be corrected. Joe sends a bounced check letter to the customer requesting a replacement check plus a $15.00 penalty (this is now included as part of the outstanding balance). Bounced checks are never redeposited.

The appropriate modeling tool to use in this situation is a data flow diagram (DFD). A DFD is a tool that shows how data enter and leave a particular process.

The process we are looking at with Joe is the handling of the bounced check. A DFD has four possible components:

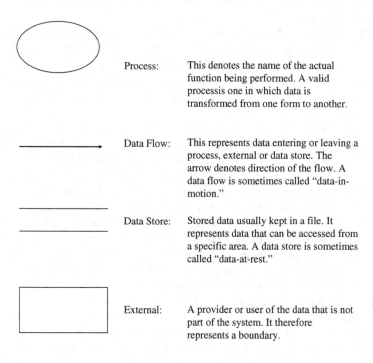

Process: This denotes the name of the actual function being performed. A valid processis one in which data is transformed from one form to another.

Data Flow: This represents data entering or leaving a process, external or data store. The arrow denotes direction of the flow. A data flow is sometimes called "data-in-motion."

Data Store: Stored data usually kept in a file. It represents data that can be accessed from a specific area. A data store is sometimes called "data-at-rest."

External: A provider or user of the data that is not part of the system. It therefore represents a boundary.

The LE of Joe's procedure using DFD tools is shown in Fig. 7.1.

Figure 7.1 shows that bounced checks arrive from the Bank, the Account Master file is updated, the Correction Department is informed, and Customers receive a letter. The Bank, Correction Department, and Customers are considered "outside"

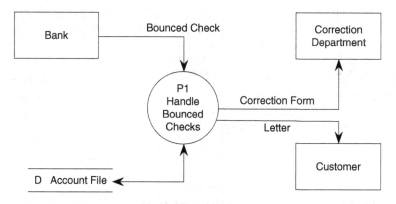

Fig. 7.1 Data flow diagram for handling bounced checks

the system and are therefore represented logically as Externals. This diagram is considered to be at the first level or "Level 1" of functional decomposition. You will find that all modeling tools employ a method to functionally decompose. DFDs use a method called "Leveling."

The question is whether we have reached the most basic parts of this process or should we level further. Many analysts suggest that a fully decomposed DFD should have only one data flow input and one data flow output. Our diagram currently has many inputs and outputs and therefore it can be leveled further. The result of functionally decomposing to the second level (Level 2) is shown in Fig. 7.2.

Notice that the functional decomposition shows us that Process 1: Handling Bounced Checks is really made up of two subprocesses called 1.1, Update Balance and 1.2, Send Letter. The box surrounding the two processes within the Externals reflects them as components of the previous or parent level. The double-sided arrow in Level 1 is now broken down to two separate arrows going in different directions because it is used to connect Processes 1.1 and 1.2. The new level is more functionally decomposed and a better representation of the LE.

Once again we must ask ourselves whether Level 2 can be further decomposed. The answer is yes. Process 1.1 has two outputs to one input. On the other hand, Process 1.2 has one input and one output and is therefore complete. Process 1.2 is said to be at the Functional Primitive, a DFD that cannot be decomposed further. Therefore, only Process 1.1 will be decomposed.

Let us decompose Process 1.1 as shown in Fig. 7.3.

Process 1.1 is now broken down into two subprocesses: 1.1.1, Update Account Master and 1.1.2, Inform Correction Department. Process 1.1.2 is a Functional Primitive since it has one input and one output. Process 1.1.1 is also considered a Functional Primitive because the "Bounced Check Packet" flow is between the two processes and is used to show connectivity only. Functional decomposition is at Level 3 and is now complete.

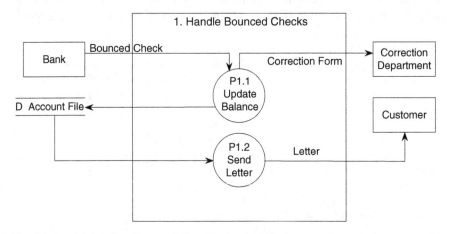

Fig. 7.2 Level 2 data flow diagram for handling bounced checks

Fig. 7.3 Level 3 data flow diagram for handling bounced checks

The result of functional decomposition is shown in Fig. 7.4.

As in long division, only the complete result, represented in Fig. 7.4, is used as the answer. The preceding steps are formulas that we use to get to the lowest, simplest representation of the logical equivalent. Levels 1–3 are used only for documentation of how the final DFD was determined.

The logical equivalent is an excellent method that allows analysts and systems designers to organize information obtained from users and to systematically derive the most fundamental representation of their process. It also alleviates unnecessary pressure to immediately understand the detailed flows and provides documentation of how the final schematic was developed.

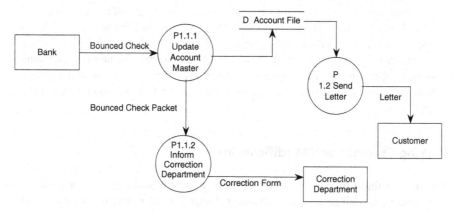

Fig. 7.4 Functionally decomposed Level 3 data flow diagram for handling bounced checks

Tools of Structured Analysis

Now that we have established the importance and goals of the logical equivalent, we can turn to a discussion of the methods available to assist the analyst. These methods serve as the tools to create the best models in any given situation and thus the most exact logical equivalent. The tools of the analyst are something like those of a surgeon, who uses only the most appropriate instruments during an operation. It is important to understand that the surgeon is sometimes faced with choices about which surgical instruments to use; particularly with new procedures, there is sometimes disagreement among surgeons about which instruments are the most effective. The choice of tools for analysis and data processing is no different; indeed, it can vary more and be more confusing. The medical profession, like many others, is governed by its own ruling bodies. The American Medical Association and the American College of Physicians and Surgeons, as well as state and federal regulators, represent a source of standards for surgeons. Such a controlling body does not exist in the data processing industry, nor does it appear likely that one will arise in the near future. Thus, the industry has tried to standardize among its own leaders. The result of such efforts has usually been that the most dominant companies and organizations create standards to which others are forced to comply. For example, Microsoft has established itself as an industry leader by virtue of its software domination. Here, Might is Right!

Since there are no real formal standards in the industry, the analysis tools discussed here will be presented on the basis of both their advantages and their shortcomings. It is important then to recognize that neither analysis tool (or methodology for that matter) can do the entire job, nor is any perfect at what it does. To determine the appropriate tool, analysts must fully understand the environment, the technical expertise of users, and the time constraints imposed on the project. By "environment" we mean the existing system and technology, computer operations, and the logistics—both technically and geographically—of the new system. The treatment of the user interface should remain consistent with the guidelines discussed in Chapter 2.

The problem of time constraints is perhaps the most critical of all. The tools you would ideally like to apply to a project may not fit the time frame allotted. What happens, then, if there is not enough time? The analyst is now faced with selecting a second choice tool that undoubtedly will not be as effective as the first one would have been. There is also the question of how tools are implemented, that is, can a hybrid of a tool be used when time constraints prevent full implementation of the desired tool.

Making Changes and Modifications

Within the subject of analysis tools is the component of maintenance modeling or how to apply modeling tools when making changes or enhancements to an existing product. Maintenance modeling falls into two categories:

1. *Pre-modeled*: where the existing system already has models that can be used to effect the new changes to the software.
2. *Legacy system*: where the existing system has never been modeled; any new modeling will therefore be incorporating analysis tools for the first time.

Pre-modeled

Simply put, a pre-modeled product is already in a structured format. A structured format is one that employs a specific format and methodology such as the data flow diagram.

The most challenging aspects of changing pre-modeled tools are

1. keeping them consistent with their prior versions and
2. implementing a version control system that provides an audit trail of the analysis changes and how they differ from the previous versions. Many professionals in the industry call this version control; however, care should be taken in specifying whether the version control is used for the maintenance of analysis tools. Unfortunately, version control can be used in other contexts, most notably in the tracking of program versions and software documentation. For these cases, special products exist in the market which provide special automated "version control" features. We are not concerned here with these products but rather with the procedures and processes that allow us to incorporate changes without losing the prior analysis documentation. This kind of procedure can be considered consistent with the long division example in which each time the values change, we simply reapply the formula (methodology) to calculate the new answer. Analysis version control must therefore have the ability to take the modifications made to the software and integrate them with all the existing models as necessary.

Being Consistent

It is difficult to change modeling methods and/or CASE tools in the middle of the life cycle of a software product. One of our main objectives then is to try avoiding doing so. How? Of course, the simple answer is to select the right tools and CASE software the first time. However, we all make mistakes, and more importantly, there are new developments in systems architecture that may make a new CASE product attractive. You would be wise to foresee this possibility and prepare for inconsistent tools implementation. The best offense here is to:

• ensure that your CASE product has the ability to transport models through an ASCII file or cut/paste method. Many have interfaces via an "export" function. Here, at least, the analyst can possibly convert the diagrams and data elements to another product.
• keep a set of diagrams and elements that can be used to establish a link going forward, that is, a set of manual information that can be re-input to another tool. This may be accomplished by simply having printed documentation of the diagrams; however, experience has shown that it is difficult to keep such information up to

date. Therefore, the analyst should ensure that there is a procedure for printing the most current diagrams and data elements.

Should the organization decide to use different tools, e.g., process dependency diagrams instead of data flow diagrams, or a different methodology such as crow's foot method in entity relational diagramming, then the analyst must implement a certain amount of reengineering. This means mapping the new modeling tools to the existing ones to ensure consistency and accuracy. This is no easy task, and it is strongly suggested that you document the diagrams so you can reconcile them.

Version Control

This book is not intended to focus on the generic aspects of version control; however, structured methods must have audit trail. When a new process is changed, a directory should be created for the previous version. The directory name typically consists of the version and date such as xyz1.21295, where xyz is the name of the product or program, 1.2 the version, and 1295 the version date. In this way previous versions can be easily recreated or viewed. Of course, saving a complete set of each version may not be feasible or may be too expensive (in terms of disk space, etc.). In these situations, it is advisable to backup the previous version in such a manner as to allow for easy restoration. In any case, a process must exist, and it is crucial that there be a procedure to do backups periodically.

Legacy Systems

Legacy systems usually reside on mainframe computers and were developed using 3GL[1] software applications, the most typical being COBOL. Unfortunately, few of these systems were developed using structured tools. Without question, these are the most common systems undergoing change today in many organizations. All software is composed of two fundamental components: processes and data. Processes are the actual logic and algorithms required by the system. Data, on the other hand, represent the information that is stored and used by the processes. The question for the analyst is, how to obtain the equivalent processes and data from the legacy system? Short of considering a complete rewrite, there are two basic approaches, namely, the data approach and the process approach.

The Data Approach

Conversion of legacy systems for purposes of structured changes requires the modeling of the existing programs to allow for the use of analysis tools. The first

---

[1] 3GL refers to Third Generation Language. These programming languages belong to a family of design that typically uses compilers to transform a higher-level language into assembly code for the target computer.

step in this endeavor is the modeling of the existing files and their related data structures. Many 3GL applications may not exist in a relational or other database format. In either case, it is necessary to collect all of the data elements that exist in the system. To accomplish this, the analyst will typically need a conversion program that will collect the elements and import them into a CASE tool. If the data are stored in a relational or database system, this can be handled through many CASE products via a process known as reverse engineering. Here, the CASE product will allow the analyst to select the incoming database, and the product will then automatically import the data elements. It is important to note that these reverse engineering features require that the incoming database is SQL (structured query language) compatible. Should the incoming data file be of a non-database format, i.e., a flat file,[2] then a conversion program will need to be used. Once again, most CASE tools will have features that will list the required input data format.

Figure 7.5 is a sample of the reengineering capabilities of a CASE tool.

Fig. 7.5 Reverse engineering using a CASE product

---

[2] A file consisting of records of a single record type, in which there is no embedded structure information governing relationships between records. Microsoft Press, Computer Dictionary, Second Edition, p. 169.

Once the data have been loaded into the CASE product, the various data models can be constructed. This process will be discussed further in Chapter 8.

Although we have shown above a tool for loading the data, the question still remains, How do we find all the data elements? Using COBOL as an example, one could take the following steps:

1. Identify all of the file description (FD) tables in the COBOL application programs. Should they exist in an external software product like Librarian, the analyst can import the tables from that source. Otherwise the actual file tables will need to be extracted and converted from the COBOL application program source. This procedure is not difficult; it is simply another step that typically requires conversion utilities.
2. Scan all working storage sections (see Fig. 7.6) for data elements that are not defined in the file description section. This occurs very often when COBOL programmers do not define the actual elements until they are read into a working storage section of the program. This situation, of course, requires further research, but it can be detected by scanning the code.
3. Look for other data elements that have been defined in working storage that should be stored as permanent data. Although this can be a difficult task, the worst case scenario would involve the storing of redundant data.
4. Once the candidate elements have been discovered, ensure that appropriate descriptions are added. This process allows the analyst to actually start defining elements so that decisions can be made during logical data modeling.

The Process Approach

The most effective way to model existing programs is the most direct way, that is, the old-fashioned way: start reading and analyzing the code. Although this approach may seem very crude, it is actually tremendously effective and productive. Almost all programming languages contain enough structure to allow for identification of input and output of files and reports. By identifying the data and reports, the analyst can establish a good data flow diagram as shown in Fig. 7.7.

```
WORKING-STORAGE SECTION.
01 PAYROLL-RECORD.
      05     NAME.
             10     INITIAL-1              PIC X.
             10     LAST-NAME             PIC X(20).
      05     DATE-OF-HIRE.
             10     MONTH-OF-HIRE         PIC 99.
             10     DAY-OF-HIRE           PIC 99.
             10     YEAR-OF-HIRE          PIC 99.
      05     PAY-NUMBER                   PIC 9(6).
```

Fig. 7.6 Working storage section of a COBOL program

```
DATA DIVISION.
FILE SECTION.
FD      PAYROLL-FILE
        LABEL RECORDS ARE OMITTED.
01      PAYROLL-RECORD.
        05    I-PAYROLL-NUMBER              PIC X(5).
        05    I-NAME                        PIC X(20).
        05    I-HOURS-WORKED                PIC 99V9.
        05    FILLER                        PIC XXX.
        05    I-PAYRATE                     PIC 99V999.
        05    I-DEPENDENTS                  PIC 99.
        05    FILLER                        PIC X(20).


FD      REPORT-FILE
        LABEL RECORDS ARE OMITTED.
01      REPORT-RECORD.
        05    O-PAYROLL-NUMBER              PIC X(5).
        05    FILLER                        PIC XX.
        05    O-NAME                        PIC X(20).
        05    FILLER                        PIC XX.
        05    O-HOURS-WORKED                PIC 99.9.
        05    FILLER                        PIC XX.
        05    O-PAYRATE                     PIC 99.999.
        05    FILLER                        PIC XX.
        05    O-DEPENDENTS                  PIC 99.
        05    FILLER                        PIC XX.
        05    O-GROSS-PAY                   PIC 999.99.
        05    FILLER                        PIC XX.
        05    O-TAX                         PIC 999.99.
        05    FILLER                        PIC XX.
        05    O-NET-PAY                     PIC 999.99.
```

Fig. 7.7 Input data and report layouts of a COBOL program

Figure 7.7 shows two file description (FD) tables that are defined in a COBOL program. The first table defines the input file layout of a payroll record and the second is the layout of the output payroll report. This is translated into a DFD as shown in Fig. 7.8.

Fig. 7.8 Translated COBOL file descriptions into a data flow diagram

In addition, depending on the program language, many input and output data and reports must be defined in the application code in specific sections of the program. Such is true in COBOL and many other 3GL products. Furthermore, many 4GL products force input and output verbs to be used when manipulating databases. This is very relevant to any products that use embedded SQL to do input/output. The main point here is that you can produce various utility programs ("quick and dirty," as they call them) to enhance the accuracy and speed of identifying an existing program's input and output processing.

Once the flows in the data flow diagram are complete, the next step is to define the actual program logic or what is typically called the process specifications (discussed later in this chapter). Once again there is no shortcut to save you going through the code program by program. There are some third-party software tools on the market that can provide assistance, but these tend to be very programming language specific. Although the manual method may seem overwhelming, it can be accomplished successfully and will often provide great long-term benefits. Many companies will bring in part-time college interns and other clerical assistance to get this done. It should be noted that a CASE tool is almost always required to provide a place to document logic. This is especially important if the CASE tool will be used to generate actual program code. Further specifics regarding analyzing legacy systems are discussed in Chapter 9.

Specification Formats

An ongoing challenge for many IS and software firms is the question: What is a good specification? Many books written about analysis tools tend to avoid answering this question directly. When addressing the quality of a process specification, we must ultimately accept the inevitable prognosis that we can no longer be exclusively graphical. Although Yourdon and DeMarco[3] argued that structured tools needed to be graphical, the essence of a specification is in its ability to define the algorithms of the application program itself. It is therefore impossible to avoid writing a form of pseudocode. Pseudocode is essentially a generic representation of how the real code must execute. Ultimately, the analyst must be capable of developing clear and technically correct algorithms. The methods and styles of process specifications are outlined in the following pages. The level of technical complexity of these specifications varies based on a number of issues:

1. The technical competence of the analyst. Ultimately, the analyst must have the ability to write algorithms to be most effective.
2. The complexity of the specification itself. The size and scope of specifications will vary and as a result so will the organization of the requirements.

---

[3] Yourdon, Ed, Modern Structured Analysis and DeMarco, Tom, Structured Analysis and System Specification focused on the importance of using graphic diagrams wherever possible.

3. The type of the specifications required. There are really two levels of spec-ifications: business and programming. The business specification is very prose-oriented and is targeted for review by a non-technical user. Its main pur-pose is to gain confirmation from the user community prior to investing in the more specific and technical programming specification. The programming spec-ification, on the other hand, needs to contain the technical definition of the algorithms and is targeted for technical designers and programmers.
4. The competence of the programming staff as well as the confidence that the analyst has in that staff. The size and capabilities of the programming resources will usually be directly proportional to the emphasis that the analyst will need to place on the specifics and quality needed for a process specification.

Although the alternative techniques for developing a process specification are further discussed in Chapter 3, Fig. 7.9 should put into perspective the approach to decide the best format and style of communication. It is important to understand that overlooking the process specification and its significance to the success of the project can have catastrophic effects on the entire development effort. Figure 7.9 reflects the type of specification suggested based on the technical skills of the users.

Figures 7.10 and 7.11 are sample business and programming specifications, respectively, that depict the flow from a user specification to the detailed program logic.

High-Level Non-Technical Users	Technically Literate Users	Very Technical Users or MIS Personnel
Business Specification in Prose	Business Specification in Prose	No need for separate Business Specification
Do not show Programming Specification	Show and review Programming Specification	Incorporate Business Spec with Programming Specification

Fig. 7.9 Types of process specifications based on user computer literacy

Client:	Date: 9/5/11
XYZ Corporation	
Application:	Supersedes:
Operations Database	
Subject:	Author:
Contact Management	A. Langer
Process:	Page:
Overview - Business Spec	1 of 2

Overview

The Contact Management Process will allow users to add, modify or delete specific contacts. Contacts will be linked to various tables including Company. A Contact refers to a person who is related to XYZ for business reasons. It can be a Client, a Vendor, a consultant, a person involved in a negotiation, etc.

Contact General Information:

The Database must allow for the centralization of all the contacts handled by all the departments in XYZ.
The database and screens will be focused on the following information component groupings:

Basic Information
This is the minimum data requirement and includes such elements as Name, Title, Organization, Phone, Fax, Address, Country, etc.

Contact Profile Information
Further qualification and related elements. Relations include:

- department
- type of client
- nature of client (primary, technical)
- interest of prospect
- importance of client
- memberships (FTUG)
- FT employee

> *This is a Business Specification which reflects the overall requirements in prose format. Its focus is to provide the user who is not technical with a document that they can authorize. This Business Specification should then point to the detailed programming logic that is shown below.*

Fig. 7.10 Sample business specification

Client: XYZ Company	Date: 9/15/11
Application: Contact Management	Supersedes: 9/5/11
Subject: Program Specification Detail	Author: A. Langer
Spec-ID FTCM01 - Add/Modify Screen Processing	Page: 1 of 1

Process Flow Description:
The user will input information in the top form. At a minimum, at least the Last Name or Contact ID will be entered. The system must check a Security indicator prior to allowing a user to modify a Contact. The Security will be by Department or Everyone. Therefore, if the Modify button is selected and the user is restricted by a different department, Display:

" Access Denied, not eligible to modify, Department Restriction"

If Security authorized, the Add/Modify Button will activate the following business rules:

If Contact-ID (cntid) not blank
    Find match and replace entered data into record
    If no match display "Invalid Contact-ID" and refresh cursor

This area actually states the algorithm required by the program. It is in a format called Pseudocode" meaning "false code." This type of logic resembles Cobol format.

If Contact-ID (cntid) Blank and Last-Name (cntlname) Blank then
    Display " Contact-ID or Last-Name must be entered"
    Place Cursor at Contact-ID (cntid) entry.

If Contact-ID (cntid) Blank and Last-Name (cntlname) + First-Name (cntfname) is Duplicate
    Display Window to show matches so that user can determine if contact already in system
    If user selects the Add Anyway button
        assume new contact with same name and assign new Contact-ID (cntid)
    else
        upon selection bring in existing data and close window.
Else
    Create new record with all new information fields and assign Contact-ID (cntid)

If Company button activated
    Prompt user for Company-ID (cmpcd) and/or Company-Name (cmpna)
    If duplicate
        link foreign-key pointer to matched company
    else
        add Company-Name (cntcmpna) to Contact Table only
        Display "You must use Company Screen to Link, Company Master File Not Updated"

Fig. 7.11 Sample programming specification

Problems and Exercises

1. Describe the concept of the logical equivalent as it relates to defining the requirements of a system.
2. What is the purpose of functional decomposition? How is the leveling of a DFD consistent with this concept?
3. How does long division depict the procedures of decomposition? Explain.
4. What is a legacy system?

5. Processes and data represent the two components of any software application. Explain the alternative approaches to obtain process and data information from a legacy system.
6. What is reverse engineering? How can it be used to build a new system?
7. Why is analysis version control important?
8. Explain the procedures for developing a DFD from an existing program.
9. What is the purpose of a process specification? Explain.
10. Outline the differences between a business specification and a programming specification. What is their relationship, if any?

Part II
Development Architecture

Creating Requirement Documents Using Analysis Tools

Chapter 7 discussed the concept of the logical equivalent, justifying and defining it by showing a functional decomposition example using data flow diagrams. In this section, we will expand upon the capabilities of the DFD by explaining its purpose, advantages, and disadvantages (described later as the good, the bad, and the ugly) and most important: how to draw and use it.

Purpose

Yourdon's original concept of the DFD was that it was a way to represent a process graphically. A process can be defined as a vehicle that changes or transforms data. The DFD therefore becomes a method of showing users strictly from a logical perspective of how data travel through their function and are transformed. The DFD should be used in lieu of a descriptive prose representation of a user's process. Indeed, many analysts are familiar with the frustrations of the meeting where users attend to provide feedback on a specification prepared in prose. These specifications are often long descriptions of the processes. We ask users to review it, but most will not have had the chance to do so before the meeting, and those who have, may not recollect all the issues. The result? Users and analysts are not in a position to properly address the needs of the system, and the meeting is less productive than planned. This typically leads to more meetings and delays. More importantly, the analyst has never provided an environment in which the user can be walked through the processes. Conventional wisdom says that people remember 100% of what they see, but only 50% of what they read. The graphical representation of the DFD can provide users with an easily understood view of the system.[1]

The DFD also establishes the boundary of a process. This is accomplished with two symbols: the terminator (external) and the data store. As we will see, both represent data that originate or end at a particular point.

---

[1] Yourdon (1989, pp. 134–135).

A.M. Langer, *Guide to Software Development*,
DOI 10.1007/978-1-4471-2300-2_8, © Springer-Verlag London Limited 2012

The DFD also serves as the first step toward the design of the system blueprint. What do we mean by a blueprint? Let us consider the steps taken to build a house. When we want to build a house, the first step is to contact a professional who knows how to do design. We call this individual an architect. The architect is responsible for listening to the homebuilder and drawing a conceptual view of the house that the homebuilder wants. The result is typically two drawings. The first is a prototype drawing of the house, representing how the house will appear to the homebuilder. The second is the blueprint which represents the engineering requirements. Although the homebuilder may look at the blueprint, it is meant primarily for the builder or contractor who will actually construct the house. What has the architect accomplished? The homebuyer has a view of the house to verify the design, and the builder has the specifications for construction.

Let us now translate this process to that of designing software. In this scenario, the analyst is the architect and the user is the homebuyer. The meeting between the architect and the homebuyer translates into the requirements session which will render two types of output: a business requirements outline and prototype of the way the system will function and a schematic represented by modeling tools for programmers. The former represents the picture of the house and the latter the blueprint for the builder. Designing and building systems, then, is no different conceptually from building a house. The DFD is one of the first—if not the first—tools that the analyst will use for drawing graphical representations of the user's requirements. It is typically used very early in the design process when the user requirements are not clearly and logically defined.

Figures 8.1 and 8.2 show the similarities between the functions of an architect and those of an analyst.

How do we begin to construct the DFD for a given process? The following five steps serve as a guideline:

1. Draw a bubble to represent the process you are about to define.
2. Ask yourself what thing(s) initiate the process: what is coming in? You will find it advantageous to be consistent in where you show process inputs. Try to model them to the left of the process. You will later be able to immediately define your

Designing the House

| Drawing | Architect | Blueprint |

Fig. 8.1 The interfaces required to design and build a house

Designing the System

| Prototype | Analyst | DFD |

Fig. 8.2 The interfaces required to design and build a system

process inputs when looking back at your DFD, especially when using them for system enhancements.

3. Determine the process outputs, or what things are coming out, and model them to the right of the process as best you can.
4. Establish all files, forms, or other components that the process needs to complete its transformation. These are usually data stores that are utilized during processing. Model these items above or below the process.
5. Name and number the process by its result. For example, if a process produces invoices, label it "Create Invoices." If the process accomplishes more than one event, label it by using the "and" conjunction. This method will allow you to determine whether the process is a functional primitive. Ultimately, the name of the process should be one that most closely associates the DFD with what the user does. Therefore, name it what the user calls it! The number of the process simply allows the analyst to identify it to the system and most importantly to establish the link to its children levels during functional decomposition.

Let us now apply this procedure to the example below:

Vendors send Mary invoices for payment. Mary stamps on the invoice the date received and matches the invoice with the original purchase order request. Invoices are placed in the accounts payable folder. Invoices that exceed thirty days are paid by check in two-week intervals.

Step 1: Draw the bubble (Fig. 8.3).
Step 2: Determine the inputs. In this example we are receiving an invoice from a vendor. The vendor is considered a terminator, since it is a boundary of the input and the user cannot control when and how the invoice will arrive. The invoice itself is represented as a data flow coming from the vendor terminator into the process (Fig. 8.4).
Step 3: Determine the outputs of the process. In this case the result of the process is that the vendor receives a check for payment (Fig. 8.5).
Step 4: Determine the "processing" items required to complete the process. In this example, the user needs to:

Fig. 8.3 A process bubble

Fig. 8.4 Terminator sending
invoice to the process

Fig. 8.5 DFD with output of
check sent to vendor

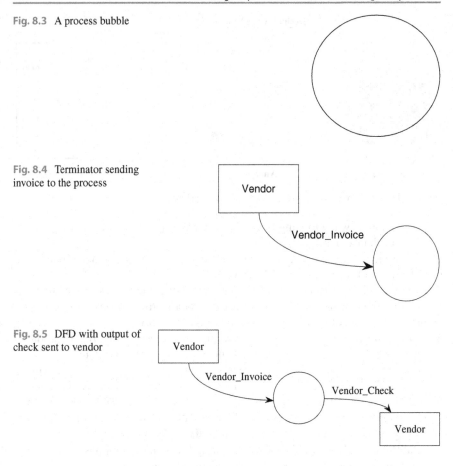

- match the invoice to the original purchase order;
- create a new account payable for the invoice in a file; and
- eventually retrieve the invoice from the account payable file for payment.

Note that the purchase order file is accessed for input (or retrieval) and there-fore is modeled with the arrow coming into the process. The accounts payable file, on the other hand, shows a two-sided arrow because entries are created (inserted) and retrieved (read) (Fig. 8.6). In addition, arrows to and from data stores may or may not contain data flow names. For reasons that will be explained later in the chapter, the inclusion of such names is not recommended.

Step 5: Name and number the process based on its output or its user definition (Fig. 8.7).

Figure 8.7 is now a complete DFD that describes the event of the user. You may notice that the procedures for stamping the invoice with the receipt date and the specifics of retrieving purchase orders and accounts payable information are not explained. These other components will be defined using other modeling tools. Once again, the DFD reflects only data flow and boundary information of a process.

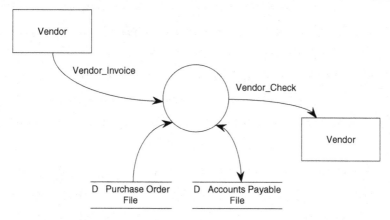

Fig. 8.6 DFD with interfacing data stores

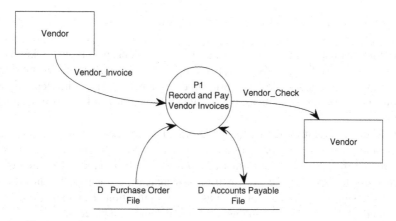

Fig. 8.7 Final named DFD

The DFD above can be leveled further to its functional primitive. The conjunction in the name of the process can sometimes help analysts to discover that there is actually more than one process within the event they are modeling. Based on the procedure outlined in Chapter 7, the event really consists of two processes: recording vendor invoices and paying vendor invoices. Therefore, P1 can be leveled as in Fig. 8.8.

Advantages of the DFD

Many opponents of the DFD argue that this procedure takes too long. You must ask yourself: What's the alternative? The DFD offers the analyst several distinct advantages. Most fundamentally, it depicts flow and boundary. The essence of knowing boundary is to first understand the extent of the process prior to beginning to define

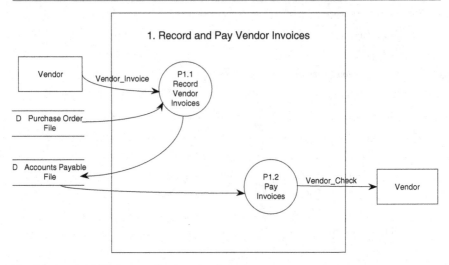

Fig. 8.8 Leveled DFD for record and pay invoices process

something that may not be complete or accurate. The concept is typically known as top-down, but the effort can also be conceived as step-by-step. The analyst must first understand the boundary and flows prior to doing anything else. The steps following this will procedurally gather more detailed information until the specification is complete.

Another important aspect of the DFD is that it represents a graphical display of the process and is therefore a usable document that can be shown to both users and programmers, serving the former as a process verification and the latter as the schematic (blueprint) of the system from a technical perspective. It can be used in JAD sessions and as part of the business specification documentation. Most importantly, it can be used for maintaining and enhancing a process.

Disadvantages of the DFD

The biggest drawback of the DFD is that it simply takes a long time to create: so long that the analyst may not receive support from management to complete it. This can be especially true when there is a lot of leveling to be performed. Therefore, many firms shy away from the DFD on the basis that it is not practical. The other disadvantage of the DFD is that it does not model time-dependent behavior well, that is, the DFD is based on very finite processes that typically have a very definable start and finish. This, of course, is not true of all processes, especially those that are event-driven. Event-driven systems will be treated more thoroughly when we discuss state transition diagrams later in this chapter.

The best solution to the time-consuming leveling dilemma is to avoid it as much as possible. That is, you should avoid starting at too high a summary level and try to get to the functional primitive as soon as you can. If in our example, for instance, the analyst had initially seen that the DFD had two processes instead of one, then the parent process could have been eliminated altogether. This would have resulted in an initial functional primitive DFD at Level 1. The only way to achieve this efficiency on a consistent basis is through practice. Practice will eventually result in the development of your own analysis style or approach. The one-in, one-out principle of the logical equivalent is an excellent way of setting up each process. Using this method, every event description that satisfies one-in, one-out will become a separate functional primitive process. Using this procedure virtually eliminates leveling. Sometimes users will request to see a summary-level DFD. In these cases the functional primitives can be easily combined or "leveled-up."

Process Flow Diagrams

While the data flow diagram provides the analyst with the LE of a process, it does not provide for the sequentiality of the processes themselves. The sequential steps of a process and the dependencies can provide an important facility to analyze the completeness of a system. This can be particularly relevant when the information gathered from users is suspect or may be inaccurate. A process flow diagram (PFD) can illuminate new processes and steps that could have been missed because it requires users to go through each phase of their system as it occurs or in an actual sequence. Having users go through their process as it actually occurs can allow them to remember things that they might otherwise miss or forget. Therefore, using process flows provides another tool that can test the completeness of the interview and LE.

Many methodologies, such as the James Martin technique, suggest that analysts should use PFDs instead of DFDs; however, it is my opinion that both models can coexist and actually compliment each other. This section will focus on how a process model is implemented and balanced against a DFD.

Components of a PFD

Historically, PFDs were called flowcharts. Flowcharts, while still valuable for certain diagramming tasks, are too clumsy and detailed to be an effective and structured modeling tool. The PFD suggested here is similar to a DFD, in that it contains processes, externals, and data flows. However, PFDs focus more on how externals, flows, and processes occur in relation to sequence and time. DFDs, on the other hand, are only focused on the net inputs and outputs of flows and the disposition of data at rest. Figure 8.9 is an example of a process flow.

Figure 8.9 shows how a PFD flows from one task to another. As with a DFD, externals are depicted by a rectangle. Flows are labeled and represent information in transition. Unlike DFDs, process flows do not necessarily require labeling of the flow arrows, and the processes themselves reflect descriptively what the step in the system is attempting to accomplish, as opposed to necessarily defining an algorithm.

Fig. 8.9 Sample process flow
diagram

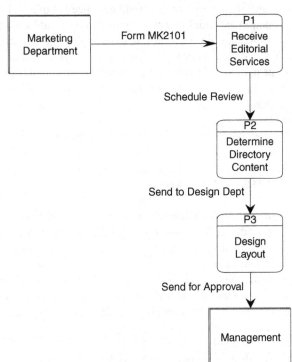

Editorial Directory Design Process Flow

DFD–PFD Compared

Perhaps the most significant difference between a DFD and a process flow is in its integration as a structured tool within the data repository. For example, a labeled data flow from a DFD must create an entry into the data dictionary or repository. Flow arrows from process flows do not. Furthermore, a functional primitive data flow points to a process specification; no such requirement exists in a process flow. Figure 8.10 represents a comparison of the editorial design process flow in DFD format.

The DFD similarity relates to the same boundaries of externals (i.e., marketing and management). The DFD flows, while similar, must be defined in the data dictionary or repository and therefore contain integrated formulas. The other notable difference is the interface of the data store "Design Information" which will eventually be defined as an entity and decomposed using logic data modeling techniques.

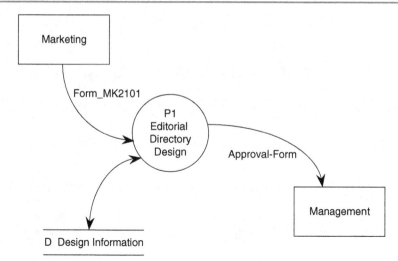

Fig. 8.10 PFD in DFD format

The question must be asked: what are the benefits of using a PFD and DFD? The answer lies in the correspondence between a process rectangle and a DFD process bubble. Process rectangles actually represent sequential steps within the DFD. It could be related to an IF statement in pseudocode or just a statement to produce a report or write information to a file. The PFD, in a sense, can provide a visual depiction of how the process specification needs to be detailed. One functional primitive DFD can thus be related to many process rectangles.

Based on the above analysis, therefore, a PFD can be justified as a tool in support of validating process specifications from within a DFD. In addition, the PFD might discover a missing link in logic that could result in the creation of a new DFD. Based on this argument, the process flow can be balanced against a DFD and its functional primitives. Finally, it represents the potential for providing a graphic display of certain levels of logic code. The balancing of the PFD to the DFD shown in Fig. 8.8 is shown in Fig. 8.11.

This example provides a view of how a DFD may contain multiple process flows. However, DFD 1.2 has a one-to-one relationship with P4 of the PFD. While P4 might be considered the same as DFD 1.2, its purpose is to describe, at a basic level, the specific order of events that take place within the event itself. There can be an argument made that every PFD component should represent a functional primitive DFD. This simply is not the case and the analyst must remember that the PFD often reflects just a graphic view of the steps (or specification) *within* a DFD functional primitive. In this way the PFD serves to validate the completeness of the DFD. Analysts should also relate each process in the PFD to a specific portion of logic in the process specification component of the structured specification.

Fig. 8.11 PFD and DFD cross-referenced

Sequence of Implementation

The question of whether the DFD should be created before or after a PFD must be discussed. In many ways, it can be left to the preference of the analyst. However, it is my preference to do the DFD first. My reason for following this sequence lies in the efficiency of creating the DFD as well as the ability to compare the DFD children against the sequential flow of the PFD. Creating the DFD first also supports the concept of decomposition, since the PFD will inevitably relate to the process specification of a functional primitive DFD. While this approach seems to be easier, there is certainly justification to do the PFD first, especially if an overview flow diagram provides a means of scoping the boundaries of an engineering process.

Data Dictionary

The data dictionary (DD) is quite simply a dictionary that defines data. We have seen that the data flow diagram represents a picture of how information flows to and from a process. As we pick up data elements during the modeling design, we effectively "throw" them into the data dictionary. Remember, all systems are composed of two components: data and processes. The DD represents the data portion.

There is a generic format followed by analysts, called DD notation. The conventional notations are listed below:

=   Equivalence
+   Concatenation
[ ] Either/Or Boundary
/   Either/Or separator
( ) Optional
{ } Iterations of
**   Comment

Equivalence (=):
The notion of equivalence does not express mathematical equality but rather indicates that the values on the right side of the equal sign represent all the possible components of the element on the left.

Concatenation (+):
This should not be confused with or compared to "plus"; it is rather the joining of two or more components. For example, Last_Name + First_Name means that these two data elements are being pieced together sequentially.

Either/Or with option separator ([/]):
Means "one of the following" and therefore represents a finite list of possible values. An example would include the definition of Country = [USA/Canada/United Kingdom/etc.].

Optional ( ):
The value is not required in the definition. A very common example is middle initial: Name = Last_Name + First_Name + (Middle_Init).

Iterations of { }:
The value between the separators occurs a specific or infinite number of times. Examples include

1{X}5   The element "X" occurs from one to five times
1{X}   The element "X" occurs from one to infinity
3{X}3   The element "X" must occur three times.

*Comments (**):*
Are used to describe the element or point the definition to the appropriate process specification should the data element not be definable in the DD. We will explain this case later in this section.

Now that we have defined the components of the DD, it is important to expand on its interface with other modeling tools, especially the DFD. If we recall the example used earlier to describe drawing a DFD, the input data flow was labeled "Vendor_Invoice" (see Fig. 8.4). The first DD rule to establish is that all labeled data flow names must be defined in the DD. Therefore, the DFD interfaces with the DD by establishing data element definitions from its labeled flows. To define Vendor_Invoice, we look at the physical invoices and ascertain from the user the required information needed by the system. It might typically be defined as follows:

Vendor_Invoice = Invoice_Number + Vendor_Invoice_Date +
            Vendor_Invoice_Name + Vendor_Invoice_Address_Line_1 +
            Vendor_Invoice_Address_Line_2 +
            Vendor_Invoice_Address_Line_3 + Vendor_State + Vendor_City
            + Vendor_ Zip_Code + Vendor_Salesperson + PO_Number +
            Vendor_Date_Shipped + Vendor_Shipped_Via +
            Vendor_Required_Date + Vendor_Terms + 1{Item-Quantity +
            Item_Description + Item_Unit_Price + Item_Amount} + Subtotal
            Sales_Tax + Shipping/Handling + Invoice_Total_Due

The above example illustrates what a vendor invoice would usually contain and what is needed to be captured by the system. Note that Vendor_Invoice is made up of component data elements which in turn need to be defined in the DD. In addition, there is a repeating group of elements {Item-Quantity + Item_Description + Item_Unit_Price + Item_Amount} which represents each line item that is a component of the total invoice. Since there is no limit to the number of items that could make-up one invoice, the upper limit of the iterations clause is left blank and therefore represents infinity. Figure 8.12 is a sample of how the physical invoice would appear.

It should be noted that many of the DD names have a qualifier of "Vendor" before the field name. This is done to ensure uniqueness in the DD as well as to document where the data element emanated from the DFD. To ensure that all data elements have been captured into the DD, we again apply functional decomposition, only this time we are searching for the functional primitive of the DD entry. We will call this functionally decomposed data element an elementary data element. An elementary data element is therefore an element that cannot be broken down any further. Let us functionally decompose Vendor_Invoice by looking to the right of the definition and picking up the data elements that have not already been defined in the DD. These elements are

Vendor_Invoice_Number	=	1 { Numeric} 5
Vendor_Invoice_Date	=	8 { Numeric }8
Vendor_Invoice_Name	=	1 { Alphanumeric } 35
Vendor_Invoice_Address_Line_1	=	1 { Alphanumeric } 25
Vendor_Invoice_Address_Line_1	=	1 { Alphanumeric } 25
Vendor_Invoice_Address_Line_1	=	1 { Alphanumeric } 25

Precision Products 1456 Emerson St Parsippany, NJ 07055-1254				**INVOICE** **INVOICE NO:** **DATE: August 15, 2011**	

To: :

SALESPERSON	P.O. NUMBER	DATE SHIPPED	SHIPPED VIA	REQUIRED DATE	TERMS
				10/5/95	

QUANTITY	DESCRIPTION	UNIT PRICE	AMOUNT
			$0.00
			$0.00
			$0.00
			$0.00
			$0.00
			$0.00
			$0.00
	SUBTOTAL		$0.00
	SALES TAX		
	SHIPPING & HANDLING		
	TOTAL DUE		$0.00

Fig. 8.12 Sample invoice form

Vendor_State	=	**All States in USA, Self Defining
Vendor_City	=	1 { Alphanumeric } 30
Vendor_Zip	=	5 { Numeric } 5 + (4 {Numeric} 4)
Vendor_Salesperson	=	1 { Alphanumeric } 20
PO_Number	=	4 { Alphanumeric } 4
Vendor_Date_Shipped	=	8 { Numeric } 8
Vendor_Shipped_Via	=	1 { Alphanumeric } 10
Vendor_Required_Date	=	8 { Numeric } 8
Vendor_Terms	=	1 { Numeric } 3
Item_Quantity	=	1 { Numeric } 5
Item_Description	=	1 { Alphanumeric } 30
Item_Unit_Price	=	** Dollars Self-Defining

Item_Amount	=	** See Process Spec xxx
Subtotal	=	** See Process Spec yyy
Sales_Tax	=	1 {Numeric }3 ** Assumed Percentage
Shipping/Handling	=	** Dollars Self-Defining
Invoice_Total_Due	=	** See Process Spec zzz

The following rules and notations apply:

1. A self-defining definition is allowed if the data definition is obvious to the firm or if it is defined in some general documentation (e.g., Standards and Reference Manual). In the case of Vendor_State an alternative would be

   Vendor_State = [AL/NY/NJ/CA....... etc.] for each state value.

2. Data elements that are derived as a result of a calculation cannot be defined in the DD, but rather point to a process specification where it can be properly identified. This also provides consistency in that all calculations and algorithms can be found in the process specification section.
3. Typically values such as numeric, alphanumeric, and alphabetic do not require further breakdown unless the firm allows for special characters. In that case, having the exact values defined is appropriate.
4. An iteration definition, where the minimum and maximum limits are the same (e.g., 8 {Numeric} 8), means that the data element is fixed (that is, must be 8 in length).

The significance of this example is that the DD itself, through a form of functional decomposition, creates new entries into the DD while finding the elementary data element. A good rule to follow is that any data element used in defining another data element must also be defined in the DD. The DD serves as the center for storing these entries and will eventually provide the data necessary to produce the stored data model.

Process Specifications

Many analysts define a process specification as everything else about the process not already included in the other modeling tools. Indeed, it must contain the remaining information that normally consists of business rules and application logic. DeMarco (1979) suggested that every functional primitive DFD point to a "Minispec" which would contain that process's application logic.[2] We will follow this rule and expand on the importance of writing good application logic. There are, of course, different styles, and few textbooks that explain the importance to the analyst of understanding how these need to be developed and presented. Like other modeling tools, each process specification style has its good, bad, and ugly.

---

[2] DeMarco, Tom, *Structured analysis and system specification*, pp. 85–86.

Pseudocode

The most detailed and regimented process specification is pseudocode or "Structured English." Its format is designed to require the analysts to have a solid understanding of how to write algorithms. The format is very "COBOL-like" and was initially designed as a way of writing functional COBOL programming specifications. The rules governing pseudocode are as follows:

- Use the Do While with an Enddo to show iteration
- Use If-Then-Else to show conditions and ensure each If has an End-If
- Be specific about initializing variables and other detail processing requirements

Pseudocode is designed to give the analyst tremendous control over the design of the code. Take the following example:

There is a requirement to calculate a 5% bonus for employees who work on the 1st shift and a 10% bonus for workers on the 2nd or 3rd shift. Management is interested in a report listing the number of employees who receive a 10% bonus. The process also produces the bonus checks.

The pseudocode would be

```
Initialize 10% counter = 0
Open Employee Master File
DoWhile more records
        If Shift = "1" then
                Bonus = Gross_Pay * .05
        Else
                If Shift = "2" or "3" then
                        Bonus = Gross_Pay * .10
                        Add 1 to Counter
                Else
                        Error Condition
        Endif
                Endif
Enddo
Print Report of 10% Bonus Employees
Print Bonus Checks
End
```

The above algorithm gives the analyst great control over how the program should be designed. For example, note that the pseudocode requires that the programmer has an error condition should a situation occur where a record does not contain a 1st, 2nd, or 3rd shift employee. This might occur should there be a new shift that was not communicated to the information systems department. Many programmers might have omitted the last "If" check as follows:

```
Initialize 10% counter = 0
Open Employee Master File
DoWhile more records
        If Shift = "1" then
                Bonus = Gross_Pay * .05
        Else
                Bonus = Gross_Pay * .10
                Add 1 to Counter
        Endif
Enddo
Print Report of 10%  Bonus Employees
Print Bonus Checks
End
```

The above algorithm simply assumes that if the employee is not on the 1st shift then they must be either a 2nd or 3rd shift employee. Without this being specified by the analyst, the programmer may have omitted this critical logic which could have resulted in a 4th shift worker receiving a 10% bonus! As mentioned earlier, each style of process specification has its advantages and disadvantages, in other words, the good, the bad, and the ugly.

The Good:

The analyst who uses this approach has practically written the program, and thus the programmer will have very little to do with regards to figuring out the logic design.

The Bad:

The algorithm is very detailed and could take a long time for the analyst to develop. Many professionals raise an interesting point: Do we need analysts to be writing process specifications to this level of detail? In addition, many programmers may be insulted and feel that an analyst does not possess the skillset to design such logic.

The Ugly:

The analyst spends the time, the programmers are not supportive and the logic is incorrect. The result here will be the "I told you so" remarks from programmers, and hostilities may grow over time.

Case

"Case"[3] is another method of communicating application logic. Although the technique does not require as much technical format as pseudocode, it still requires the

---

[3] The case method should not be confused with CASE (Computer Aided Software Engineering) products, which is software used to automate and implement modeling tools and data repositories.

analyst to provide a detailed structure to the algorithm. Using the same example as in the pseudocode discussion, we can see the differences in format:

```
Case 1st Shift
        Bonus = Gross_Pay * .05
Case 2nd or 3rd Shift
        Bonus = Gross_Pay * .10
        Add 1 to 10% Bonus Employees
Case Neither 1st, 2nd or 3rd Shift
        Error Routine
EndCase
Print Report of 10% Bonus Employees
Print Bonus Checks
End
```

The above format provides control as it still allows the analyst to specify the need for error checking; however, the exact format and order of the logic are more in the hands of the programmer. Let's now see the good, bad, and ugly of this approach:

The Good:

The analyst has provided a detailed description of the algorithm without having to know the format of logic in programming. Because of this advantage, CASE takes less time than pseudocode.

The Bad:

Although this may be difficult to imagine, the analyst may miss some of the possible conditions in the algorithm, such as forgetting a shift! This happens because the analyst is just listing conditions as opposed to writing a specification. Without formulating the logic as we did in pseudocode, the likelihood of forgetting or overlooking a condition check is increased.

The Ugly:

Case logic can be designed without concern for the sequence of the logic, that is, the actual progression of the logic as opposed to just the possibilities. Thus the logic can become more confusing because it lacks actual progressive structure. As stated previously, the possibility of missing a condition is greater because the analyst is not actually following the progression of the testing of each condition. There is thus a higher risk of the specification being incomplete.

Pre-Post Conditions

Pre-Post is based on the belief that analysts should not be responsible for the details of the logic, but rather for the overall highlights of what is needed. Therefore, the pre-post method lacks detail and expects that the programmers will provide the necessary details when developing the application software. The method has two components: pre-conditions and post-conditions. Pre-conditions represent things that are assumed true or that must exist for the algorithm to work. For example, a pre-condition might specify that the user must input the value of the variable X. On the other hand, the post-condition must define the required outputs as well as the relationships between calculated output values and their mathematical components. Suppose the algorithm calculated an output value called Total_Amount. The post-condition would state that Total_Amount is produced by multiplying quantity and price. Below is the pre-post equivalent of the bonus algorithm:

Pre-Condition 1:
> Access Employee Master file and where 1st shift = "1"

Post-Condition 1:
> Bonus is set to Gross_Pay * .05.
> Produce Bonus check.

Pre-Condition 2:
> Access Employee Master file and where 2nd shift = "2" or 3rd shift ="3"

Post-Condition 2:
> Bonus is set to Gross_Pay * .10
> Add 1 to 10% Bonus count.
> Produce Bonus check and Report of all employees who receive 10% bonuses.

Pre-Condition 3:
> Employee records does not contain a shift code equal to "1", "2", or "3"

Post-Condition 3:
> Error Message for employees without shifts = "1", "2", or "3"

As we can see, the above specification does not show how the actual algorithm should be designed or written. It requires the programmer or development team to find these details and implement the appropriate logic to handle it. Therefore, the analyst has no real input into the way the application will be designed or the way it functions.

The Good:

The analyst need not have technical knowledge to write an algorithm and does not need to spend an inordinate amount of time to develop what is deemed a programming responsibility. Therefore, less technically oriented analysts can be involved in specification development.

The Bad:

There is no control over the design of the logic, and thus the opportunity for misunderstandings and errors is much greater. The analyst and the project are much more dependent on the talent of the development staff.

The Ugly:

Perhaps, we misunderstand the specification. Since the format of pre-post conditions is less specific, there is more room for ambiguity.

Matrix

A matrix or table approach is one that shows the application logic in tabular form. Each row reflects a result of a condition, with each column representing the components of the condition to be tested. The best way to explain a matrix specification is to show an example (Fig. 8.13).

Although this is a simple example that uses the same algorithm as the other specification styles, it does show how a matrix can describe the requirements of an application without the use of sentences and pseudocode.

The Good:

The analyst can use a matrix to show complex conditions in a tabular format. The tabular format is preferred by many programmers because it is easy to read, organized, and often easy to maintain. Very often the matrix resembles the array and table formats used by many programming languages.

The Bad:

It is difficult, if not impossible, to show a complete specification in matrices. The above example supports this, in that the remaining logic of the bonus application is not shown. Therefore, the analyst must integrate one of the other specification styles to complete the specification.

The Ugly:

Matrices ae used to describe complex condition levels, where there are many "If" conditions to be tested. These complex conditions often require much more detailed analysis than shown in a matrix. The problem occurs when the analyst, feeling the matrix may suffice, does not provide enough detail. The result: conditions may be misunderstood by the programmer during development.

Bonus Percent	Shift to be tested
5% Bonus	1st Shift
10% Bonus	2nd Shift
10% Bonus	3rd Shift

Fig. 8.13 Sample matrix specification

Pseudocode	Case	Pre-Post	Matrix
Complex and detailed algorithms that need significant clarification.	The application logic is detailed but it is not necessary to develop the complete flow of the process.	Tremendous level of confidence in development staff to get the necessary application logic detail.	Large number of conditions (If statements) with an emphasis on lots of conditions before the answer is reached (i.e., complex If statements.
The analyst is also having difficulty with defining the logic.	There is more confidence in the programming staff.	The application logic is very simple and does not need further clarification.	No need for error condition checking.
Should be used when the analyst is very concerned about the aptitude of the programming staff.	The analyst wants to define all error handling conditions, but not to design them.	Few conditions ("If" statements)	Little application logic that needs to be further explained.
The analyst is very sensitive to error handling.	There are a reasonable number of "If" statements.	No need or limited error handling requirements.	

Fig. 8.14 Process specification comparisons

Conclusion:

The question must be asked again: What is a good specification? We will continue to explore this question. In this chapter we have examined the logic alternatives. Which logic method is best? It depends! We have seen from the examples that each method has its advantages and shortcomings. The best approach is to be able to use them all and to select the most appropriate one for the task at hand. To do this effectively means clearly recognizing where each style provides a benefit for the part of the system you are working with and who will be doing the development work. Figure 8.14 attempts to put the advantages and shortcomings into perspective.

State Transition Diagrams

State transition diagram (STD) was designed to model events that are time-dependent in behavior. Another definition of the STD is that it models the application alternatives for event-driven activities. An event-driven activity can be defined as any activity that depends directly on the behavior of a pre-condition which makes that event either possible or attractive. Before going any further, let's use an example to explain this definition further:

> Mary leaves her office to go home for the day. Mary lives 20 minutes walking distance from the office. When departing from the office building, she realizes that it is raining very hard. Typically, Mary would walk home; however, due

Alternative	Pre-Condition	Positive Result	Negative Result
1. Walk Home	None	Mary gets home and does not spend money	Mary gets very wet
2. Take Subway train	Must have $1.50 for Subway	Mary gets home without getting too wet.	Mary spends money and must be careful for her safety when going into the Subway
3. Take a Taxi	Must have $15.00 for the Taxi ride	Mary gets home faster and without getting wet.	It's expensive and it may be difficult to find a Taxi. There could also be a lot of traffic, resulting in delays.

Fig. 8.15 Mary's event alternatives

to the rain, she needs to make a decision at that moment about how she will go home. Therefore, an event has occurred during the application of Mary walking home which may change her decision and thus change the execution of this application.

As shown above, we have defined an event that, depending on the conditions during its execution, may have different results. To complete the example, we must examine or define what Mary's alternatives are for getting home (Fig. 8.15).

The above matrix shows us the alternative activities that Mary can choose. Two of them require a certain amount of money. All of the alternatives have positive and negative potentials that cannot be determined until executed; therefore, the decision to go with an alternative may depend on a calculation of probability. We sometimes call this a calculated risk or our "gut" feeling. Is it not true that Mary will not know whether she will be able to find a taxi until she tries? However, if Mary sees a lot of traffic in the street and not many taxis, she may determine that it is not such a good idea to take a taxi.

Much of the duplication of the scenario above falls into the study of artificial intelligence (AI) software. Therefore, AI modeling may require the use of STDs. The word "state" in STD means that an event must be in a given pre-condition before we can consider moving to another condition. In our example, Mary is in a state called "Going Home From the Office." Walking, taking a train, or taking a taxi is alternative way of getting home. Once Mary is home she has entered into a new state called "Home." We can now derive that walking, taking a train, or taking a taxi are conditions that can effect a change in state, in this example leaving the office and getting home. Figure 8.16 shows the STD for "going home."

This STD simply reflects that two states exist and that there is a condition that causes the application to move to the "Home" state. When using STDs, the analyst should

Fig. 8.16 State transition diagram for going home

1. Identify all states that exist in the system. In other words, all possible permutations of events must be defined.
2. Ensure that there is at least one condition to enter every state.
3. Ensure that there is at least one condition to leave every state.

The reasons for and approach to an STD differ greatly from those of a DFD. A DFD should be used when modeling finite, sequential processes that have a definitive beginning and end. We saw this situation in the previous examples in this chapter. The STD, on the other hand, is needed when the system effectively never ends, that is, when it simply moves from one state to another. Therefore, the question is never whether we are at the beginning or end of the process, but rather the current state of the system. Another example, one similar to that used by Yourdon in "Modern Structured Analysis," is the bank teller state diagram (Fig. 8.17).

Although you may assume that "Enter Valid Card" is the start state, an experienced analyst would know better. At any time, the automated teller is in a particular state of operation (unless it has abnormally terminated). The "Enter Valid Card" state is in the "sleep" state. It will remain in this mode until someone creates the condition to cause a change, which is actually to input a valid card. Notice that every state can be reached and every state can be left. This rule establishes perhaps the most significant difference between the DFD and STD. Therefore, a DFD should be used for finite processes and an STD where there is ongoing processing, moving from one status to another.

Let us now show a more complex example which emphasizes how the STD can uncover conditions that are not obvious or were never experienced by the user. Figure 8.18 shows matrix of states for a thermostat.

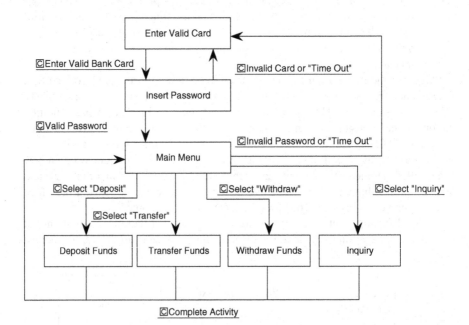

Fig. 8.17 Bank teller state transition diagram

Current State	Condition to cause a change in State	New State
Furnace Off	Temperature drops below 60 degrees	Furnace On
Furnace On	Temperature exceeds 70 degrees	Furnace Off
Air On	Temperature drops below 65 degrees	Air Off
Air Off	Temperature exceeds 75 degrees	Air On

Fig. 8.18 Thermostat states

Figure 8.19 is the STD for the states and conditions shown in Fig. 8.18.

Upon review, we notice that there are really two systems and that they do not interface with each other. Why? Suppose, for example, that the temperature went above 70 and that the system therefore went into the Furnace Off state, but that the temperature nevertheless continued to increase unexpectedly. Users expect that whenever the Furnace Off state is reached, it must be winter. In the event of a winter heat wave, everyone would get very hot. We have therefore discovered that we must have a condition to put the air on even if a heat wave had never occurred before in winter. The same situation exists for the Air Off where we expect the temperature to rise instead of falling. We will thus add two new conditions as shown in Fig. 8.20.

The STD is then modified to show how the Furnace and Air subsystems interface (Fig. 8.21).

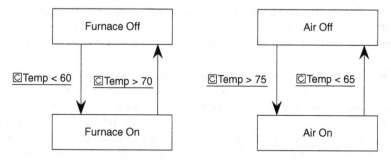

Fig. 8.19 State transition diagram based on the user-defined states

Current State	Condition to cause a change in State	New State
Furnace Off	Temperature exceeds 75 degrees	Air On
Air Off	Temperature drops below 65 degrees	Furnace On

Fig. 8.20 Additional possible states of the thermostat

Fig. 8.21 Modified state transition diagram based on modified events

Using STDs to discover missing processes (that would otherwise be omitted or added later) is very important. This advantage is why STDs are considered very effective in artificial intelligence and object-oriented analysis, where the analyst is constantly modeling event-driven, never-ending processes.

Entity Relational Diagrams

The model that depicts the relationships among the stored data is known as an entity relational diagram (ERD). The ERD is the most widely used of all modeling tools and is really the only method to reflect the system's stored data.

An entity in database design is an object of interest about which data can be collected. In a retail database application, customers, products, and suppliers might be entities. An entity can subsume a number of attributes: product attributes might be color, size, and price; customer attributes might include name, address, and credit rating.[4]

The first step in understanding an entity is to establish its roots. Since DFDs have been used to model the processes, their data stores (which may represent data files) will act as the initial entities prior to implementing logical data modeling.

It is believed, for purposes of data modeling, that an entity can be simply defined as a logical file which will reflect the data elements or fields that are components of each occurrence or record in the entity. The ERD, therefore, shows how multiple entities will interact with each other. We call this interaction the "relationship." In most instances, a relationship between two or more entities can exist only if they have at least one common data element among them. Sometimes we must force a relationship by placing a common data element between entities, just so

---

[4] Microsoft Press, Computer Dictionary, Second Edition, pg. 149.

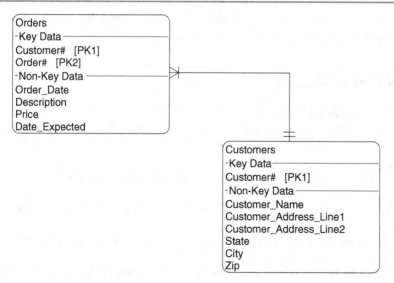

Fig. 8.22 Entity relational diagram showing the relationship between the orders and customers entities

they can communicate with each other. An ERD typically shows each entity and its connections as shown in Fig. 8.22.

Figure 8.22 shows two entities: Orders and Customers. They have a relationship because both entities contain a common data element called Customer#. Customer# is depicted as "Key Data" in the Customers entity because it must be unique for every occurrence of a customer record. It is notated as "PK1" because it is defined as a Primary Key, meaning that Customer# uniquely identifies a particular customer. In Orders, we see that Customer# is a Primary Key but it is concatenated with Order#. By "concatenation," we mean that the two elements are combined to form a primary key. Nevertheless, Customer# still has its separate identity. The line that joins the entities is known as the relationship identifier. It is modeled using the "crow's foot" method, meaning that the many relationship is shown as a crow's foot, shown in Fig. 8.22, going to the Order entity. The double vertical lines near the Customer entity signify "One and only One." What does this really mean? The proper relationship is stated:

One and only One Customer can have One to Many Orders

In English it means that Customers must have not only placed at least one order, but can also have placed more than one. "One and only One" really indicates that when a Customer is found in the Order entity, the Customer must also exist in the Customer entity. In addition, although a Customer may exist multiple times in the Order entity, it can exist in the Customer master entity only once. This relationship is also know as the association between entities and effectively identifies the common data elements and the constraints associated with their relationship. This kind of relationship between entities can be difficult to grasp, especially without benefit of a practical application.

Problems and Exercises

1. What is a functional primitive?
2. What are the advantages and disadvantages of a data flow diagram?
3. What is meant by "leveling-up?"
4. What is the purpose of the data dictionary?
5. Define each of the following data dictionary notation symbols: =, +, [ ], /, ( ), { }, **.
6. What is an elementary data element? How does it compare with a functional primitive?
7. Define the functions of a process specification. How does the process specification interface with the DFD and the DD?
8. Compare the advantages and disadvantages of each of the following process specification formats:
   - Pseudocode
   - Case
   - Pre-post condition
   - Matrix
9. What is an event-driven system? How does the program manager in Windows applications represent the behavior of an event-driven system?
10. When using an STD, what three basic things must be defined?
11. What is an entity? How does it relate to a data store of a DFD ?
12. Explain the concept of an entity relational diagram.
13. What establishes a relationship between two entities?
14. Define the term "association."

Mini-Project

You have been asked to automate the accounts payable process. During your interviews with users you identify four major events as follows:

I. Purchase Order Flow
   1. The Marketing Department sends a Purchase Order (P.O.) form for books to the accounts payable system (APS).
   2. APS assigns a P.O. # and sends the P.O.-White copy to the Vendor and files the P.O.- Pink copy in a file cabinet in P.O.#. sequence.

II. Invoice Receipt
   1. A vendor sends an invoice for payment for books purchased by APS.
   2. APS sends invoice to Marketing Department for authorization.
   3. Marketing either returns invoice to APS approved or back to the vendor if not authorized.

4. If the invoice is returned to APS it is matched up against the original P.O.-Pink. The P.O. and vendor invoice are then combined into a packet and prepared for the voucher process.

III. Voucher Initiation

1. APS receives the packet for vouchering. It begins this process by assigning a voucher number.
2. The Chief Accountant must approve vouchers > $5,000.
3. APS prepares another packet from the approved vouchers. This packet includes the P.O.-Pink, authorized invoice and approved voucher.

IV. Check Preparation

1. Typist receives the approved voucher packet and retrieves a numbered blank check to pay the vendor.
2. Typist types a two-part check (blue, green) using data from the approved voucher and enters invoice number on the check stub.
3. APS files the approved packet with the check-green in the permanent paid file.
4. The check is either picked up or mailed directly to the vendor.

Assignment

1. Provide the DFDs for the four events. Each event should be shown as a single DFD on a separate piece of paper.
2. Level each event to its functional primitives.
3. Develop the process specifications for each functional primitive DFD.

References

DeMarco, T. (1979). *Structured analysis and system specification.* Englewood Cliffs, NJ: Prentice Hall.
Yourdon, E. (1989). *Modern structured analysis.* Englewood Cliffs, NJ: Prentice Hall.

The Data

9

Introduction to Databases

Chapter 8 focused on application specifications as they relate to process. Using DFDs, PFDs, state diagrams, etc., I showed how data elements are defined in the DD. However, the process of completing the DD and building complex relational databases has further steps. This chapter focuses on how to design databases for use with e-commerce Web applications. The completion of the DD and the creation of the database schematic, called the entity relational diagram, provide developers with the data architecture component of the system. We call the process of creating this architecture logic data modeling. The process of logic data modeling not only defines the architecture, but it also provides the construct for the actual database, often called the physical database. The physical database differs from its logical counterpart in that it is subject to the rules and formats of the database product that will be used to implement the system. This means that if Oracle is used to implement the logical schema, the database must conform to the specific propri- etary formats that Oracle requires. Thus, the logical model provides the first step in planning for the physical implementation. First, we will examine the process of building the appropriate schematic. Even if a package software product is selected, the chances are that it will need to use a database product like Oracle. Thus, many of the analysis and design below will be extremely important in determining the best fit for a package.

Logic Data Modeling

Logic data modeling (LDM) is a method that examines a particular data entity and determines what data elements need to be associated with it. There are a number of procedures, some mathematically based, to determine how and what the ana- lyst needs to do. Therefore, LDM only focuses on the stored data with the intent

A.M. Langer, *Guide to Software Development*,
DOI 10.1007/978-1-4471-2300-2_9, © Springer-Verlag London Limited 2012

to design what can be defined as the "engine" of the system. Often this "engine" is called the "back-end." The design of the engine must be independent from the process and must be based on the rules of data definition theory. Listed below are the eight suggested steps to build the database blueprint. This blueprint is typically called the schema, which is defined as a logical view of the database.

1. Identify data entities
2. Select primary and alternate keys
3. Determine key business rules
4. Apply normalization to 3rd Normal Form
5. Combine user views
6. Integrate with existing data models (e.g., legacy interfaces)
7. Determine domains and triggering operations
8. De-normalize as appropriate

Prior to providing concrete examples, it is necessary to define the database terms used in this chapter. Below are the key concepts and definitions:

- *Entity*: an object of interest about which data can be collected. Larson and Larson (2000) define an entity as "a representation of a real-world person, event, or concept." For example, in an e-commerce application, customers, products, and suppliers might be entities. The chapter will provide a method of determining entities from the DFD. An entity can have many data elements associated with it, called attributes.
- *Attribute*: data elements are typically called attributes when they are associated with an entity. These attributes, or cells of an entity, belong to or "depend on" the entity.
- *Key*: a key is an attribute of an entity that uniquely identifies a row. A row is defined as a specific record in the database. Therefore, a key is an attribute that has a unique value that no other row or record can have. Typical key attributes are "Social-Security-Number," "Order-Number," etc.
- *Business rule*: this is a rule that is assumed to be true as defined by the business. Business rules govern the way keys and other processes behave within the database.
- *Normalization*: a process that eliminates data redundancy and ensures data integrity in a database.
- *User view*: the definition of the data from the perspective of the user. This means that how a data element is used, what is its business rules, and whether it is a key or not, depends largely on the user's definition. It is important that analysts understand that data definitions are not universal.
- *Domains*: this relates to a set of values or limits of occurrences within a data element or attribute of an entity. An example of a domain would be STATE, where there is a domain of 50 acceptable values (i.e., NY, NJ, and CA).
- *Triggers*: these are stored procedures or programs that are activated or *triggered* as a result of an event at the database level. In other words, an event (insert, delete, update) may require that other elements or records be changed. This change would occur by having a program stored by the database product (such as Oracle) automatically execute and update the data.

- *Cardinality*: this concept defines the relationship between two entities. This relationship is constructed based on the number of occurrences or associations that one entity has with another. For example, one customer record could have many order records. In this example, both customer and orders are separate entities.
- *Legacy systems*: these are existing applications that are in operation. Legacy applications sometimes refer to older and less sophisticated applications that need to be interfaced with newer systems or replaced completely (see Chapter 10).
- *Entity relational diagram*: a schematic of all the entities and their relationships using cardinal format. An entity relational diagram provides the blueprint of the data or the diagram of the data engine.

Logic Data Modeling Procedures

The first step in LDM is to select the entities that will be used to start the normalization process. If DFDs have been completed in accordance with the procedures outlined in Chapter 3, then all data stores that represent data files become transformed into data entities. This approach offers the major advantage of modeling process before data. If DFDs or some comparable process tool is not used, then analysts must rely on the information they can obtain from the legacy systems, such as existing data files, screens, and reports. The following example depicts how a data store from a DFD becomes an entity. The data contained in the data store called "Orders" are represented as an actual form containing many data elements. Thus, this example represents a physical form translated into an LE called a data store, which then is transformed again into an entity (Figs. 9.1 and 9.2).

Key Attributes

The next step in LDM is to select the primary and alternate keys. A primary key is defined as an attribute that will be used to identify a record or occurrence in an entity. The primary key, like any key attribute, contains a unique value. Often there is more than one attribute in an entity that contains unique values. We call an attribute that can be a primary key a *candidate* key attribute. This simply means that this attribute can serve in the role of the primary key. If there is only one candidate, then there is no issue: that candidate becomes the primary key. In the event that there is more than one candidate attribute, then one must be selected as the primary key, and the others will be called *alternate* or *secondary* key attributes. These alternate key attributes provide benefit in the physical database only. This means that they can be used to identify records in the database as an *alternative* should the primary key not be known. Take the following example. Suppose that an employee entity has two candidate keys: Social-Security-Number and Employee-ID. Employee-ID is selected as the primary key, so Social-Security-Number becomes an alternate key.

John's Parts, Inc   ORDER

1818 West Way

New York, NY 10027

ORDER NO: 12345

DATE: August 15, 2011

To: :

A. Langer & Assoc., Inc.
John St
Third Floor
White Plains, NY, 10963

P.O. NUMBER	DATE SHIPPED	SHIPPED VIA	REQUIRED DATE	TERMS
4R32	3/28/2001	UPS	4/1/2001	30 days

QUANTITY	ITEM ID	ITEM NAME	UNIT PRICE	AMOUNT
6	31	Wires	6.50	39.00
2	27	Wheel Covers	25.00	50.00
				$ 0.00
				$ 0.00
				$ 0.00
				$ 0.00
				$ 0.00
		SUBTOTAL		$ 89.00
		SALES TAX		
		SHIPPING & HANDLING		$ 5.50
		TOTAL DUE		$ 99.50

Fig. 9.1 Sample customer order form

In the logical entity, Social-Security-Number is treated as any other non-key attribute; however, in the physical database, it can be used (or indexed) to find a record. This could occur when an employee calls to ask someone in Human Resources about accrued vacation time. The Human Resource staff would ask the employee for their Employee-ID. If the employee did not know his/her Employee-ID, the Human Resource staff could ask them for their Social-Security-Number

Fig. 9.2 Transition of the
order data store into an entity

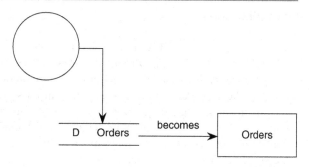

and use that information as an alternative way to locate that individual's information. It is important to note that the search on the primary key will be substantially
faster, because primary key searches use a method called direct access, as opposed
to index methods, which are significantly slower. This raises the question: When
there are multiple candidate-key attributes, which key attribute should be selected
as the primary key? The answer is the attribute that will be used most often to
find the record. This means that Employee-ID was selected as the primary key
attribute because the users determined that it was the field most often used to locate
employee information. Therefore, e-commerce analysts must ensure that they ask
users this question during the interview process. Figure 9.3 provides a graphic depiction of the employee entity showing Employee-ID as the primary key attribute and
Social-Security-Number as a non-key attribute.

There is another type of key attribute called *Foreign* keys. Foreign keys provide
a way to link tables and create relationships between them. Since foreign keys are
created during the process of normalization, I will defer discussion about them to
the section on *Normalization* in this chapter.

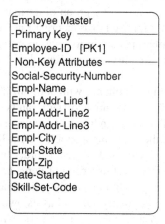

Fig. 9.3 Primary key and alternate key attributes

Normalization

While the next step in LDM is to determine key business rules, it is easier to explain the process of normalization first. That is, normalization occurs after defining key business rules in practice, but not when introducing the topic for educational purposes. Therefore, key business rules will be discussed after normalization.

Normalization, without question, is the most important aspect of LDM. As mentioned above, normalization is defined as the elimination of redundancies in an entity and ensures data integrity. It is the latter point that is critical in understanding the value of normalization in the design of e-commerce database systems. Understanding the LDM process depends largely on understanding how to implement the normalization process.

Normalization is constructed in a number of "Normal Forms." While there are five published Normal Forms, Normal Forms 4 and 5 are difficult to implement and most professionals avoid them. Therefore, this book omits Normal Forms 4 and 5. The three Normal Forms of normalization are listed below. Note that a Normal Form is notated as "NF."

1st NF: No repeating non-key attributes or group of non-key attributes.
2nd NF: No partial dependencies on a part of a concatenated key attribute.
3rd NF: No dependencies of a non-key attribute on another non-key attribute.

Each Normal Form is dependent on the one before it, that is, the process of completing normalization is predicated on the sequential satisfaction of the Normal Form preceding it. Normalization can be best explained by providing a detailed example. Using the order form provided in Fig. 9.1, we can start the process of normalization. Figure 9.4 shows the logical equivalent of the order form in entity format. In this example, the primary key is Order-Number (signified by the "PK" notation), which requires that every order have a unique Order-Number associated with it. It should also be noted that a repeating group made up of five attributes is shown in a separate box. This repeating group of attributes correlate to an area on the order form, which often is referred to as an order line item. This means that each item associated with the order appears in its own group, namely, the item identification, its name, unit price, quantity, and amount. The customer order in Fig. 9.1 shows two items associated with the Order-Number 12345.

The process of determining compliance with normalization is to evaluate whether each Normal Form or NF has been satisfied. This can be accomplished by testing each NF in turn. Thus, the first question to ask is, are we in 1st NF? The answer is no because of the existence of the repeating attributes: Item-ID, Item-Name, Quantity, Unit-Price, and Amount or as specified above an "order line item." In showing this box, the example exposes the repeating group of items that can be associated with a customer order. Another way of looking at this phenomenon is to see that within the order, there really is another entity, which has its own key identification. Since there is a repeating group of attributes, there is a 1st NF failure. *Anytime an NF fails or is violated, it results in the creation of another entity.* Whenever there is a 1st NF failure, the new entity will always have as its primary key a concatenated

Fig. 9.4 Orders entity and its associated attributes

"group" of attributes. This concatenation, or joining of multiple attributes to form a specific value, is composed of the primary key from the original entity (Orders) attached with a new key attribute from the repeating group of elements. The new key must be an attribute that controls the other group of attributes. In this example, the controlling attribute is Item-ID. After the new "key attribute" is determined, it is concatenated with the original key attribute from the Orders entity. The remaining non-key attributes will be removed from the original entity to become non-key attributes of the new entity. This new entity is shown in Fig. 9.5.

The new entity, called Order Items, has a primary key that reflects the concatenation of the original key Order-Number from the entity Orders, combined with Item-ID, which represents the controlling attribute for the repeating group. All of the other repeating attributes have now been transferred to the new entity. The new entity Order Items allows the system to store multiple order line items as required. The original entity left without this modification would have limited the number of occurrences of items artificially. For example, if the analyst/designer had defaulted to five groups of order line items, the database would always have five occurrences of the five attributes. If most orders, in reality, had fewer than five items, then

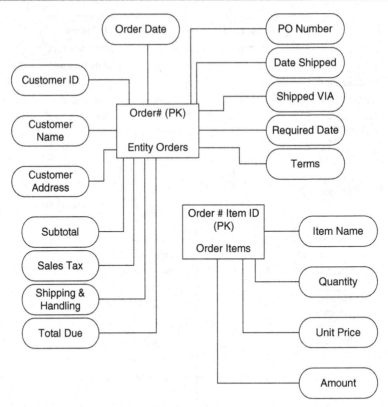

Fig. 9.5 Orders in 1st NF

significant space would be wasted. More significant is the case where the order has more than five items. In this case, a user would need to split the order into two physical orders so that the extra items could be captured. These two issues are the salient benefits of attaining entities in their 1st NF. Therefore, leaving the entity Order as is would in effect create an integrity problem.

   Once the changes to the entity Orders have been completed, and the new entity Order Item has been completed, the system is said to be a database in 1st NF. It is important to note that the new primary key of the entity Order Items is the combination of two attributes. While the two attributes maintain their independence as separate fields of data, they are utilized as one combined value for purposes of their role as a key attribute. For example, based on the data in the order form from Fig. 9.1, the entity Order Items would have two records. The first record would have the primary key of 1234531, which would be the concatenation of Order-Number (12345) with Item-ID (31). The second record would be 1234527, which is the same Order-Number, but concatenated with the second Item-ID (27). From an SQL feature perspective, while the key attribute concatenates each attribute into one address, it can be searched as separate fields. So a user could search for all the items associated with Order 12345, by simply searching on Order Items that contain an Order-Number = "12345." This exemplifies the power of versatility in the relational model. Once 1st NF has been reached, the next test must ensue, that is, testing for compliance with 2nd NF.

Second NF testing applies *only* to entities that have concatenated keys. Therefore, any entity that is in 1st NF and does not have a concatenated primary key must already be in 2nd NF. In our example, then, the entity "Orders" is already in 2nd NF because it is in 1st NF and does not have a concatenated primary key. The entity Order Items, however, is in a different category. Order Items has a concatenated primary key attribute and must be tested for compliance with 2nd NF. Second NF requires the analyst to ensure that every non-key attribute in the entity is totally dependent on all components of the primary key or all of its concatenated attributes. When we apply the test, we find that the attribute "Item-Name" is dependent only on the key attribute "Item-ID." That is, the Order-Number has no effect or control over the name of the item. This condition is considered a 2nd NF failure. Once again, a new entity must be created. The primary key of the new entity is the portion of the concatenated key that controlled the attribute that caused the failure. In other words, Item-ID is the primary key of the new entity, because "Item-Name" was wholly dependent on the attribute "Item-ID." It is worthwhile at this time to explain further the concept of attribute dependency. For one attribute to be dependent on another infers that the controlling attribute's value can change the value of the dependent attribute. Another way of explaining this is to say that the controlling attribute, which must be a key, controls the record. That is, if the Item-ID changes, then we are looking at a different Item-Name, because we are looking at a different Item record.

To complete the creation of the new entity, Items, each non-key attribute in the original entity Order Items must be tested for 2nd NF violation. Note that as a result of this testing, "Quantity" and "Amount" stay in the Order Items entity because they are dependent on both Order-Number and Item-ID. That is, the quantity associated with any given Order Items occurrence is dependent not only on the Item itself, but also on the particular order it is associated with. We call this being wholly dependent on the concatenated primary key attribute. Thus, the movement of non-key attributes is predicated on the testing of each non-key attribute against the concatenated primary key. The result of this test establishes the three entities shown in Fig. 9.6.

The results of implementing 2nd NF reflect that without it, a new Item (or Item-ID) could not have been added to the database without an order. This obviously would have caused major problems. Indeed, the addition of a new Item would have to precede the creation of that Item with a new Order. Therefore, the new entity represents the creation of a separate Item Master file.

Figure 9.6 represents Orders in 2nd NF. Once again, we must apply the next test—3rd NF to complete normalization. Third NF tests the relationship between two non-key attributes to ensure that there are no dependencies between them. Indeed, if this dependency were to exist, it would mean that one of the non-key attributes would, in effect, be a key attribute. Should this occur, the controlling non-key attribute would become the primary key of the new entity. Testing this against

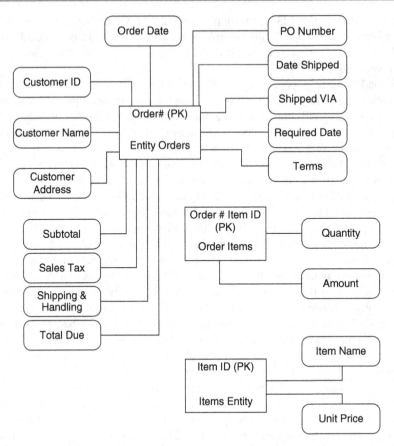

Fig. 9.6 Orders in 2nd NF

the sample entity reflects that Customer-Name and Customer-Address[1] are dependent on Customer-ID. Therefore, the entity Orders fails 3rd NF and a new entity must be created. The primary key of the new entity is the non-key attribute that controlled the other non-key attributes; in this case Customer-ID. The new entity is called Customers, and all of the non-key attributes that depend on Customer-ID are moved to that entity as shown in Fig. 9.7.

What is unique about 3rd NF failures is that the new key attribute remains as a non-key attribute in the original entity (in this case: Orders). The copy of the non-key attribute Customer-ID is called a foreign key and is created to allow the Order entity and the new Customer entity to have a relationship. A relationship between two entities can exist only if there is at least one common keyed attribute between

---

[1] Customer-Address would normally be composed of three address lines and the existence of State, City, and Zip-code. It has been omitted from this example for simplicity.

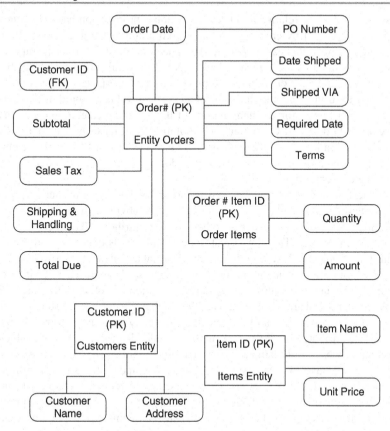

Fig. 9.7 Orders in preliminary 3rd NF

them. Understanding this concept is crucial to what normalization is intended to accomplish. Looking at Fig. 9.7, one can see that the entities Order and Order Items have a relationship because both entities have a common keyed attribute: Order-ID. The same is true in the creation of the Item entity, which resulted from a 2nd NF failure. The relationship here is between the Order Item entity and the Item entity, where both entities contain the common key attribute Item-ID. Both of these relationships resulted from the *propagation* of a key attribute from the original entity to the newly formed entity during the normalization process. By propagation, we mean that a pointer or copy of the key attribute is placed in the new entity. Propagation is implemented using foreign keys and is a natural result of the process. Note that the "PK" is followed by an "FK" signifying that the keyed attribute is the result of a propagation of the original key attribute. Such is not the case in 3rd NF. If Customer-ID were to be removed from the Orders entity, then the relationship between Orders and Customers would not exist because there would be no common keyed attribute between the two entities. Therefore, in 3rd NF, it is necessary to force the relationship because a natural propagation has not occurred. This is accomplished by creating a pointer from a non-keyed attribute to the primary keyed copy, in this case Customer-ID. The concept of a pointer is important. Foreign key structures are typically implemented internally in physical databases using indexes. Indexes, or indirect addresses, are a way of maintaining database integrity by ensuring that only one copy of an attribute value is stored. If two copies of Customer-ID were stored, changing one of them could create an integrity problem between Orders and Customers. The solution is to have the Customer-ID in Orders "point" indirectly to the Customer-ID key attribute in the Customer entity. This ensures that a Customer-ID cannot be added to the Orders entity that does not exist in the Customer master entity.

The question now is whether the entities are in 3rd NF. Upon further review, we see the answer is no! Although it is not intuitively obvious, there are three non-key attributes that are dependent on other non-key attributes. This occurs first in the Order Items entity. The non-key attribute "Amount" is dependent on the non-key attribute "Quantity." Amount represents the total calculated for each item in the order. It is not only dependent on "Quantity," but also dependent on "Unit-Price." This occurs frequently in attributes that are calculations. Such attributes are called *derived* elements and are eliminated from the database. Indeed, if we store Quantity and Unit-Price, "Amount" can be calculated separately as opposed to being stored as a separate attribute. Storing the calculation would also cause integrity problems. For example, what would happen if the quantity or unit price would change? The database would have to recalculate the change and update the Amount attribute. While this can be accomplished, and will be discussed later in this chapter, it can be problematic to maintain in the database and cause performance problems in production e-commerce systems. The Orders entity also contains two derived attributes: Subtotal and Total-Due. Again, both of these attributes are removed. The issue is whether the removal of derived attributes should be seen as a 3rd NF failure. C. J. Date (2000) views these failures as outside of 3rd NF, but in my view they represent indirect dependencies on other non-key attributes and should be included as part of the 3rd NF test. In any case, we all agree that derived elements should be removed in the process of LDM. The 3rd NF LDM is modified to reflect the removal of these three attributes as shown in Fig. 9.8.

Once 3rd NF is reached the analyst should create the entity relational diagram (ERD), which will show the relationships or connections among the entities. The relationship between entities is established through associations. Associations define the cardinality of the relationship using what is known as the crow's foot method as shown in Fig. 9.9.

The crow's foot method is only one of many formats. The method contains three key symbols:

$<$ denotes the cardinality of many occurrences

O   denotes zero occurrences

| denotes one occurrence

Fig. 9.8 Orders in second phase of 3rd NF

Fig. 9.9 The entities in ERD format using crow's feet

Therefore, the ERD in Fig. 9.9 depicts the relationships of all the entities as follows:

1. One and only one (signified by the double lines) Order record can have one to many Order Item records. It also shows that any Order in the Order Items entity must exist in the Order entity.

2. One and only one Item record can have zero to many Order Item records. The difference in this relationship and the one established between Orders and Order Items is that Items may not have a relationship with Order items, signified by the zero in the crow's foot. This would often occur when there is a new item that has not yet received any orders.

3. The Order Items entity has a primary key, which is a concatenation of two other primary keys: Order-ID from the Orders entity and Item-ID from the Items entity. This type of relationship is said to be an "associative" relationship because the entity has been created as a result of a relational problem. This relational problem exists because the Order entity has a "many-to-many" relationship with the Items entity. Thus the 1st NF failure, which created the associative entity Order Items, is really the result of a "many-to-many" situation. A many-to-many relationship violates normalization because it causes significant problems with SQL coding. Therefore, whenever a many-to-many relationship occurs between two entities, an associative entity is created which will have as its primary key the concatenation of the two primary keys from each entity. Thus, associative entities make many-to-many relationships into two one-to-many relationships so that SQL can work properly during search routines. Associative entities are usually represented with a diamond box.

4. One and only one Customer can have zero-to-many Orders, also showing that a Customer may exist who has never placed an order. As an example, this would be critical if the business were credit cards, where consumers can obtain a credit card even though they have not made a purchase. Note that the Customer-ID is linked with Orders through the use of a non-key foreign key attribute.

Limitations of Normalization

Although 3rd NF has been attained, there is a major problem with the model. The problem relates to the attribute Unit-Price in the Items entity. Should the Unit-Price of any Item change, then the calculation of historical Order Item purchases would be incorrect. Remember that the attribute "Amount" was eliminated because it was a derived element. This might suggest that normalization does not work properly! Such is not the case. First we need to evaluate whether putting "Amount" back in the ERD would solve the problem. If the Unit-Price were to change, then Amount would need to be recalculated *before* it was done. While this might seem reasonable, it really does not offer a *solution* to the problem, just a way around it. The actual problem has little to do with the attribute "Amount," but more to do with a missing attribute. The missing attribute is Order-Item-Unit-Price, which would represent the price at the time of the order. Order-Item-Unit-Price is dependent on both the Order and the Item and therefore would become a non-key attribute in the Order Items entity (i.e., it is wholly dependent on the entire concatenated primary key). The only relationship between Unit-Price and Order-Item-Unit-Price is at the time the order is entered into the system. In this situation, an application program would move the value or amount of the Unit-Price attribute into the Order-Item-Unit-Price attribute. Thereafter, there is no relationship between the two attributes. Because this is a new data element that has been discovered during normalization, it must be entered into the data dictionary. Thus, a limitation of normalization is that it cannot normalize what it does not have; it can normalize only the attributes that are presented to the formula. However, the limitation of normalization is also an advantage: the process can help the analyst recognize that a data element is missing. Therefore, normalization is a "data-based" tool that the analyst can use to reach the logical equivalent. Figure 9.10 shows the final ERD with the addition of Order-Item-Unit-Price.

The Supertype/Subtype Model

A troublesome database issue occurs in the LDM when there are records within an entity that can take on different characteristics or have many "types" of attributes. "Type" means that a portion of the attributes in a specific record can vary depending on the characteristic or identification of the row within that entity. Another way of defining type is to describe it as a group of attributes within a given record that are

Fig. 9.10 Final ERD with Order-Item-Unit-Price

different from other records of the same entity depending on the *type* of record it represents. This type is referred to as a "subtype" of the record. A subtype, therefore, is the portion of the record that deviates from the standard or "supertype" part of the record. The "supertype" portion is always the same among all the records in the entity. In other words, the "supertype" represents the global part of the attributes in an entity. Fig. 9.11 depicts the supertype/subtype relationship.

The difference between a subtype and an ordinary-type identifier (using a foreign key) is the occurrence of at least one non-key attribute that exists only in that subtype record. The major reason to create a supertype/subtype relationship is the occurrence of multiple permutations of these unique attributes that exist in just certain subtype records. Limiting these permutations of attributes within one record format can be problematic. First, it can waste storage, especially if each subtype has significant numbers of unique attributes. Second, it can create significant performance problems particularly with the querying of data. Using Fig. 9.11, we can see two ways to store these data. The first (Fig. 9.12) is a basic representation where all the permutations exist in one entity called "Educators." The "type" of row is identified by using a foreign key pointer to a validation entity called "Educator Type."

Although this representation of the data uses only one entity, it wastes storage space because *all* of the attributes of the entity are never needed by any one "type" of record. Furthermore, a user must know which attributes need to be entered for a particular type of record. This method of logic data modeling violates the concepts of normalization and entrusts the integrity of values of elements in an entity to either an application program's control (stored procedure) or to the memory of the user. Neither of these choices is particularly dependable or has proven to be a reliable method of data integrity.

On the other hand, Fig. 9.13 provides a different solution using the supertype/subtype model.

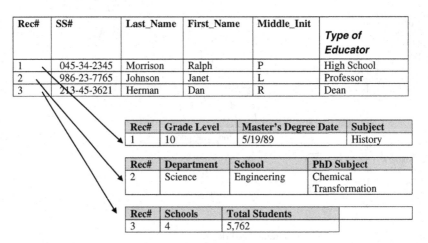

Rec#	SS#	Last_Name	First_Name	Middle_Init	Type of Educator
1	045-34-2345	Morrison	Ralph	P	High School
2	986-23-7765	Johnson	Janet	L	Professor
3	213-45-3621	Herman	Dan	R	Dean

Rec#	Grade Level	Master's Degree Date	Subject
1	10	5/19/89	History

Rec#	Department	School	PhD Subject
2	Science	Engineering	Chemical Transformation

Rec#	Schools	Total Students	
3	4	5,762	

Fig. 9.11 Supertype/subtype relationship

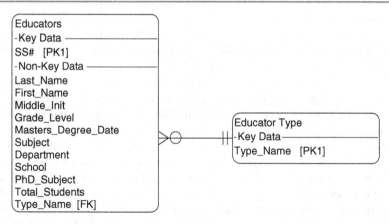

Fig. 9.12 Educator ERD using foreign key identifier

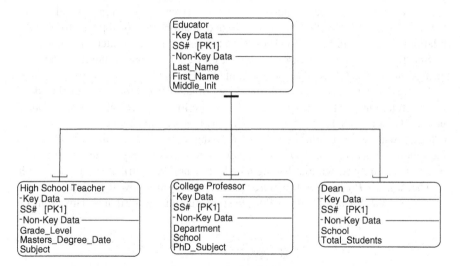

Fig. 9.13 Educator entity supertype/subtype model

This model constructs a separate entity for each type of educator, linked via a special notation in the relational model, known as the supertype/subtype relation. The relationship is mutually exclusive, meaning that the supertype entity Educator can have only one of the three subtypes for any given supertype occurrence. Therefore, the relationship of one record in a supertype must be one-to-one with only one subtype. The supertype/subtype model creates a separate subtype entity to carry only the specific attributes unique to its subtype.

There are two major benefits to this entity structure. First, the construct saves storage because it stores only the attributes it needs in each entity. Second, the subtype information can be directly addressed without accessing its related supertype. This is possible because each subtype entity contains the same primary key as its parent. This capability is significant because a user can automatically obtain the unique information from any subtype without having to search first through the supertype entity. This is particularly beneficial when the number of records in each subtype varies significantly. Suppose, for example, there are 6 million educators in the database. The Educator database would therefore contain 6 million rows. Let's say that 5 million of the educators are high school teachers, and as such, the High School subtype entity has 5 million records. Eight hundred thousand educators are professors and the remaining 200,000 educators are deans; therefore, the Professor database and Dean database have 800,000 and 200,000 records, respectively. Using the supertype/subtype model applications could access each subtype without searching through every record in the database. Furthermore, because access to one subtype does not affect the other, performance is greatly improved.

It is important to note that the supertype/subtype model is not limited to mutual exclusivity, that is, it can support multiple subtype permutations. For example, suppose an educator could be a high school teacher, college professor, and a dean at the same time or any permutation of the three types. The sample model would then be modified to show separate one-to-one relationships as opposed to the "T" relationship shown in Fig. 9.13. The alternative model is represented in Fig. 9.14.

Supertype/subtypes can cascade, that is, they can continue to iterate or decompose within each subtype. This is represented in Fig. 9.15.

Notice that in the above example the same primary key continues to link the "one-to-one" relationships between the entities. In addition, Fig. 9.15 also shows another possibility in the supertype/subtype model. This possibility reflects that a subtype can exist without containing any non-key attributes. This occurs in the example in the subtype entity *Adjunct Prof.* The "empty" entity serves only to identify the existence of the subtype, without having a dedicated non-key attribute associated with it. The *Adjunct Prof entity,* therefore, is created only to allow the other two subtypes (*Tenured Prof* and *Contract Prof*) to store their unique attributes. This example

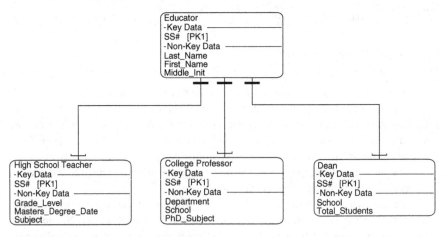

Fig. 9.14 Supertype/subtype model without mutual exclusivity

Fig. 9.15 Cascading subtypes

shows how supertype/subtype models can be constructed, and how they often have subtypes that are created for the sole purpose of identification.

Cascading subtypes can mix methods, that is, some levels may not be mutually exclusive, while other cascade levels can be mutually exclusive as shown in Fig. 9.16.

There is a controversial issue among database developers. The controversy relates to whether it is necessary to create a special attribute that identifies which entity contains the subtype entry for any given supertype. In other words, how does the database know which subtype has the continuation information? This dilemma is especially relevant when mutually exclusive relationships exist in the supertype/subtype. The question is ultimately whether the supertype/subtype model needs to contain an identifier attribute that knows which subtype holds the continuation record or is the issue resolved by the physical database product? Fleming and von Halle (1989) addressed this issue in the *Handbook of Database Design,* where they suggest that the "attribute is at least partially redundant because its meaning already is conveyed by the existence of category or subtype relationships" (p. 162). Still, the issue of redundancy may vary among physical database products. Therefore, I suggest that the logical model contains a subtype identifier for mutually exclusive supertype/subtype relationships as shown in Fig. 9.17.

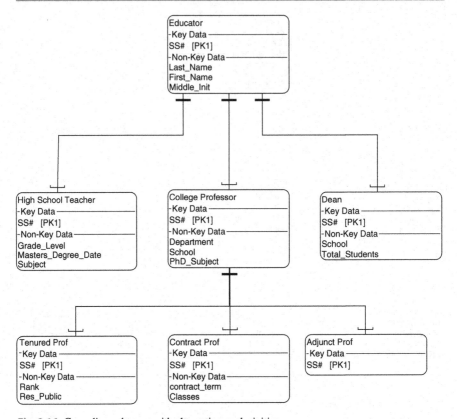

Fig. 9.16 Cascading subtypes with alternating exclusivities

Note that the above example has the subtype identifier, Professor Types as a validation entity in 3rd Normal Form.

Supertype/subtypes must also be normalized following the rules of normalization. For example, the subtype Educator Types contains elements that are not in 3rd NF. Attributes Grade_Level and Subject in the subtype entity High School Teacher can be validated using a look-up table. Department, School, and PhD_Subject can also be validated. The resulting 3rd NF ERD is shown in Fig. 9.18.

Key Business Rules

Key business rules are the rules that govern the behavior between entities when a row is inserted or deleted. These business rules are programmed at the database level using stored procedures and triggers (see Step 7: determine domains and triggering operations). These procedures are typically notated as constraints. Constraints enforce the key business rules that will be defined by the analysts and are the basis of what is meant by referential integrity, that is, the integrity based on the relations

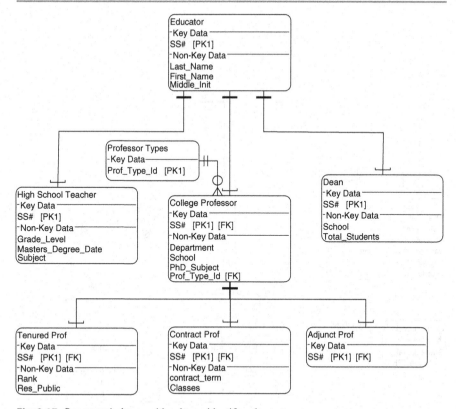

Fig. 9.17 Supertype/subtype with subtype identifier element

between tables. The process of insertion and deletion focuses on the relationship between the parent entity and the child entity. A child entity is always the entity that has the crow's foot pointing to it. Based on the ERD in Fig. 9.10 the parent–child entity relationships are as follows:

- Orders entity is the parent of Order Items entity (child).
- Customer entity is the parent of Orders entity (child).
- Items entity is the parent of Order Items entity (child).

When discussing insertion of a row, it is always from the perspective of the child entity. That is, key business rules governing the insertion of a child record concern what should be done when attempting to insert a child record that does not have a corresponding parent record. There are six alternatives:

1. *Not Allowed*: this means that the constraint is to disallow the transaction. For example, in Fig. 9.10, a user could not insert an Order Item (child) for an Order-Number that did not exist in the Orders entity (parent). Essentially, the integrity of the reference would be upheld, until the Order-Number in the Orders entity was inserted first.

2. *Add Parent*: this means that if the parent key does not exist, it will be added at the same time. Using Fig. 9.10, this would mean that the user would be prompted

Fig. 9.18   Supertype/subtype in 3rd NF

to add the Order-Number to the Orders entity before the child Item would be inserted. The difference between Not Allowed and Add Parent is that the user can enter the parent information during the insertion of the child transaction. Using this rule still enforces referential integrity.

3. *Default Value*: the use of a default value allows a "dummy" row to be inserted into the parent. An example of the use of a default occurs when collection agencies receive payments from an unknown person. The parent entity is "Account" and the child entity is "Payments." The Account entity would have a key value called "Unapplied" which would be used whenever an unidentified payment was collected. In this scenario, it is appropriate to have the dummy record because the

child transaction is really unknown, but at the same time needs to be recorded in the database. It is also useful because the user can quickly get a list of "unapplied" payments and it upholds referential integrity.

4. *Algorithm*: an algorithm is an "intelligent" default value. Using the same example as (3), suppose the user wanted to track unapplied payments by State. For example, if an unapplied payment were received in New York, the parent (Account entity) would have a record inserted with a value "Unapplied-New York." Therefore, each State would have its own default. There are also default keys that are based on sophisticated algorithms to ensure that there is an understanding to the selection of the parent's key attribute value. Again, this selection ensures referential integrity because a record is inserted at both the parent and child entities.

5. *Null*: assigning a null means that the parent does not exist. Most database products such as Oracle allow such selection, and while it is maintained within the product, it violates referential integrity because the parent is unknown.

6. *Don't Care*: this essentially says that the user is willing to accept that referential integrity does not exist in the database. The user will tell you that they never wish to balance the records in the child with those in the parent. While this happens, it should be avoided, because it creates a system without integrity.

When discussing deletion of a row, it is always from the perspective of the parent entity. That is, key business rules governing the deletion of a parent record concern what should be done when attempting to delete a parent record that has corresponding child records. There are similarly six alternatives:

1. *Not Allowed*: this means that the constraint is to disallow the deletion of the parent record. In other words if there are children records, the user cannot delete the parent. For example, if in Fig. 9.10, a user could not delete an Order (parent) if there were corresponding records in the Order Items entity (child). This action would require the user first to delete all of the Order Items or children records before allowing the parent Order to be deleted.

2. *Delete All*: this is also known as *cascading,* because the system would automatically delete all child associations with the parent entity. Using the same example as (1), the children records in Order Items would automatically be deleted. While this option ensures referential integrity, it can be dangerous because it might delete records that are otherwise important to keep.

3. *Default Value*: the use of a default value is the same as in insertion, that is, it allows a "dummy" row to be inserted into the parent. This means that the original parent is deleted, and the child records are redirected to some default value row in the parent entity. This is sometimes useful when there are many old parent records, such as old part-numbers, that are cluttering up the parent database. If keeping the child records is still important, they can be redirected to a default parent row, such as "Old Part-Number."

4. *Algorithm*: the use of the algorithm is the same as with an insertion. As in the case of (3) above, the default value might be based on the type of product or year it became obsolete.

5. *Null*: as in the case of insertion, the assigning of a null means that the parent does not exist. This creates a situation where the child records become "orphans." Referential integrity is lost.
6. *Don't Care*: same as in insertion. The database allows parent records to be deleted without checking to see if there are corresponding child records in another entity. This also results in losing referential integrity and creates "orphans."

In summary, key business rules are concerned with the behavior of primary keys during insert and delete operations. There are six alternative options within each operation (insert and delete). Four of the options uphold referential integrity, which is defined as the dependability of the relationships between items of data. Data integrity is an issue any time there is change to data, which in e-commerce systems will be frequent. Thus, the e-commerce analyst must ensure that once primary keys have been determined, it is of vital importance that users are interviewed regarding their referential integrity needs. Analysts should not make these decisions in a vacuum and need to present the advantages of referential integrity appropriately to users so that they can make intelligent and well-informed decisions.

This discussion of key business rules was predicated using examples derived from the discussion on normalization. As discussed earlier in this section, the application of normalization occurs after the determination of key business rules, especially since it may indeed affect the design of the ERD, and in the programming of stored procedures. This will be discussed further in *Determine Domains and Triggering Operations*.

Combining User Views

The application of normalization focused on breaking up or decomposing entities to include the correct placement of data. Each NF failure resulted in creating a new entity; however, there are situations where certain entities may need to be combined. This section is labeled "Combining User Views" because the meaning of data is strongly dependent on how the user defines a data element. Unfortunately, there are circumstances where data elements are called different things and defined differently by different users in different departments. The word "different" is critical to the example. In cases where we think we have two entities, we may, in fact have only one. Therefore, the process of combining user views typically results in joining two or more entities as opposed to decomposing them as done with normalization. The best way to understand this concept is to recall the earlier discussion on logical equivalents. This interpretation of the logical equivalent will focus on the data rather than the process. Suppose there are two entities created from two different departments. The first department defines the elements for an entity called "Clients" as shown in Fig. 9.19.

The second department defines an entity called "Customers" as shown in Fig. 9.20.

Fig. 9.19 The client entity

```
Clients
-Key Data ──────────────────
Client_Id  [PK1]
-Non-Key Data ──────────────
Client_Name
Client_Address
Client_Age
Client_Quality_Indicator
```

Fig. 9.20 The customer entity

```
Customers
-Key Data ──────────────────
Customer_Id  [PK1]
-Non-Key Data───────────────
Customer_Name
Customer_Address
Customer_Buyer_Indicator
Customer_Credit_Rating
```

Upon a closer analysis and review of the data element definitions, it becomes apparent that the two departments are looking at the same object. Notwithstanding whether the entity is named Client or Customer, these entities must be combined. The process of combining two or more entities is not as simple as it might sound. In the two examples, there are data elements that are the same with different names, and there are unique data elements in each entity. Each department is unaware of the other's view of the same data and by applying logical equivalencies the following single entity results as shown in Fig. 9.21.

The above example uses names that made it easier for an analyst to know they were the same data elements. In reality, such may not be the case, especially when working with legacy systems. In legacy systems, names and definitions of elements can vary significantly among departments and applications. Furthermore, the data definitions can vary significantly. Suppose Client is defined as VARCHAR2(35) and Customer as VARCHAR2(20). The solution is to take the larger definition. In

```
Customers
-Key Data  ─────────────────
Customer_Id  [PK1]
-Non-Key Data  ─────────────
Customer_Name
Customer_Address
Customer_Buyer_Indicator
Customer_Credit_Rating
Customer_Age
Customer_Quality_Indicator
```

Fig. 9.21 Combined client
and customer entity

still other scenarios, one element could be defined as alphanumeric and the other numeric. In these circumstances the decisions become more involved with user conversations. In either situation, it is important that the data elements do get combined and that users agree-to-agree. In cases where user agreement is difficult, then analysts can take advantage of a data dictionary feature called Alias. An Alias is defined as an alternate name for a data element. Multiple Aliases can point to the same data dictionary entry. Therefore, screens can display names that are Aliases for another element. This alternative can solve many problems when using different names is necessary.

Another important issue in combining user views is performance. While analysts should not be overly concerned about performance issues during LDM, it should not be ignored either. Simply put, the fewer entities, the faster the performance; therefore, the least number of entities that can be designed in the ERD the better.

Integration with Existing Data Models

The purpose of this section is to discuss specific analysis and design issues relating to how to integrate with existing database applications. The connectivity with other database systems is difficult. Indeed, many firms approach the situation by phasing each business area over time into a new redeveloped operation. In these circumstances, each phased area needs a "Legacy Link" which allows the "old" applications to work with the new phased-in software. Chapter 10 will focus on the procedures for integration of both the data and application components of package software systems. This section is limited to only those issues that affect the design of entities during LDM.

Linking entities with existing databases may force e-commerce analysts to rethink how to preserve integrity while still maintaining the physical link to other corporate data. This occurrence is a certainty with e-commerce systems given that certain portions of the data are used inside and outside the business. The following example shows how this problem occurs

> The analyst is designing a website that utilizes the company's Orders Master database. The website needs this information to allow customers to see information about their past orders for items so they can match it to a product database supplied by the e-commerce system. This feature is provided to customers to allow them to understand how items have been utilized to make their products. Unfortunately, the master Order Items database holds only orders for the past year and then stores them off-line. There is no desire by the Order department to create a historical tracking system. The ERD in Fig. 9.22 shows the relationships with the corporate Order Items database file.

Note that the Order Item Products entity has a one or zero relationship with the Order Item Master entity. This means that there can be an Order Item in the Order Item Product entity that does not exist in the Order Item entity. Not only does this violate normalization, but it also presents a serious integrity problem. For example,

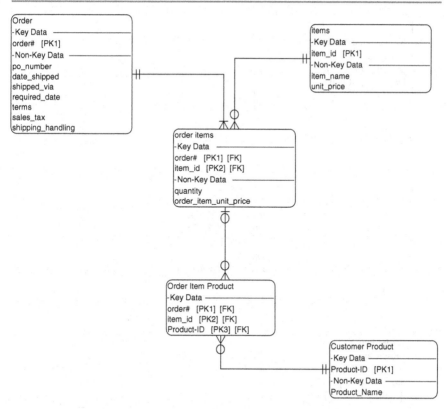

Fig. 9.22 ERD showing association between web databases and legacy employee master

if the customer wanted to display information about their products and each component Item, all Items that do not exist in the Order Item entity will display blanks, since there is no corresponding name information in the Order Item file. Obviously, this is a flaw in the database design that needs to be corrected. The remedy is to build a subsystem database that will capture all of the Order Items without purging them. This would entail a system that accesses the Order Item database and merges it with the Web version of the file. The merge conversion would compare the two files and update or add new Order Items without deleting the old ones. That is, the master Order Items would be searched daily to pick up new Order Items to add to the Web version. Although this is an extra step, it maintains integrity, normalization, and most importantly, the requirement not to modify the original Order Item database. The drawback to this solution is that the Web version may not have up-to-date Order Items information. This will depend on how often records are moved to the Web database. This can be remedied by having a replication feature, where the Web Order Item would be created at the same time as the master version. The ERD would be reconstructed as shown in Fig. 9.23.

Fig. 9.23 ERD reflecting legacy link to the Order Item entity

In Fig. 9.23 the Order Item Master and its relation to the Web Order Item entity are shown for informational purposes only. The master Order Item becomes more of an application requirement rather than a permanent part of the ERD. In order to "operationalize" this system, the analyst must first have to reconstruct the history data from the purged files or simply offer the historical data as of a certain date.

Determine Domains and Triggering Operations

The growth of the relational database model has established processes for storing certain application logic at the database level. We have already defined key business rules as the vehicle to create constraints at the key attribute level. However, there are other constraints and procedures that can occur depending on the behavior of non-key attributes. Ultimately, business rules are application logic that is coded in the database language, for example, PL_SQL for Oracle. These non-key attribute rules could enforce such actions as, If CITY is entered, the STATE must also be entered. This type of logic rule used to be enforced at the application level. Unfortunately, using application logic to enforce business rules is inefficient because it requires the code to be replicated in each application program. This process also limits control, in that the relational model allows users to "query" the database directly. Thus, business rules at the database level need to be written only once, and they govern all type of applications, including programs and queries.

As stated earlier, business rules are implemented at the database level via stored procedures. Stored procedures are offered by most database manufacturers, and although they are similar, they are not implemented using the same coding schemes. Therefore, moving stored procedures from one database to another is not trivial. In Chapter 8, the importance of having portable stored procedures and their relationship to partitioning databases across the Internet, Intranets, and wide area networks (WANs) will be discussed further. It is important to note that distributed network systems are being built under the auspices of client/server computing and may require communication among many different database vendor systems. If business rules are to be implemented at the database level, the compatibility and transportability of such code become a challenge.

Business rule implementations fall into three categories: keys, domains, and triggers. Key business rules have already been discussed as part of the normalization process. Domains represent the constraints related to an attribute's range of values. If an attribute (key or non-key) can have a range of values from one to nine, we say that range is the domain value of the attribute. This is very important information to be included and enforced at the database level through a stored procedure for the same reasons as discussed above. The third and most powerful business rule is triggers.

Triggers are defined as stored procedures that when activated "trigger" one or a set of other stored procedures to be executed. Triggers act on other entities, although in many database products, triggers are becoming powerful programming tools to provide significant capabilities at the database level rather than at the application level. Triggers resemble batch-type files which when invoked execute a "script" or set of logical statements as shown below:

```
/* Within D. B.. only authorized users can mark    */
   /* ecommerce corporation as confidential             */
   if user not in ('L','M') then
   :new.corpConfidential := 'N';
   end if;
end if;
/* Ensure user has right to make a specific users private    */
if exec= 'N' then
  :new.corpexec:= 'N';
end if;
```

This trigger was implemented in a contact management e-commerce system. The trigger is designed to allow corporate information to be marked as confidential only by specific executives. This means that an appointed executive of the corporation can enter information that is private. The second component of the trigger is programmed to automatically ensure that the executive's contacts are stored as private or confidential. These two stored procedures show how application logic executes via Oracle triggers. It is important to remember that these business rules are enforced by the database regardless of how the information is accessed.

Triggers, however, can cause problems. Because triggers can initiate activity among database files, designers must be careful that they do not impair performance. For example, suppose a trigger is written that affects 15 different database files. Should the trigger be initiated during the processing of other critical applications, it could cause significant degradation in processing and thus affect critical production systems.

The subject of business rules is very broad yet must be specific to the actual database product to be used. Since analysts may not know which database will ultimately be used, specifications for stored procedures should be developed using the specification formats presented in Chapter 3. This is even more salient in e-commerce systems given the possibility that different databases can be used across the entire system. This dilemma will be discussed in Chapter 8 as part of the integration issues facing e-commerce analysts and designers.

De-normalization

Third NF databases can often have difficulty with performance. Specifically, significant numbers of look-up tables, which are actual 3rd NF failures, create too many index links. As a result, while we have reached the integrity needed, performance becomes an unavoidable dilemma. In fact, the more integrity, the less performance. There are a number of ways to deal with the downsides of normalized databases. One is to develop data warehouses and other off-line copies of the database. Data warehousing will be discussed in Chapter 12: Data Analytics and Data Warehouses. Another alternative is to de-normalize. There are many bad ways to de-normalize. Indeed, any de-normalization hurts integrity. But there are two types of de-normalization that can be implemented without significantly hurting the integrity of the data.

The first type of de-normalization is to revisit 3rd NF failures to see if all of the validations are necessary. Third NF failures usually create tables that ensure that entered values are validated against a master list. For example, in Fig. 9.10, the Customers entity created as a result of a 3rd NF failure provides a validation to all customers associated with an Order. This means that the user cannot assign any customer, but rather only those residents in the Customer entity. The screen to select a Customer would most likely use a "drop-down" menu, which would show all of the valid Customers for selection to the Order. However, there may be look-up tables that are not as critical. For example, zipcodes may or may not be validated.

Whether zipcodes need to be validated depends on the use of zipcodes by the users. If they are just used to record a Customer's address, then it may not be necessary or worthwhile to have the zipcode validated. If, on the other hand, they are used for certain types of geographic analysis or mailing, then indeed, validation is necessary. This process—the process of reviewing the use and need for a validation table—should occur during the interview process. If this step is left out, then there is a high probability that too many non-key attributes will contain validation look-up entities that are unnecessary and hurt performance.

The second type of de-normalization is to add back "derived" attributes. While this is not the preferred method, it can be implemented without sacrificing integrity. This can be accomplished by creating triggers that automatically launch a stored procedure to recalculate a derived value when a dependent attribute has been altered. For example, if Amount is calculated based on Quantity * Unit-Price, then two triggers must be developed (one for Quantity and one for Unit-Price) which would recalculate Amount if either Quantity or Unit-Price were changed. While this solves the integrity issue, analysts must be cognizant over the performance conflict should the trigger be initiated during peak processing times. Therefore, there must be a balance between the trigger and when it is allowed to occur.

Summary

This chapter has provided the logical equivalent to the data component of the e-commerce system. The process of decomposing data is accomplished using LDM, which has eight major steps that need to be applied in order to functionally decompose the data. Data flow diagrams (DFDs) are a powerful tool to use during process analysis because they provide direct input into the LDM method. Specifically, data flows provide data definitions into the data dictionary, which is necessary to complete LDM. Furthermore, data stores in the DFD represent the major entities, which is the first step in LDM. The output of LDM is an ERD, which represents the schematic or blueprint of the database. The ERD shows the relationships among entities and the cardinality of those relationships.

The LDM also makes provisions to develop stored procedures, which are programs developed at the database level. These procedures allow "referential integrity" to be enforced without developing application programs that operate outside the data. Stored procedures can be used to enforce key business rules, domain rules, and triggers. Triggers are batch-oriented programs that automatically execute when a particular condition has occurred at the database level, typically, when an attribute has been altered in some way.

The process of LDM also allows for the de-normalization at the logical design level. This is allowed so that analysts can avoid significant known performance problems before the physical database is completed. De-normalization should occur at the user interface time, as many of the issues will depend on the user's needs.

Problems and Exercises

1. What is logical data modeling trying to accomplish?
2. Define normalization. What are the three Normal Forms?
3. What does normalization *not* do?
4. What is meant by the term "derived" data element?
5. Describe the concept of combining user views. What are the political ramifications of doing this in many organizations?
6. What are legacy links? Describe how they can be used to enforce data integrity.
7. Name and define the three types of business rules.
8. Why are stored procedures in some ways a contradiction to the rule that data and processes need to be separated?
9. What are the disadvantages of database triggers?
10. What is meant by de-normalization? Is this a responsibility of the analyst?

Mini-Project

The Physician Master File from a DFD contains the following data elements:

Data Element	Description
Social Security #	Primary Key
Physician ID	Alternate Key
Last_Name	Last Name
First_Name	First Name
Mid_Init	Middle Initial
Hospital_Resident_ID	Hospital Identification
Hospital_Resident_Name	Name of Hospital
Hospital_Addr_Line1	Hospital Address
Hospital_Addr_Line2	Hospital Address
Hospital_Addr_Line3	Hospital Address
Hospital_State	Hospital's State
Hospital_City	Hospital's City
Hospital_Zip	Hospital's Zip Code
Specialty_Type	The Physician's specialty
Specialty_Name	Description of specialty
Specialty_College	College where received degree
Specialty_Degree	Degree Name
Date_Graduated	Graduation Date for specialty
DOB	Physician's Date of Birth
Year_First_Practiced	First year in practice
Year's_Pract_Exp	Practice Experience Years
Annual_Earnings	Annual Income

Assumptions:
a. A Physician can be associated with many hospitals, but must be associated with at least one.
b. A Physician can have many specialties or have no specialty.
   Assignment: Normalize to 3rd Normal Form

References

Date, C. J. (2000). *An introduction to database systems* (7th ed.). New York: Addison-Wesley.

Fleming, C., & von Halle, B. (1989). *Handbook of relational database design.* Menlo Park, CA: Addison-Wesley.

Larson, J. A., & Larson, C. L. (2000). Data models and modelling techniques. In S. Purba (Ed.), *Data management handbook* (3rd ed.). Boca Raton, FL: CRC Press.

Legacy Systems and Integration

10

Introduction

A legacy system is an existing application system in operation. While this is an accurate definition, there is a perception that legacy systems are old and antiquated applications operating on mainframe computers. Indeed, Brodie and Stonebraker (1995) state that, "a legacy information system is any information system that significantly resists modification and evolution" (p. 3). They define typical legacy systems as

- Large application with millions of lines of code
- Usually more than 10 years old
- Written in legacy languages like COBOL
- They are built around a legacy database service (such as IBM's IMS) and some do not use a database management system. Instead they use older flat file systems such as ISAM and VSAM
- The applications are very autonomous. Legacy applications tend to operate independently from other applications, which means that there is very limited interface among application programs. When interfaces among applications are available they are usually based on export and import models of data and these interfaces lack data consistency

While many legacy systems do fit these scenarios, many do not. Those that do not can, however, be considered legacies under my original definition, that is, any application in operation. What this simply means is that there are what I call "generations" of legacy systems that can exist in any organization. Thus, the definitions of what constitutes a legacy system are much broader than Brodie and Stonebraker's descriptions. The more important issue to address is the relationship of legacy systems with package software systems. In Chapter 1, I defined package software systems as one that encompassed both internal and external applications. Thus, existing internal production systems, including third-party outsourced products, must be part of any application strategy. Furthermore, there are many legacy systems that perform external functions as well, albeit not in an Internet interface.

A.M. Langer, *Guide to Software Development*,
DOI 10.1007/978-1-4471-2300-2_10, © Springer-Verlag London Limited 2012

This chapter defines the types of legacy systems that exist and provides guidelines on how to approach their integration with package software applications. The project manager or analyst must determine whether a legacy system should be replaced, enhanced, or remain as is. This chapter also provides the procedures for dealing with each of these three choices and its effect on the overall architecture of the decision whether to make or buy a system.

Types of Legacy Systems

The types of legacy systems tend to mirror the life cycle of software development. Software development is usually defined within a framework called "generations." Most professionals agree that there are five generations of programming languages:

1. *First generation*: the first generation was known as machine language. Machine language is considered a low-level language because there it uses binary symbols to communicate instructions to the hardware. These binary symbols form a one-to-one relationship between a machine language command and a machine activity, that is, one machine language command performs one machine instruction. It is rare that any legacy systems have first-generation software.

2. *Second generation*: this generation comprises assembler programming languages. Assembler languages are proprietary software that translates a higher-level coding scheme into more than one machine language instruction. Therefore, it was necessary to design an assembler, which would translate the symbolic codes into machine instructions. Mainframe shops may still have a considerable amount of assembly code that exists, particularly with applications that perform intricate algorithms and calculations.

3. *Third generation*: this language continued the growth of high-level symbolic languages that had translators into machine code. Examples of third-generation languages are COBOL, FORTRAN, BASIC, RPG, and C. These languages use more English-like commands and have a higher ratio of machine language produced from one instruction. Third-generation languages tend to be more specialized. For example, FORTRAN is better suited for mathematical and scientific calculations. Therefore, many insurance companies have FORTRAN because of the high concentration on actuarial mathematic calculations. COBOL, on the other hand, was designed as the business language and has special features to allow it to manipulate file and database information. There are more COBOL applications that exist than any other programming languages. Most mainframe legacy systems still have COBOL applications. RPG is yet another specialized language that was designed for use on IBM's mid-range machines. These machines include the System 36, System 38, and AS/400 computers.

4. *Fourth generation*: these programming languages are less procedural than third-generation languages. In addition, the symbols are more English-like and emphasize more about desired output results than how the programming statements need to be written. As a result of this feature, many less technical programmers have learned how to program using fourth-generation languages (4GLs). The

most powerful features of 4GLs include query of databases, code generation, and graphic screen generation abilities. Such languages include Visual Basic, C++, Powerbuilder, Delphi, and many others. Furthermore, 4GLs also include what is known as *query languages* because they contain English-like questions that are used to directly produce results by directly accessing relational databases. The most popular 4GL query language is Structured Query Language (SQL).

5. *Fifth generation*: these programming languages combine what is known as rule-based code generation, component management, and visual programming techniques. The rule-based code generation became popular in the late 1980s with the creation of artificial intelligence software. This software uses an approach called knowledge-based programming, which means that the developer does not tell the computer how to solve problems, but rather the problem (Stair & Reynolds, 1999). The program figures out how to solve the problem. While knowledge-based programming has become popular in specialized applications, such as in the medical industry, it has not been as popular in business.

Most legacy applications will either be third-generation or fourth-generation language systems, therefore, analysts need to have a process and methodology to determine how to integrate package software technology with these applications.

Third-Generation Language Legacy System Integration

As previously discussed, most third-generation language legacy systems were developed using COBOL. COBOL was developed to provide a method of forcing programmers to self-document their code so that other programmers could maintain it. Unfortunately, COBOL requires what is known as a file description (FD) table. The FD defines the record layout for every file used by the COBOL program. In other words, every file is described within the program and must match the format of the actual physical data file. This means that any change to a file structure must be synchronized with every COBOL program that uses that data file. Thus, COBOL is somewhat eclectic: there is no real separation of the data description and the program logic. In COBOL programs, a change in data format could necessitate a change in the program code. That is why COBOL programs suffer from large degrees of coupling of code. Coupling is defined as the reliance of one piece of the code on another.

COBOL programs may or may not use a relational database as its source of data. I earlier defined two other common formats called ISAM and VSAM, which are flat file formats, meaning that all data elements are contained in one record as opposed to multiple files as is the case in the relational database model. However, many COBOL legacy systems have been converted to work with relational databases such as IBM's DB2. In this situation the FD tables interface with the database's file manager so that the two entities can communicate with each other. Figure 10.1 depicts the interface between program and database.

Employee Payroll File Description Table in COBOL Program

```
DATA DIVISION.
FILE SECTION.
FD      PAYROLL-FILE
        LABEL RECORDS ARE OMITTED.
01      PAYROLL-RECORD.
        05      I-PAYROLL-NUMBER              PIC X(5).
        05      I-NAME                        PIC X(20).
        05      I-HOURS-WORKED                        PIC 99V9.
        05      FILLER                        PIC XXX.
        05      I-PAYRATE                             PIC 99V999.
        05      I-DEPENDENTS                  PIC 99.
        05      FILLER                        PIC X(20).
```

Employee Payroll Entity

Payroll-Number (PK)
L-Name F-Name Hours-Worked PayRate Dependents

Fig. 10.1 COBOL file description interface with database manager

Notwithstanding whether the COBOL legacy is using a database interface or flat files the analyst needs to determine whether to replace the application, enhance it, or leave it as is.

Replacing Third-Generation Legacy Systems

When replacing third-generation legacies, analysts must focus on both the data and processes. Because of the age of these systems, it is likely that there will be little documentation available, and the amount available will most likely be outdated. Indeed, the lack of proper documentation is the major reason why legacy systems are slow to be replaced: rewriting code without documentation can be an overwhelming and time-consuming task. Unfortunately, all things must eventually be replaced. Delaying replacement leads to legacy systems that keep businesses from remaining competitive. The following sections provide a step-by-step approach to COBOL-based legacies.

Approaches to Logic Reconstruction

The best way to reconstruct the logic in COBOL applications is to separate the data from the processes. This can be accomplished by creating data flow diagrams (DFDs) for each program. Having a DFD will result in defining all of the inputs and outputs of the application. This is accomplished by following the tasks below:

1. Print the source code (actual COBOL written code) from each application. Each application will contain an "FD" section that defines all of the inputs and outputs of the program. These will represent the data stores of the data flow diagrams (Fig. 10.2).
2. DFDs should be decomposed so that they are at the functional primitive level (one-in and one-out, preferred). This provides functional decomposition for the old application and sets the framing for how it will be decomposed into an object-oriented (OO) solution.
3. By reviewing the code, write the process specifications for each functional primitive.
4. Follow the steps as outlined in Chapter 8 to determine which functional primitive DFDs become methods of a particular class.
5. Capture all of the data elements or attributes required by each functional primitive DFD. These attributes are added to the data dictionary (DD).
6. Take each major data store and create an entity. Do normalization and logic data modeling in accordance with the procedures in Chapter 4, combining these elements with the package software system as appropriate.
7. Data stores that represent reports should be compared against sample outputs. These reports will need to be redeveloped using a report writer such as Crystal's report writer or a data warehouse product.
8. Examine all existing data files and/or databases in the legacy system. Compare these elements against those discovered during the logic reconstruction. In

```
FD      REPORT-FILE
        LABEL RECORDS ARE OMITTED.
01      REPORT-RECORD.
        05      O-PAYROLL-NUMBER            PIC X(5).
        05      FILLER                      PIC XX.
        05      O-NAME                      PIC X(20).
        05      FILLER                      PIC XX.
        05      O-HOURS-WORKED              PIC 99.9.
        05      FILLER                      PIC XX.
        05      O-PAYRATE                   PIC 99.999.
        05      FILLER                      PIC XX.
        05      O-DEPENDENTS                PIC 99.
        05      FILLER                      PIC XX.
        05      O-GROSS-PAY                 PIC 999.99.
        05      FILLER                      PIC XX.
        05      O-TAX                       PIC 999.99.
        05      FILLER                      PIC XX.
        05      O-NET-PAY                   PIC 999.99.
```

Fig. 10.2 COBOL file description tables

third-generation products there will be many data elements or fields that are redundant or used as logic "flags." Logic flags consists of fields used to store a value that depicts a certain state of the data. For example, suppose a record has been updated by a particular program. One method of knowing that this occurred is to have the application program set a certain field with a code that identifies that it has been updated. This method would not be necessary in a relational database product because file managers automatically keep logs on the last time a record has been updated. This example illustrates how different third-generation legacy technology differs from more contemporary technologies.

There is no question that replacing third-generation legacies is time-consuming. However, the procedures outlined above will prove to be accurate and effective. In many situations, users will decide that it makes sense to reexamine their legacy processes, especially when the decision has been made to rewrite the program and integrate it with package software system. We call this business process reengineering. Business process reengineering is therefore synonymous with enhancing the legacy system (see Chapter 11).

Enhancing Third-Generation Legacy Systems

Business process reengineering (BPR) is one of the more popular methodologies used to enhance third-generation applications. A more formal definition of BPR is "a requirement to study fundamental business processes, independent of organization units and information systems support, to determine if the underlying business processes can be significantly streamlined and improved."[1] BPR is not just rebuilding the existing applications for the sake of applying new technology to older systems, but also an event that allows for the application of new procedures designed around the object-oriented systems paradigm. In this scenario, however, BPR is used to enhance existing applications without rewriting them in another generation language. Instead, the analyst needs to make changes to the system that will make it function more like an object component, even though it is written in a third-generation language. In order to accomplish this task, it is necessary for the analyst to create the essential components of the legacy operation. Essential components represent the core business requirements of a unit. Another way of defining core business requirements is to view essential components as the reasons why the unit exists, what does it do, and for what reasons. For example, Fig. 10.3 depicts the essential components of a bank.

Once the essential components have been created then the legacy applications need to be placed in the appropriate component so that it can be linked with its related package software applications.

The first step in applying successful BPR to legacy applications is to develop an approach to define the existing system and extracting its data elements and

---

[1] Whitten, Jeffrey, Bentley, Lonnie, Barlow, Victor. Systems Analysis and Design Methods, Third Edition, pg. 238.

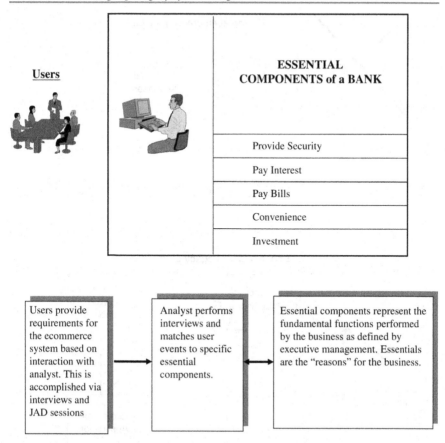

Fig. 10.3 Essential components of a bank

applications. Once again, this is similar to the process described above when replacing third-generation legacy applications in that the data need to be captured into the data repository and the applications need to be defined and compared to a new model based on essential components.

Data Element Enhancements

The analyst will need to design conversion programs that will access the data files that are not in relational database format and place them in a data repository. The ultimate focus is to replace all of the existing data files in the legacy with relational databases that can be linked with package software databases. This methodology differs from replacing legacies. In replacement engineering, data files are integrated directly into a package software system. This means that the legacy data will often be used to enhance the package software databases. However, the process of enhancing legacy systems means that the legacy data will remain separate but converted into the relational model. For legacies that already have relational databases,

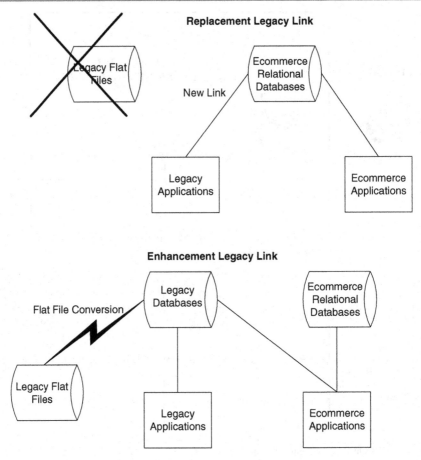

Fig. 10.4 Replacing vs. enhancing legacy data

there is no restructuring required beyond setting up links with the package software database. Figure 10.4 reflects the difference between replacing legacy data and
enhancing it.

Another interesting difference between the two approaches is that enhanced legacies will likely have intentional data redundancy. This means that the same element
may indeed exist in multiple databases; a violation of 3rd Normal Form. However,
the redundancy must exist for the sake of maintaining separate identities of the systems. Duplicate elements may take on different formats. The most obvious is where
a data element has alias, meaning that an element has many different names, but the
same attributes. Another type is the same element name, but with different attributes.
The third type, and the most challenging, is the duplicate elements that have different names and different attributes. While duplicate data elements may exist in
enhanced legacy applications that are integrated with the package software product,
it is still important to identify duplicate data relationships. This can be accomplished

by documenting data relationships in a CASE tool and in the database's physical data dictionary where aliases can exist.

Application Enhancements

BPR typically involves a methodology called business area analysis (BAA). The purpose of BAA is to

- establish the various legacy business areas that will be linked with the package software system
- reengineer the new and old requirements of each business area
- develop requirements that provide an OO perspective of each legacy business area, meaning that there is no need to map its requirements to the existing physical organization structure
- define the links that create relationships among all the legacy business areas and the package software business areas

This is accomplished by mapping business areas to specific essential component. Applications designed for the package software system must also be mapped to an essential component. Once this has occurred, the legacy applications and package software applications must be designed to share common processes and databases as shown in Fig. 10.5. BPR is discussed further in Chapter 11.

Once the legacy and package software applications have been placed in their appropriate essential component they will need to be linked, that is, communicate with each other to complete the integration of the internal and external systems. Linking occurs in two ways: parameter messaging and database. Parameter messaging requires that the legacy programs be modified to receive data in the form of parameters. This allows the application system to deliver information directly to the legacy program. Conversely, the legacy program may need to return information back to the package software system. Therefore, legacy applications need to be enhanced so they can actually format and send a data message to the package software system. A database interface is essentially the same concept except that it occurs differently. Instead of the application sending the data directly to another program, it forwards it as a record in a database file. The legacy program that returns the data also needs to be modified to forward messages to a database.

There are advantages and disadvantages of using either methods. First, parameters use little overhead and are easy to program. They do not provide reusable data, that is, once a message has been received it is no longer available to another program. Parameters are also limited in size. Databases, on the other hand, allow programs to send the information to multiple destinations because it can be read many times. Unfortunately, it is difficult to control what applications or queries can access the data, which does raise questions about how secure the data are. Furthermore, applications must remember to delete a record in the database if it is no longer required. Figure 10.6 reflects the two methods of transferring data between legacy systems and package software applications.

Once the legacy and the new package software applications have all been mapped to the essential components, analysts can use a CRUD diagram to assist them in

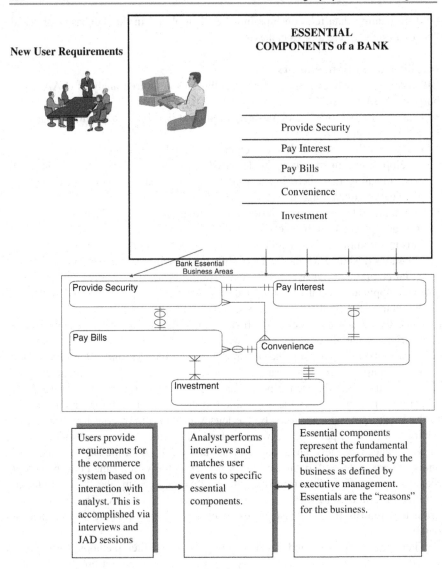

Fig. 10.5 BPR legacy modeling using essential components

reconciling whether all of the data and processes have been found. The importance of the CRUD diagram is that it ensures

- that an essential component has complete control over its data,
- that all of the entities are accessible by at least one process, and
- that processes are accessing data (Fig. 10.7).

While CRUD is not 100% accurate, it certainly uncovers potential problems as shown above. Even if BPR is not used, the CRUD diagram is an excellent tool to use

Fig. 10.6 Linking data
between legacy and package
software systems

Legacy Link Using a Parameter

Legacy Link using a Database

Processes or Business Function / Data Subject or Entity	Process Orders	Validate Products	Shipping	Commission
Customers	R		R,U	
Orders	C, U		U	R
Items	R	C,U,D	R	R
Inventory	R,U	C,U	U	
Expense Section				
Market Person	R			U

Fig. 10.7 Sample CRUD diagram

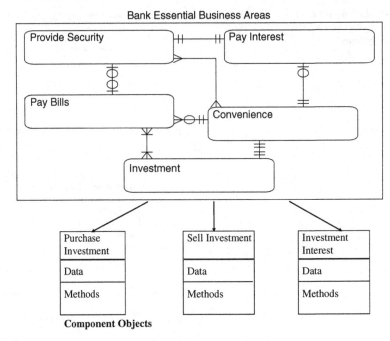

Fig. 10.8 Essential component object diagrams

to determine the processes and data needed for an essential component or an object. Once the CRUD diagram is finalized, the objects and classes would then be created as shown in Fig. 10.8; some of these objects are still in the form of a third-generation COBOL program while others might be in a JAVA-based package software format. CRUD is discussed in more detail in Chapter 11.

"Leaving As Is"—Third-Generation Legacy Systems

Moving to an object-oriented and client/server paradigm from a third-generation product like COBOL may not be feasible. The language design of third-generation procedural programs may result in conceptual gaps between procedural and object-oriented philosophies. For example, distributed object-oriented programs require more detailed technical infrastructure knowledge and graphics manipulation than was required in older legacy systems. Native object-oriented features such as inheritance, polymorphism, and encapsulation do not apply in traditional third-generation procedural design. It is difficult, if not impossible to introduce new object concepts and philosophies during a direct COBOL to JAVA migration. If the translation is attempted without significant restructuring (as discussed earlier in this chapter) then the resulting product will likely contain slower code that is more difficult to maintain.

Fig. 10.9 "As is" legacy links

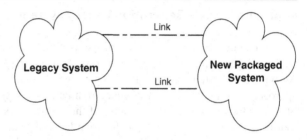

There can also be a cultural divide that occurs. Veteran COBOL programmers and newer JAVA developers do not understand each other's technologies. This scenario will often create bias during any conversion effort. Furthermore, COBOL programmers learning new technology can present them with self-specified threats to their cultural status. Furthermore, COBOL and RPG applications have benefited from the more lengthy testing, debugging, and overall refinement than newer programming generations. While JAVA is more dynamic, it is less stable, and the procedure of debugging and fixing problems are very different than for COBOL or RPG. Therefore, the analyst will leave the legacy "as is" and create only package software links for passing information that is required between the two systems. While this is similar to the "linking" proposed for enhancing legacy systems, it is different because legacy programs are not enhanced, except for the external links needed to pass information. This is graphically shown in Fig. 10.9.

Using parameters or databases to link connecting information is still relevant, but analysts must be cognizant that legacy data formats will not be changed. This means that the legacy applications will continue to use their original file formats. Another concept used to describe "links" is called "bridges." The word suggests that the link serves to connect a gap between the package software system and the legacy applications. Bridging can also imply temporary link. Very often "as is" can be seen as a temporary condition because legacy conversions cannot occur all at once, so it is typically planned in phases. However, while parts of the system are being converted, some portions may need temporary bridges until it is time to actually enhance them. One can visualize this as a temporary "road block" or detour that occurs when there is construction on a highway.

Fourth-Generation Language Legacy System Integration

Integrating fourth-generation legacy systems with package software technology is much easier than third-generation languages. The reasons are twofold. First, most fourth-generation implementations are already using a relational database, so conversion of data to the package software system is less complex. Second, fourth-generation language applications typically use SQL-based code, so conversion to an object-oriented system is also less involved.

Replacing Fourth-Generation Legacy Systems

As stated above, replacement of fourth-generation language systems is less complex than third-generation languages with respect to the package software conversion. As with any system replacement, separating data and process is the suggested approach. Fortunately, in fourth-generation language systems, process and data are likely to already be separate, because of the nature of its architecture. Specifically, fourth-generation languages typically use relational databases, which architecturally separate data and process. Therefore, replacing the legacy is more about examining the existing processes and determining where the applications need to be reengineered.

Approaches to Logic Reconstruction

The best approach to logic analysis is to print out the source code of the programs. If the source is written in SQL, then the analyst should search for all SELECT statements. SQL SELECT FROM statements define the databases that the program is using as shown in Fig. 10.10.

As in third-generation languages' logic reconstruction, the analyst should produce a DFD for every program as follows:

1. SELECT statements define all inputs and outputs that a program uses. Each SELECT statement file will be represented by a DFD data store. Reviewing the logic of the application program will reveal whether the data are being created, read, updated, or deleted (CRUD).
2. DFDs should be decomposed to the functional primitive level so that the framework to an object-oriented system is established.
3. For each DFD copy the relevant SQL code, making modifications where necessary to provide more object-oriented functionality to the program. This means that the decomposition of the code will likely require that some new logic be added to transform it to a method. This is shown in Fig. 10.11.
4. Examine existing system objects and determine if functional primitive DFDs belong to an existing class as a new method or whether it truly represents a new object in the package software system.
5. Capture all of the data elements required by the new methods and add them to their respective object. Ensure that the package software DD is updated appropriately.
6. Determine whether any new objects need to become a reusable component in the third-party (TP) monitor (middleware), a reusable component in the client application, or as a stored procedure at the database level.

```
Select    IdNo, Last-Name, First-Name
from      employee
where     IDNo = "054475643"
```

Fig. 10.10 SELECT statements in a fourth-generation language application

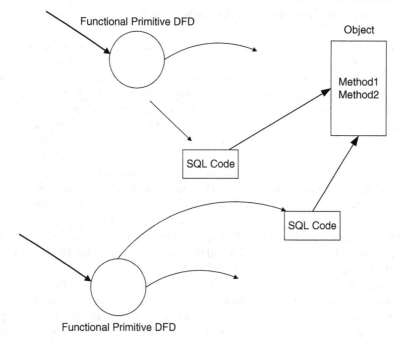

Fig. 10.11 SQL code transition to object method

7. Examine the legacy databases and do logic data modeling to place the entities in 3rd Normal Form (3NF).
8. Combine and integrate data elements with package software databases, ensuring that each data field from the legacy system is properly matched with package software data elements. New elements must be added to the appropriate entity or require that new entities be created for them.
9. Link new entities with existing models using 3rd Normal Form referential integrity rules.
10. Determine which data elements are redundant, such as calculations. These data elements will be removed; however, logic to their calculations may need to be added as a method as shown in Fig. 10.12.

Fig. 10.12 Transition of redundant data elements to process specifications

Enhancing Fourth-Generation Legacy Systems

Enhancing fourth-generation language legacy systems is really the process of converting it to an object-oriented client/server system. BPR (business process reengineering) is also used on fourth-generation language legacy systems to accomplish this transition. The process, as one might expect, is much easier than for third-generation languages; however, the process of determining essential components is the same in both types of systems. Once essential components are established, the existing applications need to be decomposed and realigned as appropriate. This is accomplished by using BAA, as it was used for third-generation legacy applications. The fact that fourth-generation languages are less procedural than third-generation languages greatly assists this transition. Fourth-generation language systems, by simply looking at the SQL SELECT statements, can identify which data files are used by the application. Using logic modularity rules, an analyst can establish cohesive classes based on applications that use the same data. This can be accomplished without using DFDs, although reengineering using DFDs is always a more thorough method for analysts to follow.

Linkage of fourth-generation language legacy and package software applications needs to be accomplished after application reengineering is completed. As with third-generation language systems, this can be accomplished either using a data parameter or by creating a special database. However, with fourth-generation languages it is likely that application integration will occur using databases, since both systems use them in their native architectures. An analyst will most likely find that application communication with fourth-generation languages will not always require separate databases to be designed solely for the purpose of system linkage. The more attractive solution to integration is to identify the data elements that are common between the two systems so it can be shared in a central database available to all applications as shown in Fig. 10.13.

The use of CRUD in fourth-generation languages is used less, but is certainly applicable and should be implemented by the analyst if he/she feels that the code is too procedural. In other words, the code architecture resembles third generation as opposed to fourth generation.

Fig. 10.13
Fourth-generation language
legacy shared database
architecture

"Leaving As Is"—Fourth-Generation Legacy Systems

The process of limiting integration to just the sharing of data is similar to the design architecture that I used for third-generation language systems. Indeed, the architecture of linking separate and distinct software systems can only be accomplished by sharing common data. Once again these data can be shared either using a data parameter or using a data file.

Because many fourth-generation language systems utilize the same architecture as a package software system (three-tier client/server using Windows NT/2000 or UNIX/LINUX), it is sometimes advantageous to make use of certain operating system-level communication facilities. For example, UNIX allows applications to pass data using an operating system facility called a "pipe." A pipe resembles a parameter, in that it allows an application to pass a message or data to another application without creating an actual new data structure, like a database. Furthermore, a pipe uses an access method called "FIFO" (first-in, first-out), which is the same access criteria used by parameters. FIFO also requires that once the data are read, it cannot be read again. The major advantage of using a pipe is that the message/data can be stored long after the application that created the message has terminated in memory. Thus linkage of information among package software and fourth-generation language applications can be accomplished in RAM at execution time, which is called "intra-application communication." This capability reduces overhead as well as the need for separate modules to be designed that would just handle data communication as shown in Fig. 10.14.

Hybrid Methods: The Gateway Approach

Thus far in this chapter, I have focused on the interface between a specific type of legacy and a package software system. Each type was defined with respect to its "generation" type. In reality, however, legacy systems are not that self-defined. Many large organizations have "legacy layers," meaning that multiple generations exist throughout the enterprise. In this case, attempting to integrate each generation with a central package software system is difficult and time-consuming. Indeed, migrating and integrating legacy systems are difficult enough. In these complex models, another method used for migration of legacy applications is a "hybrid"

Fig. 10.14 Intra-application communication using a UNIX pipe

Fig. 10.15 Gateway architecture for legacy integration

approach called "Gateway." The gateway approach means that there will be a software module that mediates requests between the package software system and the legacy applications. In many ways, a gateway performs similar tasks as a TP system. Thus, the gateway acts as a broker between applications. Specifically gateways:

- Separate yet integrate components from different generation languages. It allows for the linkages among multiple generation language systems
- Translates requests and data between multiple components
- Coordinates between multiple components to ensure update consistency. This means that the gateway will ensure that redundant data elements are synchronized

Typical gateway architectures would be designed as shown in Fig. 10.15.

The most beneficial role of the gateway is that it allows for the phasing of legacy components. The infrastructure provides for an incremental approach to conversion by establishing a consistent update process for both data and applications.

Incremental Application Integration

A gateway establishes a transparency for graphical user interfaces (GUIs), character-based interfaces, and automated interfaces (batch updates) to appear the same as the

Global Packaged System Interface
for
Viewing Order Status

Gateway

System 1
Character-Based Legacy
Sysytem
for
Viewing Order Status

System 2
GUI Legacy
Sysytem for
Viewing Order
Status

Fig. 10.16 Application functions of legacy gateways

package software system. Hence, the gateway insulates the legacy system so that its interface with the package software systems seems seamless. This is accomplished through an interface that translates requests for process functions and routes them to their appropriate application, regardless of the generation of the software and its particular phase in the package software migration. Figure 10.16 depicts the process functions of the gateway system.

The most salient benefit of the gateway approach is its consistency with the object-oriented paradigm and the concept of application reusability. Specifically, it allows any module to behave "like" a reusable component notwithstanding its technical design. Under this architectural philosophy, a particular program, let's say a third-generation language system, may eventually be replaced and placed into the gateway, with temporary bridges built until the overall migration is completed. This procedure also supports a more "global" view of the enterprise as opposed to just focusing on a particular subsystem. Figure 10.17 depicts the concept of process integration using the gateway architecture.

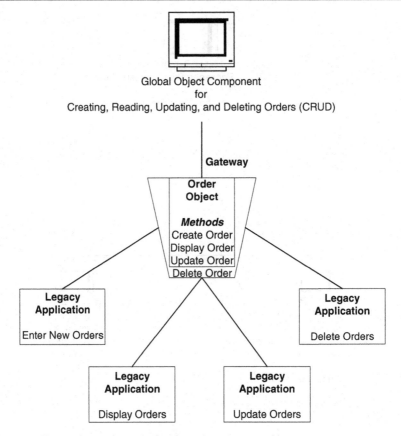

Fig. 10.17 Process integration and migration using gateway architecture

Incremental Data Integration

Incremental data integration focuses on the challenge of keeping multiple sets of data coordinated throughout a package software system.

The two primary issues relating to data integration focus on queries and updates. Queries involve the access of complete information about a data set (collection of related data elements) across multiple systems. Much of the query challenges can be addressed by using a data warehouse or data mining architecture. This will be discussed in detail in Chapter 12. The gateway would serve as the infrastructure that would determine how many copies of the data exist and its location.

The more difficult and more important concept of data integration is the ability of the gateway to coordinate multiple updates across databases and flat file systems. This means that the changing of a data element in one component would "trigger" an automatic update to the other components. There are four scenarios that could exist regarding the different definitions of data elements:

1. The data elements in each system have the same name. This at least allows analysts to identify how many copies of the element exist in the system.
2. The data elements do not match up by name. This requires that the analyst design a "mapping" algorithm that tracks the corresponding name of each alias.
3. Data elements match by name but not by attribute. In this case the analyst must propagate updates to the data element by tracking the different attribute definitions it has across systems. These differences can vary dramatically. The most obvious is element length. If the length of the data element is shorter than the one that has been updated then there is the problem of field truncation. This means that either the beginning value or the ending value of the string will be lost when the value is propagated to the system with the shorter length definition. On the other hand, if the target is longer, then the process must populate either the beginning or end of the string so that the element has a complete value. This is graphically depicted in Fig. 10.18.

   Furthermore, the same data element might have different data types, meaning that one is alphanumeric and the other numeric. In this case, analysts need to know that certain values (e.g., a leading zero) will not be stored in the same way depending on its data type classification.
4. There is not a one-to-one relationship among data elements. This suggests that a data element in one system may be based on the results of a calculation (a derived data element). This would require a more in-depth analysis and mapping often solved by creating a stored procedure that replicates the business rule to calculate the data element's value. So in this case there might be simple copies of the element moved from one system to another as well as one data element value that needs to first be calculated and then be propagated across multiple systems.

Fig. 10.18 Propagating data elements with different field lengths

Fig. 10.19 Propagation of
calculated data elements

**System Calculates Total Amount as
Quantity * Price and does not Store Total
Amount as an Element**

Quantity   Price

**Program "Triggers" stored
procedure to update Derived
Data Element stored in
Legacy System**

Legacy Data Element Total-Amount

Total-Amount

For example, if the data element "Total-Amount" is entered in one system but calculated as Quantity * Price in another, the propagation of the values is very complex. First, the analyst must know whether the calculated value is performed first before the resultant value, in this case, Total-Amount is reentered in another system. If this is true, then the propagation is much easier; once the calculation is made then the result is copied to the "entered" element. The converse is much more complex. If the Total-Amount was entered, but the values of Quantity and Price were not, then it would be very difficult to propagate until both Quantity and Price were entered. The example is further complicated if adjustments are made to the Quantity, Price, or Total-Amount. For any change, the systems would need to automatically be "triggered" to recalculate the values to ensure they are in synchronization. Figure 10.19 graphically shows this process.

Converting Legacy Character-Based Screens

It would be naïve to assume that most legacy systems do not have character-based screens. Character-based screens are those that do not make use of the GUI. While most character-based screens in existence emanate from third-generation language mainframe implementations there are also many early fourth-generation language systems that preceded the GUI paradigm. Unfortunately, character-based screens often do not map easily to its GUI counterparts. The analyst must be especially careful not to attempt to simply duplicate the screens in the legacy software. Figure 10.20 shows a typical character-based legacy screen. Note that there can be up to four Contract/PO's as shown in the upper right-hand corner. The user is required to enter each Contract/PO on a separate screen.

	Bill of Lading Container		Screen 1 of 4

B/L:____ SCAC: _____	VESSEL: _____		Total: ____
	VOYAGE: _____		CTN: ____

PO Information

Contract/PO: _____	Tot Unit: _____
Item: _____	GWT: _____
Style: _____	CBM: _____
Stat: _____	O/F Chrg: _____
Orig Country: _____	Con Rate: _____

Activities

Activity	Descr	Date	Location

Fig. 10.20 Character-based user screen

On the other hand, the replacement GUI screen in Fig. 10.21 takes advantage of the view bar that allows for scrolling in a window. Therefore, the GUI version requires only one physical screen, as opposed to four.

The Challenge with Encoded Legacy Screen Values

In most legacy character-based screens, a common practice was used to create codes that represented another, more meaningful data value. For example, numeric codes (1, 2, 3, 4, etc.) might be used to represent product colors such as blue, green, and dark red. Legacy applications used codes because they reduced the number of characters needed to type in the value on a screen. The technology to implement common GUI features such as drop-down menus and pop-up windows was not available. Indeed, many people used codes just from habit or had to use them in order to implement computer systems. When transitioning to a GUI system, especially on the Web, it is wise to phase-out any data elements that are in an encoded form unless the codes are user-defined and are meaningful within the industry or business area. This essentially means that certain codes, like State (NY, CT, CA, etc.), are industry standards that are required by the business, as opposed to those created to aid in the implementation of software—like color codes. In the latter case, the color name itself is unique and would be stored in an entity with just its descriptive name, as

![Screenshot of B/L Container GUI screen]

Fig. 10.21   Transformed character-based screen to GUI screen

Fig. 10.22   Encoded value GUI screen transition

opposed to a code, which then identifies the actual description. Figure 10.22 shows the character-based and GUI screen transition.

Changing character-based screens that contain encoded values has a trickle-down effect on the data dictionary and then on logic data modeling. First, the elimination of a coded value inevitably deletes a data element from the data dictionary. Second, codes are often key attributes, which become primary keys of entities. The

Legacy Representation of Color Entity with Encoded Value

Color-Code
Color Name

Sample Value Listing

Color Code	Name
01	Red
02	Blue
03	Lavender

Legacy Representation of Color Entity without Encoded Value

Color-Name

Sample Value Listing

Color Name
Red
Blue
Lavender

Fig. 10.23 Transition to encoded databases

elimination of the code, therefore, will eliminate the primary key of the entity. The new primary key will likely be the element name. These changes must then be made to the entity relational diagram (ERD) and placed in production (see Fig. 10.23).

Third, the elimination of codes affects previous stored procedures that use queries against the coded vales. Therefore, analysts must be sure to reengineer all queries that use the codes. This transition will add tremendous value since encoded elements typically add unnecessary overhead and time delays to queries. Finally, the elimination of encoded values will free up considerable space and index overhead. This will result in an increase in performance of the legacy system.

Legacy Migration Methodology

As stated earlier, all legacy systems inevitably must reach the end of their original life cycle. Therefore, notwithstanding whether certain components will remain "as is" or enhanced, eventually IT management must plan for migration to another system. The issue that this section addresses is how to establish a migration life cycle that takes into consideration an incremental approach to replacement of various legacy components within an enterprise computer system. The previous sections provided a framework of what can be done with legacy systems and their integration with other systems. This section provides a step-by-step template of procedures to follow that can assist the analysts on the schedule of legacy migration including temporary and permanent integration. This approach is an incremental one, so analysts can use it as a checklist of the progression they have made in the legacy migration life cycle. In all there are 12 steps as follows:

1. Analyze the existing legacy systems
2. Decompose legacy systems to determine schedules of migration and linkage strategies
3. Design "as is" links
4. Design legacy enhancements
5. Design legacy replacements
6. Design and integrate new databases
7. Determine new infrastructure and environment, including gateways
8. Implement enhancements
9. Implement links
10. Migrate legacy databases
11. Migrate replacement legacy applications
12. Incrementally cutover to new systems

The above steps are graphically depicted in Fig. 10.24.

Note that there are two streams of steps, that is, steps 3–5 and 8–10 that can occur in parallel. These steps encompass the three types of legacy migration choices that can be made: replacement, enhancement, and "as is." While this life cycle seems simple, in reality it is a significant challenge for most migrations to plan, manage, and modify these steps and their interactions. Indeed, creating a migration plan and

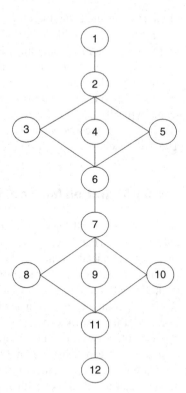

Fig. 10.24 Legacy migration
life cycle

adequately coordinating the incremental and parallel steps is a difficult project. The subsequent sections will provide more details for each of these 12 steps.

Step 1: Analyze the Existing Legacy Systems

It is obviously important that analysts fully understand all of the existing legacy components that exist in the system. The objective is to provide the requirements of each system and how it relates to the system. Analysts must remember that little to no documentation will be available to fully represent the architecture of the legacy system. However, analysts should compile as much information that is available including but not limited to:

- user and programming documentation
- existing users, software developers, and managers
- required inputs and outputs and known services of the legacy system
- any historical perspective on the history of the system itself

Regardless of what existing information and documentation is available, certain aspects of reverse engineering must be used. Various CASE (computer-aided software engineering) tools should be used that allows analysts to create a repository of data and certain levels of code analysis, particularly for third-generation language migrations. The analyst should create DFDs and PFDs for process analysis and logic data modeling (LDM) and entity relational diagramming (ERD) for representation of the data. The analyst should also determine which legacy components are decomposable and non-decomposable. Inevitably, regardless of whether the decision is to replace immediately, enhance, or leave "as is," ultimately little of the existing code will survive the ultimate migration of a legacy system (Brodie & Stonebraker, 1995).

Step 2: Decompose Legacy Systems to Determine Schedules of Migration and Linkage Strategies

The gradual migration of legacy systems is easily accomplished when analysts utilize decomposition engineering. Previous chapters have outlined the process of functional decomposition, which is based on the breaking down of a system into its functional components. Decomposition, which results in components, also allows for reusability of code. Since the fundamental premises of a package system are reusability, the process of decomposition is a mandatory part of the life cycle of any legacy migration. Thus, analysts should decompose all DFDs to functional primitives. Process analysis continues with the writing of process specifications for each functional primitive. These functional primitives will either be rewritten from the existing code or documentation or recreated from analyzing the functionality of the program. Analysts need to remove all dependency logic that links modules from the legacy code because it represents coupling among the programs. Module dependencies can typically be identified by finding *procedure calls* from within the legacy code. Ultimately, each of these process specifications will become methods.

Eventually all methods will be mapped to classes and identify the attributes that each class needs. While this sounds simple, there will be a number of processes for which decomposition will be problematic. This will typically occur for legacy code that is too eclectic and needs to simply be reengineered. In these cases, analysts may want to interview users to understand the functionality that is required, as opposed to relying solely on the written legacy code.

From a data perspective, entity relational diagrams (ERDs) need to undergo normalization. Remember that the DD and ERD produced in Step 1 is a mirror of the existing system, which most likely will not be in 3rd Normal Form. Thus this step will result in the propagation of new entities and even new data elements. Furthermore, data redundancies will be discovered as well as derived elements that should be removed from the logic model. However, while these steps are taking place, analysts need to be cognizant that the process of normalization represents the total new blueprint of how the data should have been originally engineered. The actual removal of elements or reconstruction of the physical database needs to be a phased plan in accordance with the overall legacy migration effort. Thus Step 2 provides the decomposed framework, but not the schedule of implementation.

Finally, analysts must always be aware of the challenges of decomposition, particularly overdecomposition, meaning that too many classes have been formed that will ultimately hurt system performance. There needs to be a mix of decomposed levels, which will serve as the basis of the new migration architecture.

Step 3: Design "As Is" Links

This step involves determining and designing what components will remain untouched except for linkages that are necessary with other package software components. These modules are determined not to be part of the initial migration plans, however, they need to function *within* the package software system infrastructure and are therefore part of its architecture. Part of the decision needs to include how data will be migrated into the package software framework. In most cases, "as is" components continue to use their legacy data sources. Consideration must be given to how legacy data will be communicated to other components in the package software system. Analysts need to consider either a parameter-based communication systems, or a centrally shared database repository as outlined earlier.

Step 4: Design Legacy Enhancements

This step determines which modules will be enhanced. BPR (business process reengineering) will be used to design new features and functions in each business area. Analysts should identify essential components and determine what changes need to be employed to make the existing system behave more like an object-oriented system. Common processes and databases also need to be mapped so that shared resources can be designed between legacy and package software systems.

New linkages will also be needed and the analyst must determine whether to use parameters or databases or both to implement the communication among application systems.

User screens may also need to be updated as necessary, especially to remove encoded values or moving certain character-based screens to GUI. Many of the enhancements to a legacy application are implemented based on the analysis performed in Step 1. Any modifications will need to eventually operate on newer platforms once the total migration of legacy systems is completed. Analysts need to be cognizant that additional requirements mean increasing risk, which should be avoided when possible. However, during enhancement consideration it is almost impossible to ignore new requirements. Therefore, analysts need to focus on risk assessment as part of the life cycle of legacy migration.

Step 5: Design Legacy Replacements

Analysts must focus on how to reconstruct logic in a later generation of software architecture. Therefore, it is important to understand the differences in generation language design. This chapter provided two types of legacy software systems: third-generation and fourth-generation languages. Third-generation languages were depicted as being more procedural and more difficult to convert.

Analysts must design the target applications so they will operate in accordance with the business rules and processes that will be supported in the new systems environment. Because of this integration, most replacement legacy migrations require significant reengineering activities. These activities necessitate the inclusion of new business rules that may have evolved since the legacy system was placed in production. Furthermore, new business rules can be created simply by the requirement of being a package software system.

Another important component of legacy migration is screen design. When replacing legacy systems, analysts must view the migration as assimilation, that is, the old system is becoming part of the new one. As a result, all existing package software screens need to be reviewed so that designers can determine whether they need to be modified to adopt some of the legacy functionality. This is not to suggest that all of the legacy system screens will be absorbed into the existing package software system. Rather, there will be a combination of new and absorbed functionalities added to the target environment.

Step 6: Design and Integrate New Databases

From an enterprise perspective, analysts must gather all of the permutations of legacy systems that exist and seek to provide a plan on how to integrate the data into one source. For "as is" solutions, legacy data files will most likely remain separate from the package software system until the complete legacy is migrated. However, the process of enhancing and replacing legacy data should have the objective of creating one central database source that will serve the entire package software enterprise system. Indeed, a central data source reduces data redundancy and significantly increases data integrity.

The process of data integration can only be accomplished by "combining user views," which is the process of matching up the multiple data element definitions that overlap and identifying data redundancies and alternative definitions. This can only be completed by creating a repository of data elements and by representing the data graphically using an ERD. Once each system is represented in this fashion then the analyst must perform logic data modeling as prescribed in Chapter 9. The result will be the creation of one central database system cluster that can provide the type of integration necessary for successfully package software implementations.

While this is the goal for all analysts, the road to successful implementation is challenging. First, the process of normalization will require that some data elements be deleted (e.g., encoded values) while others will need to be added. Second, full data integration cannot be attained until all replacement screens are complete. Third, applications must be redesigned so that the centrality of the data source is assumed to exist. Since this process may be very time-consuming, it may not be feasible to attempt a full database migration at one time. Therefore, the legacy data may need to be logically partitioned to facilitate incremental database migration. Thus, there will be legacy data subsets that are created to remain independent of the central database until some later migration phase is deemed feasible. Of course this strategy requires the design of temporary "bridges" that allows the entire package software system to appear cohesive to users.

Another important factor in planning data migration is to determine how much is really known about the legacy data itself. The less knowledge available, the longer the period where legacy data and package software data need to run separately and in parallel.

Step 7: Determine New Infrastructure and Environment, Including Gateways

Prior to the migration of any system, the necessary hardware and software infrastructure must be planned and installed. A common error in legacy migration is not factoring the time and effort to provide this infrastructure. Furthermore this process, which may create a new network environment, needs to determine the placement of software in a three-tier client/server platform. This means that further decomposition may be required of all processes, especially object classes. You may recall in Chapter 8 that classes may undergo further decomposition depending on the need to distribute application across the network.

Another important factor is performance. In many instances it is difficult for network engineers to predict performance in large application system environments. It may be necessary to plan for several benchmarks in performance early in the design phase. Benchmarking is the process of setting up an environment that replicates a production network so that modifications can be made, if necessary, to the design of the system to increase performance.

Another decision that must be made at this juncture is whether a gateway infrastructure will be created to mediate legacy layers. This decision, of course, is highly dependent on the migration life cycle; the more legacy layers that will be phased in over time, the higher the chances that a gateway processor for data and applications will be necessary. The decision to go with a gateway is significant, not only from the perspective of software design, but from network infrastructure as well. Constructing a gateway can be very costly. It involves writing the system from scratch or tailoring a commercial product to meet the migration requirements. It is also costly because of the amount of additional hardware necessary to optimize the performance of the gateway servers. However, the benefits of a gateway are real, as it could provide a dependable structure to slowly migrate all components in the new systems environment.

Step 8: Implement Enhancements

This step requires a schedule of when legacy enhancements will be implemented and become part of the production system. Many analysts suggest that the simplest modules go into production first so that any unexpected problems can be dealt with quickly and efficiently. Furthermore, simple modules tend to have small consequences should there be a problem in processing or performance. There are some other aspects of coordination, however. For example, enhancements that feed off the same data or use the same subsystems should obviously be implemented at one time.

Another factor in the decision of which enhanced components go first relates to the effects it has on other subsystems. This means that the priority may indeed be influenced by what other systems need or are dependent upon from other systems. Another issue could be the nature of the legacy links. Should a link be very complex or dependent on other subsystem enhancements, its schedule could be affected. Finally, the nature of the enhancements has much to do with the decision as opposed to just the application's complexity. There may be simple enhancements that are crucial for the package software system and vice versa.

Step 9: Implement Links

As I alluded to in Step 8, the determination of legacy links greatly affects the scheduling of the migration cycle. Once the determination is made in Step 8, the related legacy links must be put in place. This could also mean that the gateway, if designed, must also be in operation since many links might be filtered through the gateway infrastructure. So, the implementation of legacy links relates to both hardware and software. Notwithstanding whether a gateway is in place, database links often require separate servers. In many cases because these servers interface with the Internet, there is a need to install firewalls to ensure security protection.

From a software perspective, legacy links can almost be treated like conversion programs. There needs to be substantial testing done to ensure that they work properly. Once legacy links are in production, like data conversions, they tend to keep working. It is also important to ensure that legacy links are documented. Indeed, any link will eventually be changed based on the incremental migration schedule. Remember that most legacy links are accomplished by building temporary "bridges." The concept of temporary can be dangerous, in that many of these links, over time, tend to be more permanent. That is, their temporary life can sometimes extend beyond the predicted life of a permanent component. The message here should be that legacy links, while they are a temporary solution, should be designed under the same intensity and adherence to quality as any other software development component.

Step 10: Migrate Legacy Databases

The migration of data is so complex that it should be handled as a separate and distinct step in the migration life cycle. Data affect everything in the system and often if it is not migrated properly it can cause immense problems. First, the analyst must decide on the phasing of data based on the schedule of application migration. Hopefully, the process of data migration should be done in parallel to Steps 8 and 9.

The most challenging aspect of data migration is the physical steps in the process. Migrating new entities and schema changes are complex. For example, changes to databases require that the tables be "dropped," meaning that they are taken off-line. Data dictionaries need to be updated and changes to stored procedures and triggers are extremely time-consuming. Most problematic is the process of quality assurance. While some testing can be done in a controlled environment, most of the final testing must be done once the system is actually in production. Therefore, the coordination with users to test the system early is critical. Furthermore, there must be backup procedures in case the database migration does not work properly. This means that there is an alternate fail-safe plan to reinstall the old system should major problems arise. Finally, a programming team should be ready to deal with any problems that arise that do not warrant reinstalling the old version. This might include the discovery of application "bugs" that can be fixed within a reasonable period and are not deemed critical to operations (which means there is usually a "workaround" for the problem). Analysts must understand that this process must be followed each time a new database migration takes place!

Database migration is even more complex when there is a gateway. The reason is that the gateway, from an incremental perspective, contains more and more database responsibilities each time there is a migration. Therefore, for every migration, the amount of data that can be potentially affected grows larger. In addition, the number of data that becomes integrated usually grows exponentially, so the planning and conversion process becomes a critical path to successful migration life cycles. Since the migration of legacy databases becomes so much more difficult as the project progresses, the end of the life cycle becomes even more challenging to reach. That is why many migrations have never been completed!

Step 11: Migrate Replacement Legacy Applications

Once the database migration is completed, then the remainder of the legacy applications can be migrated to the new system. These applications are usually the replacement components, which have been reengineered in the object-oriented paradigm. These programs, then, have been designed to operate against the target databases with the new functionality required for the package software system. Since replacement applications usually do not create links, there is typically little effect on gateway operations. What is more challenging is the quality assurance process. Users need to be aware that the code is relatively new and will contain problems regardless of the amount of pre-production testing that has been performed. In any event, programmers, database administrators, and quality assurance personnel should be on call for weeks after system cutover.

Step 12: Incrementally Cutover to New Systems

As discussed above, testing and application turnover are two areas that frequently are overlooked. Because projects typically run over budget and schedule, the final procedures like testing and verification are usually shortened. The results of this decision can be devastating to successful legacy migrations. Because of the size and complexity of many package software systems, to go "cold turkey" is unrealistic and irresponsible. Therefore, an analyst should consider providing test scenarios that provide more confidence that the system is ready to be cutover. This approach is called "acceptance testing" and requires that users be involved in the determination of what tests must be performed before the system is ready to go live. Thus, acceptance test plans can be defined as the set of tests that if passed will establish that the software can be used in production. Acceptance tests need to be established early in the product life cycle and should begin during the analysis phase. It is only logical then that the development of acceptance test plans should involve analysts. As with requirements development, the analyst must participate with the user community. Only users can make the final decision about the content and scope of the test plans. The design and development of acceptance test plans should not be confused with the testing phase of the software development life cycle.

Another perspective on acceptance testing is that it becomes a formal checklist that defines the minimal criteria for incrementally migrating systems. However, one must work with the understanding that no new product will ever be fault-free. The permutations of testing everything would make the timetable for completion unacceptable and cost prohibitive. Therefore, the acceptance test plan is a strategy to get the most important components tested completely enough for production. Figure 10.25 represents a sample acceptance test plan.

Quality Assurance
Acceptance Test Plan

Product: Contact - Using Enter Key

Number:

Test Plan #: 1G

Vendor:

QA Technician:

Date:

Test No.	Condition Being Tested	Expected Results	Actual Results	Comply Y/N	Comments
1	Enter LAST NAME for a new contact, press enter key. Repeat and enter FIRST NAME, press enter key	Should accept and prompt for COMPANY SITE			
2	Select COMPANY Site from picklist	Should accept and prompt for next field			
3	Enter LAST NAME and FIRST NAME for a CONTACT that is already in the System.	Should accept and prompt for COMPANY SITE			

Fig. 10.25 Acceptance test plan

Problems and Exercises

1. What is a legacy? Explain.
2. Describe the five generation languages. What increases with each generation?
3. What are essential components?
4. What does the object-oriented paradigm mean?
5. How does object orientation relate to business area analysis?
6. What is a legacy link?
7. Explain the notion of logic reconstruction.
8. What is a UNIX pipe?
9. Explain how legacy integration operates through gateway architecture.
10. What is propagation?
11. What is the essential difference between character-based screens and GUI?
12. What is an encoded value?

References

Brodie, M. L., & Stonebraker, M. (1995). *Migrating legacy systems: Gateways, interfaces and the incremental approach*. San Francesco, CA: Morgan Kaufmann Publishers, Inc.

Stair, R. M., & Reynolds, C. W. (1999). *Principles of information systems* (4th ed.). Cambridge, MA: Course Technology.

Business Process Reengineering

11

Business process reengineering (BPR) in Chapter 10 was specifically discussed in relation to legacy applications. This chapter provides further methods on actually replacing legacy systems as part of the redesign for a new system. That is, rather than create legacy links, replace the old application with the new system altogether. This approach can often be an attractive alternative because a packaged solution might indeed contain many of the features and functions of the legacy. The object-oriented (OO) paradigm is again the way to accomplish this analysis, particularly using the essential components that were outlined in Chapter 10. The essential components first require the establishment of the core business requirements and then the mapping of the functionality of the organization or business unit to these components.

Many chief information officers (CIOs) today are confronted with a corporate mission to reengineer their existing applications and apply a more sophisticated and structured approach to develop what is known as the "enterprise" system. The enterprise system is composed of one common data repository for all of the organization's data. The typical enterprise configuration includes the OO paradigm and the client/server model as shown in Fig. 11.1.

The mission of BPR is to take an existing system, which is typically based on older technology and developed on the basis discussed in Chapter 9 (where the analyst is on the outside looking in), and reengineer it into one integrated system. Much has been written about the approaches or methodologies to use when applying BPR, especially by Jacobson. The focus of this book is to provide direction from a practitioner's perspective, that is, something that can realistically be applied within the typical resources and constraints that exist in most information system (IS) organizations of today.

A.M. Langer, *Guide to Software Development*,
DOI 10.1007/978-1-4471-2300-2_11, © Springer-Verlag London Limited 2012

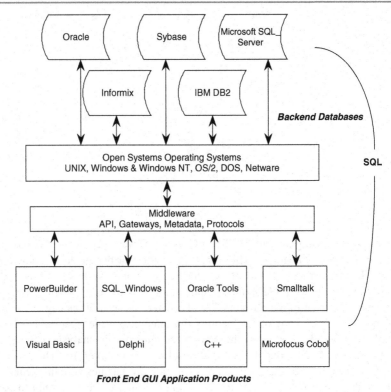

Fig. 11.1 Client/server three-tier architecture

Analyzing Legacy Systems for Replacement

The first step in applying successful BPR is to develop an approach to define the existing system and extracting its existing data elements and applications. The data need to be captured into the data repository and the applications need to be defined and compared to a new model based on essential components. Our assumption in this section is that the legacy system resides on an IBM mainframe computer. The data are stored in a VSAM format (non-database files) and the applications have been developed in COBOL. There are no central libraries or repositories of data or programs.

Data Elements

The analyst team will need to design conversion programs that will access the data files and place them in a data repository. Once all the data elements are loaded, the more rigorous process of identifying duplicate elements becomes the major effort. Duplicate elements may take on different forms. The most obvious is the same element with the same name and attributes. Another type is the same element name, but with different attributes. The third type, and the most challenging, is the duplicate elements that have different names and different attributes. This third type can be related to our discussion about combining user views. In any event, users and analysts will need to begin the laborious process of taking each element and building a data repository.

Applications

Application documentation is more problematic but again resembles the procedures followed using flow diagrams. This means that each existing application must be flowed and included as part of a new reengineered process. Although this procedure may sound straightforward, it is not. BPR typically involves a methodology called business area analysis (BAA). The purpose of BAA is to

- establish various business areas that make-up the enterprise;
- breakdown the business areas to their required data and process portions;
- reengineer the new and old requirements of each business area;
- develop requirements that provide an OO perspective of each business area, meaning that there is no need to map its needs to the existing physical organization structure; and
- define the links that create relationships among all of the business areas.

A business area should be developed in the same manner as depicted in Chapter 10, where we established the essential components of a bank. Each component is a business area that needs to be reengineered into its equivalent OO and client/server enterprise system. Therefore, each essential component must be functionally decomposed to its reusable parts.

Combining Structured and Object Techniques

Once the essential components or business areas have been completed and agreed to by the user community, it is time to develop the actual architecture of the new reengineered system. What modeling tools should we use? The answer is that we should be ready to use all of them when required. Figure 11.2 is a schematic of the reengineering process within a business area.

Like OO paradigm, BPR also uses the object concept to develop cohesive and reusable processes. We use the example from Chapter 10 to demonstrate how this maps to business areas. Once the business areas are defined, the structured tools should be used to define all data and processes. BPR supports the concept that the data for a business area should be determined before the processes. You may recall that the same data represented an excellent method for creating cohesive modules. By using the same data, functional primitive DFDs and STDs can be mapped to their appropriate business area.

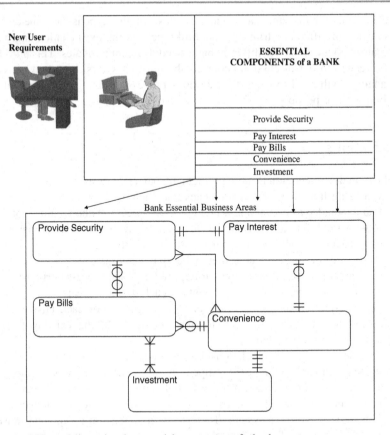

Fig. 11.2 BPR modeling using the essential components of a bank

Logical data modeling and the ERD will need to be completed prior to creating the permanent objects and classes that belong to each business area. Normalization must be applied to the required entities, which will not only have the legacy data elements, but also those added as part of the reengineering analysis process.

Prior to mapping the processes and data to their logical objects, the analyst can use another tool to assist in the reconciliation that all data and processes have been found. The tool is called an Association Matrix or a CRUD diagram. CRUD stands for the four functions that can be performed on any entity: Create, Read, Update, or Delete (archive). The importance of the CRUD diagram is that it ensures (Fig. 11.3):

- that an object has complete control over its data,
- that a data file is accessed by at least one process, and
- that processes are accessing data.

CRUD matrix in Fig. 11.3 tells us a lot about the status and activities of our business area data and processes:

Processes or Business Function / Data Subject or Entity	New Orders	New Products	Shipping	Sales Commission
Customers	R		R, U	
Orders	C, U		U	R
Items	R	C, U, D	R	R
Inventory	R,U	C, U	U	
Expense Category				
Salesperson	R			U

Fig. 11.3 Sample CRUD diagram

- Only the Items entity has enough component processes to control its objects data, that is, by spelling CRUD its processes have the minimum capabilities to control the cycle of any data element. Although this does not ensure that processes are not missing, it is a good indicator that the analysis has covered the life cycle of an entity.
- The Expense Category is not accessed by any process. This means that we have a file that the system is not using. This is an excellent indicator that processes are missing.
- The Customer, Expense Category, and Salesperson data are created and deleted by some other processes or business area. This could be a situation where the physical location of a business function is not where it logically should be processing. The analyst should look for the missing processes to complete the spelling of CRUD before finalizing both the processes and data of any business area.

Even if BPR is not used, the CRUD diagram is an excellent tool used to determine the processes and data needed for an object. Once the CRUD diagram is finalized, the objects and classes can be created as in Fig. 11.4.

It is important to recognize that many of the objects that are developed during BPR may become reusable components of other business area classes. If there are additions to an object as a result of reviewing a new business area, then the object's data and methods may need to be updated. The best approach to track these objects is through an integrated CASE tool, although any level of automation can be feasible.

Dealing with End Users

When applying BPR, analysts need to formulate a plan for how users and user groups will be interviewed. Most importantly, since reengineering implies change, change means discussions that must lead to decisions. Coordination of these decisions is critical, and it can get out of hand quickly. For this reason, the analyst should attempt to organize BPR using multiple JAD sessions. The sessions should be focused first on each individual business area. Prior to actually holding the session,

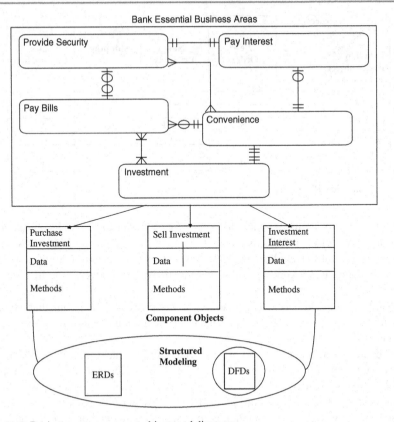

Fig. 11.4 Business area component objects and diagrams

analysts and facilitators should educate users on the techniques and reasons for BPR. Analysts should not be afraid to show users the business area schematic and explain the concepts of essential components and how they eventually can become reusable objects. This means that there may be a need to hold a one-day training session for the users who will be involved in the JADs. This suggestion is consistent with the concept of having users prepared before they attend a meeting.

JAD sessions should be organized to have session leaders who can provide walkthroughs of the existing functions. While these walkthroughs take place, the adjustments and missing functionalities can be added to the business area. The issues concerning the selection of key personnel are extremely important, especially when selecting decision makers. Because of the volume of information being discussed, it is advisable to have more than one scribe available. This minimizes the risk of not capturing important business rules.

After each business area is completed, the links to the other business components must be handled. These should also take place via JADs and typically use the session leaders as attendees. Session leaders tend to have enough information at this point from the JAD sessions to determine the necessary links for each business area.

The use of prototypes for each JAD is highly recommended because it will provide the best vehicle to get agreement on the new system. This suggests that an integrated CASE product is almost a necessity for creating a successful BPR project.

Information Systems Issues

BPR is implemented on existing systems. Existing systems have IS staffs and constraints that must be addressed as part of the process. Since the current view of BPR is to create an open systems client/server enterprise system, the physical requirements of the network are critical during analysis. Remember, RAD means the combining of analysis, design, and development into multiple iterative steps. In order to take the objects and classes developed from the JAD sessions, the analyst must start breaking up the data and methods of the classes into its related client and server functions. You may recall that if the client and server processing portions of an object must reside on separate hardware components then the object/class must be separated or further decomposed into separate physical modules (Fig. 11.5).

We have emphasized the importance of analysts being involved with the network design for client/server systems. BPR thus requires that the network design be completed as soon as possible and ideally before analysis starts. This will be difficult since many of the network decisions may be altered depending on how the objects become distributed across the network. In addition, the back-end database stored procedures (business rules, triggers, etc.) and middleware software components must be defined while the analysis specification is being finalized.

IT personnel must also be heavily involved in the JAD sessions to clarify questions about the existing system processes. This will involve discussions about the amount of data processed as well as the difficulty or ease of getting additional information from the suggestions brought up during the JADs. IT can also disclose the details of the equipment choices and how these may affect the requirements being discussed. Such input may enable quicker decisions based on predetermined IS constraints.

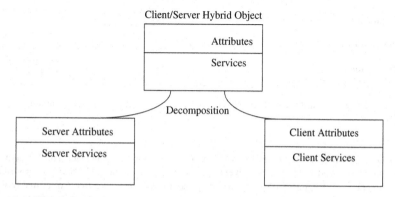

Fig. 11.5 Client/server hybrid model

Finally, IT will be required to establish the information about the existing data and processes. They will most likely be responsible for the conversion of the data as well as for clarifying the meaning of many of the data elements in question. You may assume that many of the legacy data element definitions will be unknown and as a result analysts and programmers will be spending time together figuring out what such elements do in the system. Existing process review means looking at the current application programs and how they function in the system. Most of this work will be required from IT programmers and legacy designers (if they are still around!). Since our assumption was that the existing system was developed under COBOL, there will be a more difficult mapping of how a 3GL (third-generation language[1]) is designed as opposed to today's 4GL (fourth-generation language[2]) products.

System Development Life Cycle (SDLC)

BPR changes the steps in the typical IS SDLC. The traditional SDLC is based on the waterfall approach as was shown in Chapter 1 (Fig. 11.6).

The problem with the waterfall approach is that it is unrealistic (as discussed in Chapter 1) and that it does not conform to the requirements of the OO life cycle. Therefore, IS must modify its SDLC to conform to the OO and client/server needs of BPR. The OO client/server life cycle resembles a spiral as shown in Fig. 11.7.

The spiral life cycle reflects a much larger allocation of time spent on design than in the traditional life cycle, because much of the development time is spent designing the objects for product reuse. Although this may appear unduly time-consuming,

Activity		March	April	May	June	July	August	Sept	Oct
Feasibility		▨							
Analysis			▨						
Design				▨					
Development					▨				
Quality Assurance							▨		
Implementation									▨

Fig. 11.6 The classic waterfall SDLC showing each phase dependent on the completion of the previous one

---

[1] A generation language refers to the level of the programming language. Third-generation languages were considered high-level development systems that included C, Pascal, and COBOL.
[2] Fourth-generation languages typically include programming languages that work directly with database systems and contain simpler program instructions than its predecessor languages.

Fig. 11.7 Object-oriented software life cycle

there is a heavy payback in BPR if it is done correctly. Remember that the spiral life cycle is applied to the development of each object since it is a cohesive component within itself. The more reusable the object, the more spiral the effort becomes with a particular emphasis on the analysis/design phase.

Pilot Applications

Many analysts opt to have a pilot application as part of the BPR effort. The purpose of the pilot is to get users excited about the benefits of creating the new system. Because an actual application is developed, IS must be involved to ensure that the pilot is successful. How can success be evaluated? The first real decision in a pilot is to select an existing application that is not working favorably and one that can demonstrate enough advantages of the OO GUI and client/server environment to pique the interest of users. Below is a suggested strategy:

- Focus on an application that can demonstrate the flexibility of the GUI front-end.
- Select an application that accesses existing corporate data to show the users how easily the data can be reached. Analysts should avoid an application that gets involved with massive updates or large data queries, as this is inviting an unexpected delay in processing. Such exercises tend to involve much study and experience with the corporate network of information, and this expertise may not be available.
- Select an application that has a relatively short development time when using a GUI product. Do not try an application that might be more involved when using a client/server model.

The pilot application not only has the potential to generate more interest, but it also allows users to be more creative and understanding of the requirements of BPR.

Downsizing System Components

After the business areas and interfaces among them have been completed, the analyst and development must decide on a strategy for implementation. To attempt to convert an entire enterprise-level system in one project is very dangerous and

Bank Legacy System

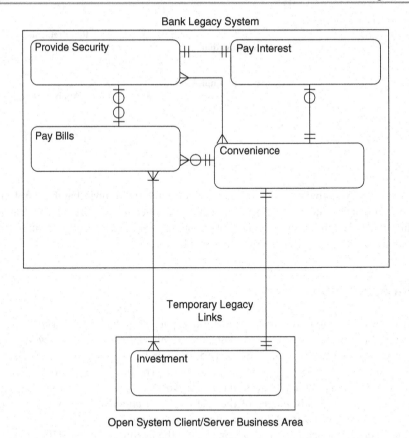

Open System Client/Server Business Area

Fig. 11.8 Legacy links of a business area

very unlikely to succeed. The user community also needs to be involved with this decision since many business units can convert only at certain times of the year due to various seasonal business requirements. Therefore, the analyst must plan to migrate applications in pieces. It is only logical to do this migration by business area and to develop temporary legacy links back to the main system. Most organizations are doing just this by purchasing open systems hardware and moving complete self-contained business areas independently onto the new platforms (Fig. 11.8).

As each business area is converted to the open systems architecture, the temporary legacy links will be deleted and incorporated into the new system.

Transactions vs. Data Warehousing

Our sample system is categorized as a transaction-based operation, that is, the system was designed to maximize its performance based on the processing of transactions. This type of systems must perform under the stress of many users who are using the system for production purposes. The limit of these systems is that they do not provide the end user with on-line data comparisons and what-if analysis in a productive and robust environment. Such systems were designed in the early 1980s and were called decision support systems (DSSs). Today's robust software goes even further than the awkward DSSs, and users want the same level of flexibility with their enterprise solutions. The problem is simple: You cannot maximize your transactions performance while maximizing your DSS functionality. The result is many client/server systems have had trouble performing at the same level as the legacy systems. SQL-based queries that are issued during peak-time enterprise processing can cause significant slowdown in processing. In most cases such delays are simply unacceptable. In fact, GUI applications will never outperform VSAM transaction-based mainframe systems. This sounds like a disappointing state of affairs for users. The remedy is to separate the transaction processing from the DSS functionality and improve transaction processing to an acceptable user level. This is accomplished by creating a data warehouse environment. A data warehouse is an archive of the database off-loaded usually to a separate machine to provide DSS capabilities to those that need to query information.

The problem with data warehousing is the currency of the data, since off-loaded information is typically not performed real time. Therefore, users must agree to use "old" data. Many organizations have provided data warehousing capabilities within hours of the input or update of information. Nevertheless, data warehousing can work only if the user community can settle on aged data that they cannot change. There are products such as SAS that provide specific tools to create data warehouse databases. Often the data are not fully normalized because the user cannot change

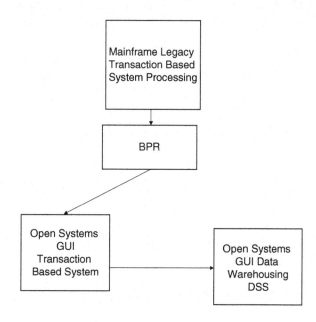

Fig. 11.9 Transaction/data warehouse BPR solution

the information. This results in a more efficient and accessible database because the information is stored in a flatter format (fewer database files). Almost every database manufacturer will be providing data warehouse capabilities in their next release. The analyst must be involved in determining which applications (usually reporting and inquiry operations) are candidates for the warehouse function. Analysts and IS personnel must take care in explaining the role of the data warehouse to the users so that they can use it effectively. Data warehouses are discussed further in Chapter 12 (Fig. 11.9).

Problems and Exercises

1. Explain the objectives of BPR.
2. How is BPR consistent with the object and client/server models?
3. What is a business area?
4. Explain the relationship between BPR and structured tools.
5. What is a CRUD diagram?
6. How should BPR be introduced to users and IS personnel?
7. What is SDLC? Why is it called a waterfall approach?
8. Compare SDLC with OOLC.
9. What is the significance of the spiral approach and how does it support the development of reusable objects?
10. Describe the procedures to implement a pilot application. Why is this so important in BPR?
11. Describe the philosophy of reengineering an enterprise system.
12. What is the difference between a transaction database and a data warehouse?

Data Analytics and Data Warehouses

Introduction

This chapter focuses on how to extract information from package software systems. This information will be used for decision support system (DSS) purposes and typically be presented to the user in an on-line display format or as a report. The concept behind DSS is that it deals with data "after the fact," meaning that the data are no longer in a production mode, but rather in a storage mode where it can be used for different forms of analytical processing. The major benefit of operating on processed data is that it cannot be changed and therefore can be accessed without concern for data integrity. Another salient issue is that because the data are not subject to change it can be copied multiple times, allowing for some interesting performance improvements and "flattening" of the data stored in the relational database. The referential integrity that was attained in a production database does not maximize performance for the query of data for reporting purposes. Almost all systems today need to determine how best to extract information for what is now being called "data analytics," that is, the ability to understand and analyze the information contained in application software systems. Increasingly, CIOs are being held responsible for providing this information.

In order to maximize the efficiency of accessing and analyzing data it is necessary to separate it from the production system. This is accomplished by creating copies of the data solely for decision support analysis. There are a number of different ways to do this separation. One way is data warehousing, where data are reformatted from one or more data sources and placed in a special repository for analytical processing. Another approach is to create data marts. While similar to a data warehouse, data marts are defined as more strategic in nature and more specifically organized to support the gathering of departmental data. Data warehouses can be composed of many data marts. Still another method is called data mining, in which multiple definitions of data from different systems are collected and analyzed for similarities. Data mining provides more artificial intelligence features and can perform advanced analysis against multiple data warehouses and data marts, especially when the data

A.M. Langer, *Guide to Software Development*,
DOI 10.1007/978-1-4471-2300-2_12, © Springer-Verlag London Limited 2012

come from multiple computer systems. All of these alternatives will be examined in this chapter and its relationship to the analysis and design of package software systems. In order to provide effective data warehouses, data marts, and data mining, it is necessary to understand how to obtain the data that are needed to populate these data structures.

A major component of creating effective repositories of data for DSS or data analytics is how to extract the information through database query. In order to accomplish this effectively, it is important to understand the transaction processing system, since some transactions might need to be captured when they occur as opposed to after they have updated database files. Furthermore, the process of creating reports and screen displays needs to be included as part of the analyst's specification. Some reports are precoded, while others are generated through user-initiated query applications.

Data Warehousing Concepts

Operational databases are those that are designed to track business events in real time. In operational databases, processing data usually correlates to cost while the completion of the data's process relates to revenue. I have shown in Chapter 11 that the data in operational databases are accessed at the detailed level, where individual records are created, read, updated, or deleted (CRUD). Entities in the relational model are constantly updated to ensure that the integrity of the data is preserved and that no historical information on the entity's previous status is stored.

Data warehouses, on the other hand, can capture both completed events *and* their original transactions. This allows data warehouse implementations with the ability to characterize more about how the data were produced at a much more detailed and granular level than usually available in operational databases. However, it is also important to remember that data warehouses are static snapshots on historical events. As a result, they are often not in sink with an operational database, which always reflects the current aggregate picture of the data. This has both advantages and disadvantages. From an advantage point of view, a data warehouse can contain multiple copies of the same data. Each set could represent the same data at a different moment in time, or could represent different views of the same data, or any combination of all of these. Figure 12.1 depicts the relationship between a data warehouse and the operational databases in a package software system.

The issue of data synchronization between the operational databases and the data warehouses is significant. The ultimate consideration when designing a data warehouse system relates to the age of the data in the warehouse and how often these data need to be refreshed. For example, if an accounting department needs to produce a report by the 15th of every month on the previous month's activity, then the data refresh would need to occur sometime after the end of the previous month and before the 15th of the new month. On the other hand, if a daily report were needed on the previous day's activities, then an evening refresh would be required. Data refreshment requires that the data from the operational database be copied to the

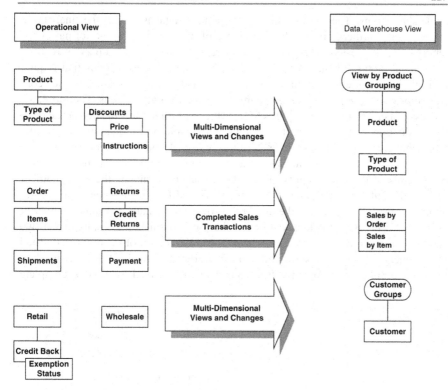

Fig. 12.1 Operational and data warehouse databases

warehouse. Unfortunately, this may not be the end of the data refresh procedure, since the format of the data in the warehouse may be very different from that of the operational system. Thus, there is typically a need for the data to be reformatted so that it can be fed into the warehouse structure directly. Because a data warehouse might be an aggregation of the operational data, it can be necessary to perform mathematical computations on the ported data to produce derived data information. You might recall that derived data are a violation of normalization and not allowed in the operational database. Therefore, data warehouses are de-normalized models of the operational systems and will typically contain data elements that were removed through 3rd Normal Form implementation.

Performance Benefits of Data Warehouses

The advantages of developing a warehouse are many. First, it allows users to analyze data without interfering with the operational systems. This is a significant benefit because of the inherent problems associated with SQL. When queries are produced against an operational database to produce reports they often require what is known as database joins. These joins create intermediate databases until the final report is produced. Furthermore, the final database of these joins is in the format of the report being requested. This means that a report from an SQL query is really a subschema picture of the original database. Issuing complex queries that require multiple joins can easily tie up an operational database, thus creating serious confrontations between production personnel and support organizations. Therefore, the process of performing DSS requires SQL, which in turn hinders the performance of the production system. Figure 12.2 shows an example of the quantity of dynamic tables that can be produced as a result of a simple SQL join statement.

Figure 12.2 shows how an SQL PROJECT statement creates a subset schema of columns of the parent entity. Thus, the subschema contains the same number of records, but fewer columns or attributes. The SELECT statement also creates another entity, which reduces the number of rows, but contains the same number of attributes as the parent database. Finally, the join combines the results of the two subschemas to produce a third entity, which is in the format of the report requested by the query. This sample shows how much overhead is involved with the production of a simple report. When voluminous data are involved the time to complete

Fig. 12.2 Dynamic SQL table joins

the query is even more significant. Indeed, some queries have been known to run over 24 h! Therefore, data warehouse solutions should be the preferred method for analyzing data rather than using standard SQL directly against production databases.

Concept of Multiple Dimensions

Data warehousing has often been referred to as a three-dimensional way of representing data. The three dimensions are seen as a cube of data. Each cell is viewed as a box within an array. This cube represents one data warehouse aggregation (combination) and provides a number of ways to view the data. Figure 12.3 shows a data warehouse aggregation of three viewable dimensions of information. The relational table is two-dimensional; it contains rows and columns, which are synonymous with records and attributes. The corresponding multidimensional cube reflects a three-attribute dimensional view of the data. The two-dimensional part is Orders and Items, with the third dimension being Markets. Figure 12.4 reflects another third dimension, the addition of the price attribute to the array. From a reporting perspective, a user could query for Orders and Items, which would only use two of the three

Item	Market	Period	Quatity
Books	New York	Q1	1200
Books	New York	Q4	300
Books	St. Louis	Q2	568
Books	St. Louis	Q3	985
Books	Los Angeles	Q2	3500
DVDs	Los Angeles	Q1	5440
DVDs	Austin	Q4	1500

Fig. 12.3 Relational table and multidimensional cubes with three aggregations

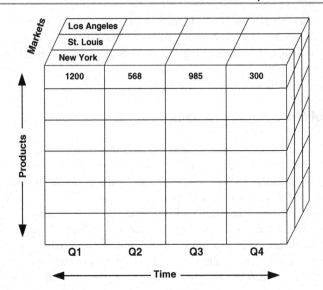

Fig. 12.4   Relational table and multidimensional cubes with four aggregations

dimensions, or ask for Orders by Item within Market. To use all the dimensions available, the user could search on Orders, by Item within Market by Price.

These examples picture the data warehouse from a logical perspective, that is, the cube does not exist physically, just conceptually. From a physical perspective, data warehouses use a standard data structure called the star schema. The star schema contains the main table in the center of the star, and each node represents another dimension of the data as shown in Fig. 12.5.

The star schema in Fig. 12.5 allows for queries to be performed based on an Order. In many ways it resembles an ERD in an operational database. However, most star schemas start with a multidimensioned center (concatenated primary key), so that query time is enormously reduced because there are less joins. Figures 12.6, 12.7, and 12.8 show how the number of tables is dramatically reduced as the number of primary key concatenations in the center table increases. It is important to recognize that more key concatenations in the center table greatly reduces the types of searchers that can be performed on the data, that is, the flatter the schema the less dimensions available to view the data. For example, in Fig. 12.8, there are no nodes in the star schema because there are no dimensions. Therefore, a user can only query the data warehouse to view Items within Orders, by Market and Price. It is also important to recognize that Fig. 12.8 contains no validation or look-up tables, which are normally used to validate the data of certain data elements. Data validation is not required in a warehouse architecture because the data are read-only, that is, records cannot be inserted, updated, or deleted. This is significant because this structure greatly improves data access performance. The removal of validation tables eliminates index pointers and the need for multiple joins of tables,

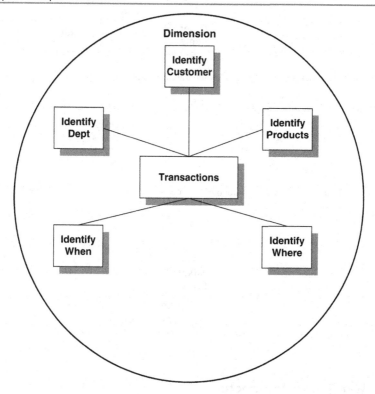

Fig. 12.5 Star schema

which simply reduces overhead and increases the performance of report queries. Figures 12.6–12.8 also depict the number of dynamic searches that are needed to produce one report. It is also feasible to design package software data warehouses that contain all four types of star schemas. This could occur if there were four departments who had three different fixed views of how they wanted the data to be represented to them.

Because there can be multiple copies of data in a data warehouse environment, there is an advantage to create more schemas that represent the data as it is needed for a specific report or analysis, as opposed to designing an elaborate star schema that allows for multiple views of the data. The reason for this position is simple: why design a data warehouse that resembles an operation database? Another way of looking at this model is to conceptualize that every data warehouse is nothing more than a view of data for a specific user view. The more alternative searches you offer the user, the less attractive the model is from a performance perspective. However, multiple warehouses require multiple conversions from the operational systems. So, the analyst must balance the design taking into consideration both performance and overhead issues.

Fig. 12.6 Prices, order items and market as separate warehouses

Fig. 12.7 Order items and market warehouses combined

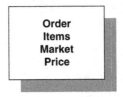

Fig. 12.8 Prices, order items and market as one warehouse

Data Warehouse Architecture

The first step in creating a package software decision support system is designing the data warehouse structure. This structure, or architecture, provides a framework for identifying how data will be utilized within the package software system. A basic data warehouse architecture is shown in Fig. 12.9.

The fundamental characteristics of the basic data warehouse architecture are as follows:

- Data are extracted from operational databases, flat files, and other data sources.
- The data from all of the source systems are first integrated and transformed into another format before being loaded into the actual data warehouse.
- The data warehouse can only be used for read-only activities for DSS.
- Users obtain access to the data warehouse through a front-end application tool, usually supplied by the warehouse vendor.

Extracting Data from the Source

The data warehouse process starts with identifying the source of the data needed for the DSS. These will typically come from two places: (1) the operational databases that exist in the new package software system and (2) the data files that exist in legacy systems. The most difficult part of the process is to identify the meaning

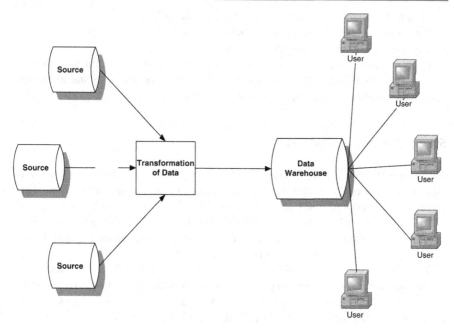

Fig. 12.9 Basic data warehouse architecture

of the data elements in each system so they can be transformed properly into the data warehouse. This can only be accomplished by first creating a central repository of the data—typically by using a CASE (computer-aided software engineering) tool. Porting data into a central repository is easier when working with relational databases because they are better documented and can be reverse engineered into a CASE tool. However, legacy data are more challenging because of their lack of documentation and less conventional data formats. Notwithstanding the format of the source data, the process to define the operational data is time-consuming but extremely valuable for the project to be successful. Many data warehouse products, like Sagent, provide their own metadata dictionaries that can be used instead of a CASE tool. These metadata libraries store the relationships that exist among the different yet related databases in the production systems. Analysts also need to extract data from third-party products that are part of the operational system. For example, a weekly stock price file that is integrated in to the production system. In any event, most data warehouse systems can extract data from multiple databases from multiple systems.

Many operational systems can be categorized as "transaction processing" based. This means that they are heavily geared toward capturing transactions that occur throughout the day. Typically, transaction processing systems are those that take orders, ship them, and then record financial information. Transaction processing systems have the following characteristics:

• High transaction rate
• Constantly changing

- Data redundancy is avoided in order to ensure integrity
- Optimized indexes to ensure SQL query efficiency
- Two-phase commit architecture to ensure recoverability.

DSSs using data warehouses provide tremendous advantages for transaction processing systems because they can reformat data into dimensions so that users can better understand the meaning and results of the transactions.

Staging the Extracted Data

As previously stated, a significant component of the data warehouse product is a load server that compiles the data and establishes the links among duplicate data elements. Furthermore, the load server allows for the definition of elements, especially for those attributes that have complex meanings. These attributes are called intelligent keys where portions of the attribute have special meanings. This is shown in Fig. 12.10 for a Part Number data element.

The load server has the ability to store information about the Part Number so the warehouse can easily identify the data element's components during a query. Overall, the load server prepares the raw data and creates a new repository of information in the format required by the data warehouse schema.

Read-Only Activities

As previously stated, the data warehouse is a read-only copy of operational data. The philosophy is that operational data and DSS data are inherently different. Specifically, DSS provides easy to understand formats of data so that analytical information can be created to support better tactical and strategic business decisions within the company. These analytical processes require that historical data be kept in

Fig. 12.10 Encoded data elements

different views, unlike the single normalized view required in operational databases. Indeed, one database format alone cannot efficiently provide for both types of functional need. Thus, at the core of all warehouse products is a read-only database that represents the primary component of information analysis.

Front-End Tools

In most data warehouse systems, the data access infrastructure makes up the next most important component of the DSS architecture. This data access is composed of front-end query tools and application programs that provide useful and accessible decision support information from the data warehouse. Thus, analysts need to design the warehouse schemas, query logic, and applications to create a useful data warehouse environment that operates under the auspices of the production systems. The important component of application and query support are the third-party applications that are provided with the purchase of the data warehouse. Most warehouse products, like SAS, Sagent, and Oracle, all come with sophisticated developer tool kits that allow for the generation of advanced query and application development. These add-on application products do not, however, provide the proper analysis and design process to determine what they need to do.

Types of Data Warehouse Architecture

Thus far we have only looked as what can be called a "generic" data warehouse architecture. However, there are more sophisticated design considerations when formulating a package software enterprise warehouse system. Figure 12.11 depicts a slightly more complex data warehouse that loads data into what is known as business area. A business area represents a defined segment of the organization and is based on perceived business similarities. These similarities could be based on where income is derived, type of clients, etc. Therefore, each business has its own view and use for a warehouse. All of these multiple warehouses are derived from one enterprise warehouse that has been ported from the integration of multiple data sources.

In Fig. 12.11, data are extracted from various source systems and integrated and transformed before being loaded into an enterprise data warehouse. These data are then restructured, redesigned, and moved into separate business area warehouses, which are then used for DSS. The major benefits of using a business area architecture is to:

- ensure that all business areas are deriving data from a central warehouse system;
- create subwarehouses that can better facilitate the needs of smaller departments;
- provide access to different user communities. Internal, consumers, and customers all have different business area needs and access authorization criteria; and
- ensure that the timing of the data is consistent across all warehouses. In this way comparisons of data across the enterprise are consistent.

Fig. 12.11 Business area data warehouses

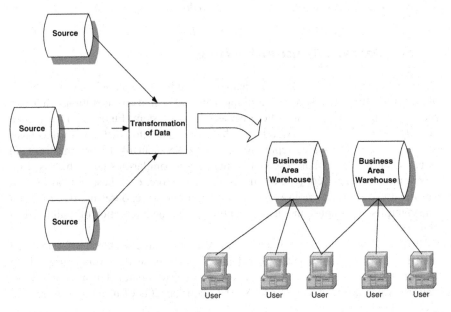

Fig. 12.12 Direct business area data warehouse

Another hybrid version of the business area model is to create separate area warehouses directly from the load server as shown in Fig. 12.12. While this architecture does not contain a central enterprise data warehouse, it has all of the constructs that represent a true data warehouse. Obviously, the advantage is the time and space

Fig. 12.13 Integrated relational data warehouse

saving of creating an intermediate enterprise data warehouse. This model is advantageous when there is little need for a centralized warehouse and when there are multiple updates of the warehouse from multiple source files.

Still another intricate architecture is shown in Fig. 12.13. This model creates an integrated relational database in 3rd Normal Form. The data that come from source operational systems remain read-only; however, new data can be added to the integrated database directly from users. The purpose of these updates is to provide additional data that facilitate expanded decision support activities. Sometimes this process also helps to "clean-up" bad data. Once the new data have been entered, the data are transformed into a data warehouse.

The Package Software Decision Support Life Cycle

The system development life cycle (SDLC) for package software DSS focuses on data, as opposed to processing and functionality. As a result of the elimination of many process-oriented steps, the DSS life cycle is much faster and less complex than its traditional counterpart. The main activity for the analysts is to take data from various sources and platforms and provide multiple strategic views of the data in another infrastructure.

The phases of the package software DSS are as follows:
1. Planning
2. Gathering data requirements and modeling
3. Physical database design and development
4. Data mapping and transformation

   5. Data extraction and load
   6. Automating the data management process
   7. Application development and reporting
   8. Data validation and testing
   9. Training
  10. Rollout

Phase 1: Planning

The planning phase in package software DSS is very similar to the project life cycle
and entails the creation of a project plan and realistic time estimates. Planning,
like that for any project, includes defining the project scope, plan, resources, tasks,
timeliness, and deliverables. Figure 12.14 depicts the project planning components.

Furthermore, the DSS will require changes to the network infrastructure.
Therefore, there will be technical infrastructure design that needs to be implemented
while formulating the proper DSS environment. The technical components include
capacity planning, archival strategies, data refresh/update strategies, and operations
and job scheduling.

Phase 2: Gathering Data Requirements and Modeling

During this phase the analyst must understand the business needs and data requirements of the users of the system. Because package software systems are composed
of internal users, customers, and consumers, the data modeling requirements for
data warehouses will vary depending on the different user views. Essentially, data
requirements will involve the process of identifying what elements are needed for
DSS by each group of users. The assumption should be that normalized databases
exist, legacy links have been made, and intermediate transaction processing systems
are in place. If a central repository of all data elements is in a CASE product, then
identifying the components of the warehouse will be much easier and productive.
Unlike regular data gathering, analysts should be looking at what users need to see
in the form of screen displays and printed reports. Thus, it is the output that identifies what is needed for the data warehouse. Therefore, the analyst does not need
to use process models like DFDs to model the data warehouse, rather the specification will consist of query screens for data access, sample reports, and screen display
views. The reports and screen displays need to be in prototype form so that users
can validate that the information and format are correct. Another interesting aspect
of data warehouse design is to determine what users might want to see in addition to
what they have already identified. Basically, most users will want to see the reports
and screen displays that they are used to having from their existing system. However,
data warehousing allows so much more that the analysts need to consider what users
might want to see given the robust power of the data warehouse query software.
While this activity might seem counter to my previous position that analysts should

Fig. 12.14 DSS project planning components

never create requirements, I do believe that the analyst must at least inform, usually through demonstrations, the power of the data warehouse to each user constituency. Obviously, this process may not be practical for consumers, except where the marketing department is involved with focus groups. Analysts must remember to inform users that data warehouses do not contain current data. While designing real-time data warehouses is possible, it is unlikely and difficult to implement.

What is most important, however, is not the reports and displays, but the strategy of designing the data warehouse (or data mart) architecture. Reports can usually be modified without great pain, but schema design is more complicated. This process requires that the analyst determine which type of warehouse designs to use. Remember that there can be multiple data warehouses produced from multiple sources, so the options for design are many-to-many as shown in Fig. 12.15.

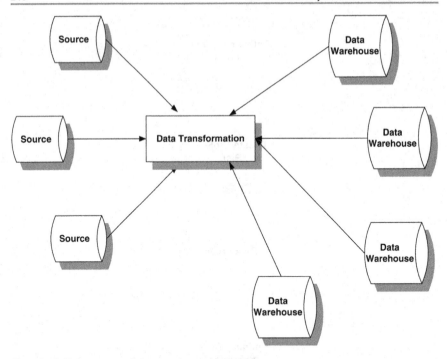

Fig. 12.15 Data source and data warehouse relationships

Notwithstanding the relationships between data sources and data warehouses, it is important to focus on the schema design, that is, what is the design of the star schema. There are essentially three approaches. The first approach suggests that the data warehouse contains a star schema that resembles the report or screen display. This design was discussed earlier in this chapter. The advantage of this approach is that data are already placed in the format required so there is little need for data manipulation. As a result, the production of the reports and displays is very efficient. Furthermore, there is little that the user needs to do other than just selecting the option to produce the report. The bad news is that the warehouse is very limited because all it can do is produce the report. The economies of scale for creating the report in a data warehouse form may seem like overkill, unless the process of obtaining the data in one central repository has significant time saving for the user. Figure 12.16 shows a data warehouse report schema.

The second approach is to create sophisticated star schemas that support a grouping of needs. Each schema would contain a central table that provides a data repository required by a group of users. Each node would provide the supplemental data that might be needed depending on the user group and the report subject. The benefit of this model is somewhat obvious in that it allows warehouses to serve multiple needs and provides for more DSS analysis of the data. The downsides are also obvious; users need more knowledge on how to query the data and therefore need

Order Analysis Report					
Order #	Item ID	Market	Price	Salesperson	Date Shipped
14387	A5567	West	120.00	Joe Smith	3/15/2001

Fig. 12.16 Data warehouse report schema

training and an understanding of what data are available for analysis. In addition, the performance of the reports and displays will vary depending on the level of sophistication of the queries that are afforded to the end users. Figure 12.17 depicts a star schema for group user query.

The third approach comes back to the earlier example of the enterprise-level data warehouse. Rather than having multiple warehouses serving many users, one central complex star schema can be designed to afford the needs of an entire organization, group, or department. These types of data warehouses will contain the most nodes on the schema and look very much like a 3rd Normal Form database. The advantage

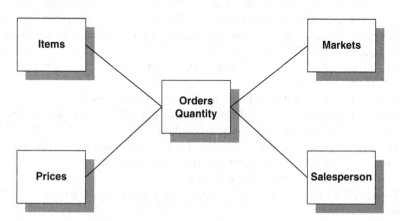

Fig. 12.17 User group star schema

is that data are copied once per cycle to one data warehouse thus ensuring that all the data represent the same time period. The downside is that the warehouse becomes voluminous and requires significant data query manipulation in order to extract the needed information.

Another challenge in the movement of data from operations sources to data warehouses is derived elements. I previously discussed the handling of derived data as being a violation of 3rd Normal Form and a database redundancy. As a result, all derived data elements were removed from the production database. However, because data warehouses are read-only, there is no need to eliminate derived data. In fact, warehouses that contain derivations will be much more efficient for query and report production. The question to answer is how to populate derived data back into the database. If a CASE tool was used to produce the normalized operational database, then there is a good chance that derived elements might exist in the data dictionary. You might recall in my earlier chapter that many derived elements are first placed in the data dictionary and defined in a process specification. Thus, the identity of these derived data elements and their calculations can be extracted from the data dictionary. Unfortunately, such is not the case when dealing with legacy databases and flat file systems. In these situations, the analyst must reconcile each report and screen display against the existing data dictionary to determine where derived elements exist. Furthermore, just identifying them is not enough—analysts must work with users to understand how they are derived. Once all derived elements have been discovered and defined they need to be added to the metadata dictionary usually provided with a data warehouse product. The use of metadata (data that define data) will be discussed later in this chapter; however, its use is important when integrating derived data elements in the data warehouse. The metadata repository will allow analysts to store the calculation formula. When the data warehouse is produced (or refreshed), a triggering operation will examine the data and calculate the derived values as set forth in the metadata repository. The process of calculating derived data elements is shown in Fig. 12.18.

There may also be derived data elements that cannot be directly calculated from the supplied data sources. This means that the derived elements must be calculated outside the data warehouse domain and then imported directly into the data warehouse. This is shown in Fig. 12.19.

In summary, the data gathering and modeling phase must address the following key questions:

• What will be the number and design of the data warehouses?
• How will data be reflected in the data warehouse model, particularly the derived data, which do not exist in the production database?
• Is there a CASE tool that will allow for the transformation of derived data elements from a data dictionary to the data warehouse?
• How often does data need to be refreshed?

Figure 12.20 reflects the major steps that analysts must complete in this phase.

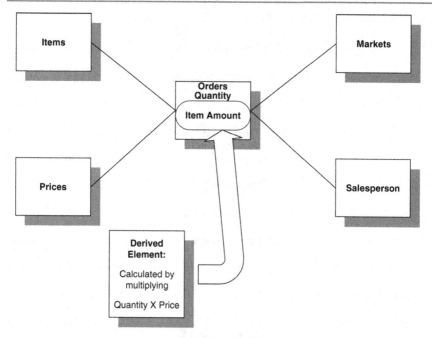

Fig. 12.18 Adding derived data elements to the data warehouse

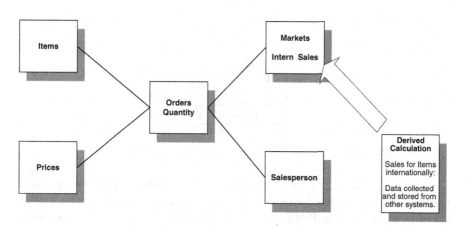

Fig. 12.19 Porting derived data elements directly into a data warehouse

Phase 3: Physical Database Design and Development

The physical database design entails a number of steps that enable the database to operate efficiently. There are three main components involved in the physical design process: fact tables, dimension tables, and look-up tables.

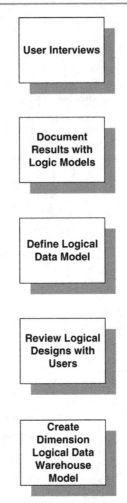

Fig. 12.20 DSS gathering data requirements and data modeling components

Fact tables, which are sometimes known as major tables, contain the quantitative or factual data about a business. It is, in effect, the information for which users are doing the query (Poe, 1996). Fact table information is often numerical measurements of data that contain many attributes and sometimes millions of occurrences. For example, a marketing database can contain data on various sales for the company. Dimension tables or minor tables, on the other hand, are smaller than fact tables and hold descriptive data that reflect various dimensions of the facts—like month, year, and region. In the previous example, dimensions of sales could be product, markets, etc. Figure 12.21 reflects the marketing data warehouse with dimension tables.

Thus, the combination of fact tables and dimension tables provides for the basis of the initial star schema. This star schema can then allow users to scan the data

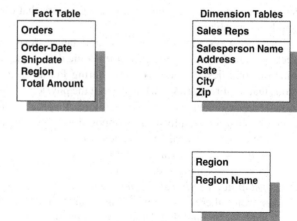

Fig. 12.21 Fact and dimensional data warehouse tables

and with the appropriate database constraints provide interesting analysis of the information. Look-up tables are another type of dimension table. They provide fill-in information used to describe possible values that certain fact data need. They represent entities that are similar to 3rd Normal Form validation tables. An example of a look-up table is the available colors of a particular model car. Figure 12.22

Fig. 12.22 Fact, dimensions, and look-up date warehouse tables

shows a combined star schema physical database that combines facts, dimensions, and look-up tables.

In many ways, much of the physical database design concepts discussed in this section could be considered part of the logic data modeling phase (Phase 2). While much of this design could be done during Phase 2, there are some related decisions that require more knowledge about the physical environment, that is, the actual data warehouse environment. Furthermore, the process of de-normalization is often accomplished during physical as opposed to logical database design. Beyond just database design, the analyst also needs to

1. *Identify the actual primary and secondary key structures*: sometimes this could involve de-normalized data elements.
2. *Develop aggregation strategies*: aggregation is the process of accumulating fact data from other transactions. This means that a derived data element transaction could be generated that depicts the results of many detailed transactions.
3. *Creating indexing strategies*: indexes are separate tables that are internally created to improve look-up performance. An index is an indirect address that points to where specific information exists in the database, without having to search every record. Figure 12.23 depicts an index look-up table. Any field can be indexed so that query speed to access that information can be dramatically increased.
4. *Develop partition tables*: partitioning is the process of breaking up physical databases into many different storage areas. Logically, these multiple partitions are treated as one database, but physically are distributed on many different areas of a disk or across multiple physical hard disks. The benefit of partitioning is purely performance. Partitioning of data maximizes performance of the data warehouse when particular parts of the data are needed by specific users. So, in

Fig. 12.23 Index tables

theory, two users can be using the same logical data warehouse, yet be accessing two separate physical partitions of the same database.

5. *Performing capacity planning*: analysts must determine the amount of storage space and processor speed that they will need in order to provide an efficient data warehouse environment. Analysts should not do this configuration alone; network architects must be involved to assist in the determination as to what processor types might best handle the load and perceived growth of the data warehouse. The key input needed from the analyst is the number of records that will be estimated in each data warehouse. There are two components that are needed to determine space requirements. The first, which was covered in an earlier chapter, calculates the size of each data warehouse record by multiplying the total number of maximum characters in each attribute within a record. By maximum I mean the largest size for all VARCHAR2 (variable length) data elements. The result of this calculation will establish each record size. The analysts need to then calculate the database size by multiplying this total record size by the estimated number of records in the data warehouse (see Fig. 12.24).

This last step might not be that easy, but sometimes estimating maximum data warehouse sizes (i.e., the largest it could be) is the safest calculation. Furthermore, analysts must take into consideration the needs for temporary storage that are required during SQL JOINS, PROJECTS, and SELECTS of data from tables. Remember that SQL-based queries generate dynamic database tables for reporting. Thus, analysts need to consider doubling or even tripling the storage requirements of the host data warehouse. This is why partitioning can be so effective; it allows network architects to scale storage by attaching more physical hard disks. The issue of how many processors to have, the memory size, and disk access speeds needs to

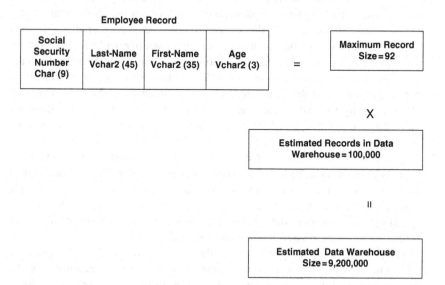

Fig. 12.24 Sample data warehouse size calculation

be determined by the proper network professionals, but heavily based on the input supplied by the analyst.

Phase 4: Data Mapping and Transformation

The data mapping and transformation phase is one where the analyst must locate the source of the data in the operational systems, do analysis to understand the types of data migrations and transformations that need to occur, and map the source data to target data warehouses. This phase ultimately determines what the source data will be, how it will be converted, and where the data will be ported. The specific steps within this phase are as follows:

1. *Defining the data sources*: much of this activity can be accelerated if the analyst has loaded the data elements of each system into a central CASE tool repository. Other factor is the extent of legacy data that exist in the system and the nature of how the data are stored. Furthermore, the amount of data redundancy and derived data elements all play a factor in the time requirements to ascertain where the data are and how they are defined.

2. *Determining file layouts*: once data sources have been defined, the analyst must clearly understand the file layouts of these systems and how the files interrelate with each other within a particular source repository. For example, a file that contains fact data may be linked to another table in the same system that provides validation information. Thus, the analyst needs to understand the schema of each source system. If the source is a relational database, then the best approach is to generate (if not available) an entity relational diagram (ERD). The ERD will expose the referential integrity that exists at the database level and expose those relationships that have been implemented at the application level. It might also expose data redundancies. If the system is a flat file legacy application, then the analyst should print out the file description tables (particularly if the system is written in COBOL). The file description tables will identify all of the data elements in each file. By creating a simple template or utility program, analysts can determine where duplicate elements exist among these flat files. This will allow the analyst to understand how the files link to one another, where there are redundancies, and how to schematically look at the system from a dimensional and relational perspective.

3. *Mapping source data to target data*: once the source systems and schematic have been identified, the analyst needs to map or identify the source data to the data warehouse star schemas. This can be accomplished by creating a matrix that shows source elements and their attributes as well as their corresponding data warehouse data elements. Figure 12.25 shows a sample matching source-to-target matrix developed using a spreadsheet program.

4. *Develop transformation specifications*: the matrix shown in Fig. 12.25 is only one component of what is called the transformation specification. Another name for a transformation specification is conversion document. A conversion document provides the requirements for a programmer to develop a utility program

Source Data Element	Attribute	Source Table	Data Warehouse Data Element	Attribute	Target Table
Company	Char(3)	Items	Company-Name	Vchar2(15)	Company
Designator	Char(15)	Items	Vendor-Style	Char(18)	PO-Item
Group-ID	Char(10)	Items	Dept-No	Char(2)	Purchase-Order
Frt-Term	Char(3)	PO			
Final-Dest	Vchar2(30)	PO	Freight-Terms	Char(1)	PO-Header
Purchase-Term	Char(4)	Contract			
Discharge-Point	Char(30)	Contract	Import-Whse-No	Char(4)	PO-Header
Arrive-By-Date	Date	Contract	FOB-Terms	Char(1)	PO-Detail
			Cancel-Date	Date	PO-Detail
Sup-Approval	Char(30)	Import	Whse-Message	Char(60)	Header-Mess
Coord-Item	Vchar(80)	Merchandise	Item-Message	Char(80)	PO-Detail

Fig. 12.25 Source-to-target data element mapping matrix

that prepares, moves, and transforms source data to a data staging file. The data staging file is an intermediate data store that is created for actual transport to the data warehouse.

5. *Reviewing the update cycle*: this process establishes the refresh cycle required for each data warehouse. Refresh cycles define when a cycle begins, when it ends, and how long it runs. It is also important for the analyst to have some idea about how long a refresh cycle might take. This can be determined best by running tests on sample source files and then forecasting the total update time based on the results of the test. The determination of conversion time could be critical since the update cycle needs to complete prior to the user wanting to see the data results. Therefore, if an update cycle runs every 24 h, then the update cycle needs to complete by the beginning of the next morning. While this might sound like plenty of time, many large-scale update cycles can take substantial time to complete. The time to complete also heavily depends on the amount of data manipulation that occurs during the conversion of data from source to target.

6. *Developing strategies for archival*: this step entails the decision of what portions of warehouse data can be archived or deleted from the DSS. Typically, this becomes more of an issue when looking at transaction-based information. The decision is to determine when dated transactions, which are used to formulate results of the data, are no longer providing enough value to keep them actively stored in the live data warehouse. The reason for purging certain transaction is because of the performance degradation that is caused during warehouse queries. Sooner or later, historical transaction data need to be removed from the active warehouse. Analysts have two options. Option one is to generate a summary transaction record that might represent a group of detailed transactions. This

means that the summary transaction would provide a view of the meanings of the detailed transactions. Figure 12.26 provides an example of representing detailed transactions in a summary record. If this option is selected then the detailed trans-actions can be deleted or archived. The creation of summary records may also require that specific program changes be made to query applications so that a summary record can be appropriately identified from a detailed transaction. The second option is to just create a separate file of purged transactions that can be accessed using a different set of query applications. This purged file would typi-cally be resident on a separate processor so that it would not conflict with normal data warehouse activities. Regardless of which option is used, the analyst needs to create specifications that identify the conditions for purging data and where the data are to be stored. Both options also require the development of specific query applications that can access purged data when needed.

7. *Review security requirements*: once the data warehouse is in place, the analyst must integrate security requirements into the specification. Unlike many security issues, because data warehouses are read-only, there are no concerns about the creation of illegal or dangerous records. However, data warehouse information is

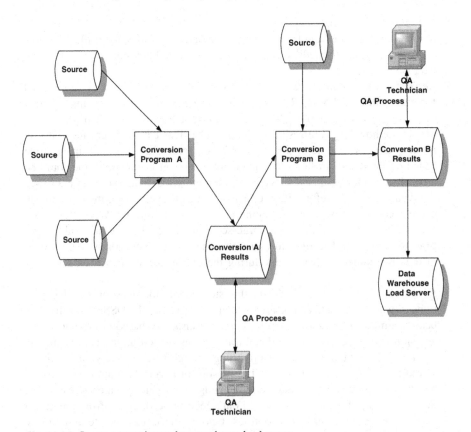

Fig. 12.26 Source conversion to data warehouse load server

still proprietary and could provide valuable information for those with malicious or illegal intensions. Thus, securing data warehouses from unauthorized use is a key component of data warehouse design. This is especially important because most accesses to data warehouses in package software systems will occur via the Web, either from an Intranet or from an Internet. So who has access to what features in a Web-based data warehouse query becomes very important in the design of the warehouse system. Much of the design issues covered in Chapter 11 are relevant in data warehouse development as well. Therefore, analysts should review the security requirements of the data warehouse using the same approach as in any other system.

8. *Capacity plan review*: once the data mapping and conversion methodologies have been completed, the analyst will have a much better perspective on the specific capacity requirements. This step simply suggests that the capacity planning and space determination is an iterative process in which the analyst and network architects will fine-tune the capacity needs as each phase in the life cycle is completed.

Phase 5: Populating the Data Warehouse

This phase involves the actual extract, conversion, and population of the target data warehouses. This is typically accomplished with a combination of conversion and update software supplied with the data warehouse vendor's product and with the development of specific conversion programs designed by the analyst. The steps involved with completing the population of data warehouse data are as follows:

1. *Loading and staging the data*: this step may involve an intermediate program that begins the process of building a repository of data where the data warehouse software will extract the information from. While many data warehouse products will allow for the loading of data directly from an operational database or file system, this is often not recommended. Accessing operational data are usually not a best practice for data architects.

2. *Converting and integrating data*: this step entails the execution of the actual conversion programs and the integration of multiple data sources. The process involves the confirmation that multiple data source migrations have been completed and the execution of one or more conversion programs (that migrate the data as per the specification) has occurred. This step should result in the formation of a warehouse load server that is ready for testing before being moved to the live data warehouse. Figure 12.26 shows the process.

3. *Testing and load*: the test and load phase is the final step to creating the data warehouse. The test part of this step is to provide various reconciliation results that provide assurance that data have been converted to specification. For the most part, the testing should be consistent with audit-trail philosophies including the verification that the number of records read, written, and transferred is correct. If records are rejected for whatever reason, these should also be reported. The load portion of this step involves the actual porting of the data into the warehouse for

use by users. There should also be an audit-trail report specifying that the process of final load has been successful.

4. *Capacity review*: once again, the analyst should review the capacity needs of the system after the final data warehouses have been created, since the storage at the time of completion will represent the actual storage prior to query operations on the data.

Phase 6: Automating the Data Management Process

While much of the work has been performed to generate the data warehouse, there is a need to create automated processes that refresh the information on a periodic basis. The periods may vary depending on the type and number of data warehouses that have been designed. Thus, once the first data extraction is completed and data warehouses are created, the analyst needs to design automated utilities that migrate new data to a preexisting data warehouse. These utilities must be automatically activated based on time and/or conditions. They must also activate the application operations that are part of the life cycle of refreshing data, namely, data mapping, conversion, extraction, and load. When subsequent or ongoing refresh is in place, data will be replaced in the load server and ultimately in the data warehouse. The procedures for verifying that this process has occurred properly also involve the creation of utility applications that report on the outcomes of each automated step, each time the refresh occurs.

There also needs for an automatic backup and restore process should data become corrupt or damaged because of a hardware failure. There is typically a backup/restore feature available in data warehouse products as well as from third-party vendors. Restoration procedures must be designed and tested in order to ensure that data warehouse information can be restored correctly and within the time constraints set forth by the user communities. Of course, all automated processes need to be tested, therefore, the analyst needs to design test case scenarios that will assist in the verification that data can be backed-up and restored correctly.

Phase 7: Application Development and Reporting

This phase focuses on the delivery of output from the data warehouse. DSS application development is usually accomplished by using special data access tools to design and prebuild reports. Indeed, the tools selected to generate reports are critical to the success of any data warehouse. Analysts need to determine the environment to support data access and information analysis rather than just selecting a front-end software package. There are several steps that are required to understand the complexities of providing a reporting environment for users in a package software environment. The first issue to address is the ways in which users can receive information from the data warehouse. There are four types of reporting as follows:

1. *Parameter-based ad hoc*: this allows users to enter particular information that will act as a parameter into the report application. Parameters often consist of date information or domain constraints like department or group. Users, while changing parameters, are not creating new reports, but rather modifying existing reports within a predefined range of choices.
2. *Display access*: this involves the display of reports on the Web or some other central place on the system. The important concept here is that reports are generated as needed but assumed to be effective in a view-only mode.
3. *Complete ad hoc*: the user interacts directly with the data warehouse using the query tools that support the warehouse product. Thus, users will need to be trained on how to issue queries and how to manipulate the data in the warehouse. While this option provides the most versatility, it is also the most difficult report to use successfully. The problem is whether users can really master the query tool, be knowledgeable on how the data are stored, and can appropriately test their results. Indeed, the largest risk for users is generating reports that are not accurate.
4. *Hard copy*: these are predefined and developed by the analyst. They typically have a fixed format and are printed and forwarded to the appropriate requester.

There are also a number of ways that users need to navigate through a package software DSS. This is based on user needs, similar to my earlier definition of user categories. The three primary methods are as follows:

1. *Executive*: allows executives to get predefined reports quickly and on a regular basis.
2. *Structured decision support*: contains predefined and ad hoc reports and outputs. Thus, structured decision support provides another level of analysis offered to the user community. This hybrid approach is usually required by middle-tier users like line managers and supervisors, where there is a clear need to generate what-if analysis in a dynamic day-to-day environment.
3. *Unstructured decision support*: these users have access to all types of reports, but prefer to design ad hoc reports from scratch and use them when they are needed for a particular analysis. These users are more activity-based on the information they need.

The level and categories of users vary in how they use reports. What reports are needed by users also depend heavily on whether they are internal, customers, or consumers. Typically, internal users are those who can be trained to use unstructured techniques to access data warehouse information. Figure 12.27 represents another view of how certain types of users utilize report options.

Report Access and Analysis

A data warehouse is not an automated method of getting the information you want without working to find it. Users should not be disillusioned about what a data warehouse product will afford them to do. Misunderstanding the commitment that data warehouses require, both from designers and users, is a critical factor for success (Poe, 1996). Figure 12.28 depicts the sequential steps that users should follow when using DSS and when analyzing their data.

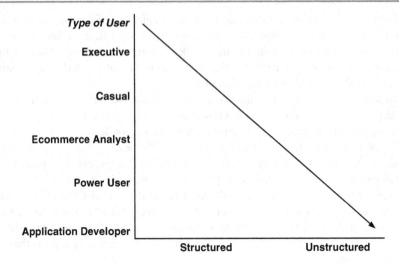

Fig. 12.27 Types of users and their report access preferences

Report Access and Analysis Sequence
1. Understand and Visualize the Data Warehouse
2. Understand how to formulate a request
3. Understand how the request is processed
4. Learn how to present results
5. Understand how to perform advanced analysis
6. Formulate how to communicate results and findings

Fig. 12.28 Report access and analysis sequence

The viewing of the reports is another important component of analysis of DSS. Users may want to specify what format they want to view the data. Thus, analysts need to provide options for users where they can select from a fixed menu of display options. While tabular and cross-tabular reports are most common, graphical output is also a common way of analyzing what reports are telling users about their data. Figure 12.29 shows various types of data warehouse report presentations.

Listed below is the most common report functions that DSS should provide to users:

- Changing the axis: this allows users to swap rows and columns
- Changing sort order
- Adding and deleting subtotals and other information breaks
- Creating color reports highlighting certain variables
- Format options for fonts, styles, sizes, and colors
- Graphical display of information should support line graphs, dimensional and stacked bars, pie, scatter, bubble, tape and area
- Ability to change graph axis labels, colors, and titles

Types of Query Tools

There are a number of types of queries that allow for the production and viewing of the information that has been defined herein. There are four types of query tools:

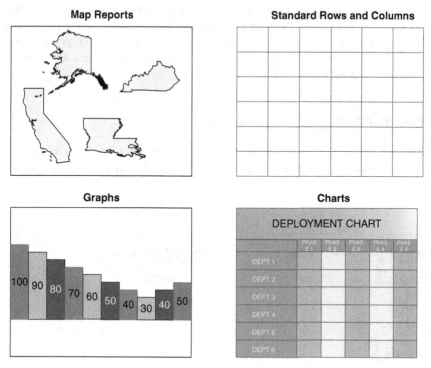

Fig. 12.29 Data warehouse report presentations

Fig. 12.30 Report writer DSS

1. *Report writers*: these are third-party products that access the data warehouse directly and produce reports based on SQL-type queries. Examples of third-party report writers are Crystal Reports and Cognos (see Fig. 12.30).
2. *Multidimensional database management systems (MDBMS)*: these tools create a subset database that can be populated by both operational systems and data warehouses. These databases are usually multidimensional and are often defined as on-line analytical processing (OLAP) systems. They allow for specialized reporting of data in an aggregate form that can support advanced data mining activities (see Fig. 12.31).
3. *Advanced DSS tools*: advanced tools are very similar to report writers except that they support more advanced query capabilities and dimensional analysis. They specifically support access to multiple data warehouses from one query.
4. *Executive information systems (EISs)*: EIS represents a higher level of DSS. These systems contain advanced metadata facilities that can create sophisticated and predefined analysis of data. EIS also supports artificial intelligence activities, which are fundamental infrastructures to the support of trend analysis and decision-making alternatives (see Fig. 12.32).

Phase 8: Data Validation and Testing

While I have mentioned that testing must occur throughout the data warehouse implementation, there is a need to have a central test plan strategy. Although each

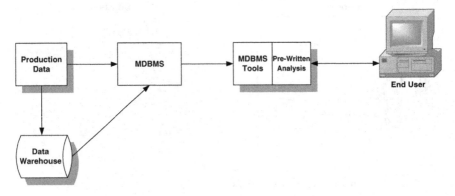

Fig. 12.31 MDBMS DSS architecture

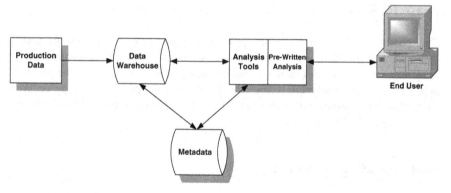

Fig. 12.32 EIS DSS architecture

phase has a quality assurance process, the entire data warehouse life cycle requires integrated test scripts. These scripts establish what the expected results should be from each previous life cycle step. Sometimes this is best accomplished by having reports that provide reconciliation of what the warehouse contains. However, analysts should also suggest that users review the output reports. Users should be encouraged to hand check certain reports until they are satisfied that the system is calculating and collecting information based on their requirements. All too often we see users who just accept what the output of a report tells them!

Furthermore, analysts should plan for change—for change is inevitable with DSS (package software systems). Change is not only modifications to the reporting, it's the addition or changing of what data need to be supplied to the data warehouse and in what form. In addition, new systems are added and need to be integrated into the overall data warehouse schema. With this in mind, analysts need to design and maintain sophisticated testing systems that can be reused each time a change is made to the warehouse infrastructure or transformation process.

Phase 9: Training

While this might not be the actual responsibility of the analyst, it is important to plan for the training of users with the objective of teaching them how to work with the data warehouse. Notwithstanding that predesigned reports do not require much data warehouse knowledge from the users, most systems will always have "super users" who want to do advanced analysis on the DSS. The training phase of the DSS life cycle includes the following considerations:
- Understanding the scope of information in the data warehouse
- Training on the front-end tools and how to write queries
- Understanding of how to use existing reports and how to modify them
- Train the trainer concepts so users can eventually own the responsibility of training new employees or other users

Phase 10: Rollout

This phase essentially involves the process of going live. It requires the actual deployment of the data warehouse into the production network environment, creating user support infrastructures including adding new users, creating the physical procedures for users to request new reports and options, providing the procedures for backup and restore, and creating a team to troubleshoot problems that inevitably occur early in the DSS rollout.

Understanding Metadata

Metadata is data about data. Metadata is the fundamental component that allows data warehouse systems to provide the complex information that users require. There are two primary forms of metadata: operational and DSS. Operational metadata contains the information about where the data are in the production systems and/or in the staged database system prior to conversion. The DSS metadata establishes a catalog of the data in the data warehouse and maps these data to the query applications. Figure 12.33 depicts the metadata architecture.

Therefore, the metadata infrastructure provides the front-end users with the ability to manipulate the data without working directly with the data. That is, the user works directly with the metadata, which in turn operates on the data warehouse attributes. Thus, the metadata provides a higher level of abstraction about the data. This abstraction allows for the ease of use of operating with the database.

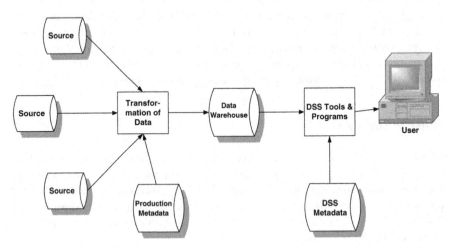

Fig. 12.33 Metadata architecture

Problems and Exercises

1. What is a data warehouse?
2. What are the advantages and disadvantages of using data warehouses?
3. Describe the concept of data aggregation.
4. What is a star schema?
5. Explain the different types of data warehouses and how they should be used.
6. Describe the relationship between the concept of decision support systems and data warehouses.
7. How does data mapping relate to data warehousing?
8. What are fact tables and dimension tables?
9. What is a source-to-target element mapping matrix?
10. Describe the process of populating a data warehouse.
11. What are the different types of reporting and analytics available via warehouses?
12. What is metadata?

Reference

Poe, V. (1996). *Building a data warehouse for decision support.* Upper Saddle River, NJ: Prentice-Hall.

Documentation and Acceptance Testing

13

Many IT organizations are faced with the ongoing issue of good product documentation. Documentation has been classically defined as having two components: user documentation and technical documentation. User documentation consists of the necessary instructions required for users to operate and maintain the system. Technical documentation, on the other hand, contains detailed information about the inner components of the product itself. Technical documentation should be designed to provide developers with the ability to support and maintain the system from a programming and engineering perspective.

Once analysis and design is completed, user documentation can be developed as a parallel function with the rest of the product life cycle components. This means that the screens and reports can be used from the design phase to build the documentation on the inputs, queries, and output reports of the system. If the software is a GUI product, then the user documentation must also adhere to the standard Help facility, which is included in these types of products. Although analysts may be involved with providing information to the documentation team, it is not their responsibility to produce user documentation.

A major part of the technical documentation should be the product of the analyst's work. All of the tools used by the analyst to formulate the logical equivalent must remain as the schematic or blueprint of the product. It is not advisable to try to provide other documentation. First, there rarely is enough time, and second, it should not be necessary. Remember, the concept of using modeling tools was compared to the creation and maintenance of an architect's blueprint in which the schematic had to be self-documenting. There are, however, other components of technical documentation. This technical documentation relates to the physical software development itself. Programming source code, product libraries, and version control are examples of technical product documentation that should be the responsibility of the programming team.

A.M. Langer, *Guide to Software Development*,
DOI 10.1007/978-1-4471-2300-2_13, © Springer-Verlag London Limited 2012

Acceptance Test Plans

Acceptance test plans can be defined as the set of tests that if passed will establish that the software can be used in production. Acceptance tests need to be established early in the product life cycle and should begin during the analysis phase. It is only then logical that the development of acceptance test plans should involve analysts. As with requirements development, the analyst must participate with the user community. Only users can make the final decision about the content and scope of the test plans. The design and development of acceptance test plans should not be confused with the testing phase of the software development life cycle. Testing should be defined as the carrying out or execution of the acceptance test plans themselves.

The analysis and design of acceptance test plans is often overlooked in many IT organizations. This is because it is viewed inappropriately as a testing method rather than as a way of developing better systems. The question then is, why and how do acceptance test plans improve software quality?

Quality During Analysis

If acceptance test planning is conducted as a step in analysis, then the issue of how to best test the requirements becomes part of making decisions about overall system requirements. Specifically, if a user wants something that can be difficult to test and maintain, it may force them to rethink the requirement and alter its focus. What better time to do this than when the requirement itself is being discussed? Remember, a strong part of quality software is how easy that software is to maintain.

Cannot Test 100% of Everything

One must work with the understanding that no new product will ever be fault free. The permutations of testing everything would make the timetable for completion unacceptable and the costs prohibitive. The acceptance test plan is a strategy to get the most important components tested completely enough for production. The testing of software can be compared to the auditing of a company. Accounting firms that conduct an audit for a public company must sign a statement that the books and records of their client are materially correct, meaning that there are no significant discrepancies in the stated numbers. Accounting firms know that they cannot test everything in their client's books and records to be 100% confident that the numbers are correct. Therefore, auditors apply strategic methods like statistical sampling in order to be "comfortable" that the risk of a significant difference is improbable. Software verification is no different. Analysts and users must together decide on the minimum tests necessary to provide comfort to going live with the system. It is unfair to leave this responsibility solely with the user. Having the analyst or programmer do this alone is equally unfair. The wise strategy is to have acceptance test plans developed by the analyst along with input from the user and verification by programming as follows:

1. As each part of a system is functionally decomposed using the various modeling tools, the analyst should develop generic test plans that are based on typical standard logic tests (e.g., Account_Number must be numeric). The analyst and users should then meet to refine the test plans by focusing on how many permutations are required for each logical test. Users should also be encouraged to establish new tests that are missing from the plan. It is highly recommended that the analyst not wait for the entire analysis to be completed before working with acceptance test plan generation Tailoring an acceptance test plan specifically to the needs of a group of users is a good technique. This means that as the analyst completes the interviews with each user or user group, the acceptance test plans should be completed for the specifications developed for them. This philosophy is also good because it avoids the process of meeting again and rehashing old information.
2. The analyst develops inter part tests necessary to ensure that each component properly links with the other.
3. Once the acceptance test plans are approved by users, development must design tests that focus on product-specific validation. These include operating system and program tests to ensure that the operating environment is working correctly. Users and analysts need not be involved with this step as it represents the testing from an engineering perspective. Quality assurance personnel who are part of the development team should be involved in these test designs as these professionals are specifically trained to provide intricate testing that involves the mathematical aspects of finding errors. Once again, quality assurance and testers should not be confused or combined with the role the analyst and users play in the design of acceptance test plans.

More Efficient Development

Providing development personnel with the acceptance test plans is a somewhat controversial idea. Many IS professionals would object to doing so, arguing that the testing of software quality should not be carried out by programmers. However, programmers who are given the test plans are not being asked to do the testing but rather to understand what the user perceives as the most important operational qualities of the system. If the programmer is aware of the specific focus of the tests, then he/she should direct the development to ensure that such errors do not occur. In essence, we are trying to focus the programmer on the most important aspects of the system. To ask programmers to treat each component of a program in an equal manner is unfair, especially since they have no perspective on how to make the decision. If the programmer is especially focused on the tests, there should be fewer errors detected during the test review, thus supporting a more efficient development effort. Focusing on the tests does not suggest, however, that the programmer is free to ignore the other quality areas of the program.

Now that we have established the reasons and processes of developing acceptance test plans, the analyst must provide a format for its use. The format must be user friendly so that users can participate. The format must include a record of each iteration of the test, allowing for better documentation and audit trail. The test plans should be in a machine-readable format so that changes can be made. Figure 13.1 is a sample acceptance test plan.

This particular test plan assumes that no data are on the screen and that the operator will only use the enter key (as opposed to a mouse). Each condition to be tested and its expected result must be listed. The tester will then execute each test number and fill in the results along with any comments. The test plan is then reviewed for completeness. If the test plan fails, the test will be performed again after the software is fixed. Each test iteration is part of the documentation of the testing process. Users and analysts should periodically review the test plans when the system goes live. This procedure will allow the test plans to be "fine-tuned" should any critical errors occur when the system goes into production.

Designing acceptance test plans is not a trivial task, for either the user or the analyst; however, good test plans can make the difference in the ultimate quality of the software. When GUI products are tested, the number of test iterations increases substantially. For example, the test plan above is focused only on data entry (as opposed to changing existing data) and when the operator uses the enter key. Because this is GUI, operators can enter data by using the enter key, a mouse, or the tab key. Therefore, the analyst will need to repeat the same test plan two more times, one when the operator uses a mouse and the other when a tab key is used.

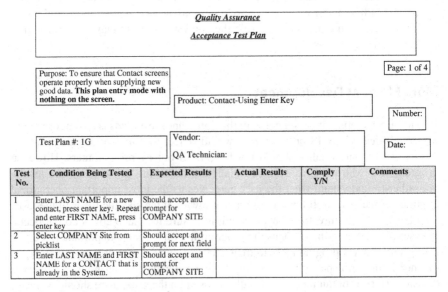

Fig. 13.1 Sample acceptance test plan

Budget Process

We have continued to expand the role of the analyst in the life cycle of systems development. Analysts must develop the ability to view an upcoming project and submit an accurate budget for their time and effort. The best approach here is to list the generic tasks that are typically performed by an analyst and then attempt to provide an estimate of the requirements, not only for each task, but also for each system component within the task. Below is a step-by-step process that can be followed.

Establish the Task List

The analyst should begin the budget by listing the three standard tasks:
- Interviewing
- Modeling
- Acceptance test planning

Each of these tasks will then need to be expanded depending on the scope of the project.

Interviewing

The analyst will need to assess the number of users on the project and whether there will be a need for JAD sessions. Once this schedule is put together, the analyst should arrange for pre-meetings to assess the user skill sets, as this will affect the strategy and time frame of the user interface process. Analysts should employ a weighted criterion when budgeting time. Although there is no exact science to doing this, Fig. 13.2 is a suggested template to follow.

Figure 13.2 does not include the specific budget for each session, as this would require the analyst to have pre-meetings to assess the number of functions in each component and then budget the time necessary. The user interviewing tasks should take into consideration an estimate for the number of iterations. More detailed sessions can require three to four iterations before final approval is accomplished. The number of hours (or whatever time period is chosen) should be based on a novice user. Note that if the user(s) is knowledgeable, then there may actually be a reduction

Task: User Interviewing

Sub-Task	Expected Hours	User Skill Set Weight .75 – Knowledgeable 1.75 – Amateur 1.00 – Novice	Weighted Hours
Selection of Users			
Determine JAD Sessions			
Pre-Meetings			
Individual Meetings			
JAD Sessions			

Fig. 13.2 User interview budget worksheet

in the budgeted time whereas amateurs (those that know a little) may substantially increase the time frame. The latter situation is due to the likelihood that amateur users will tend to get off track and in general have more questions. The ultimate budget for JAD sessions must be based on a composite of the levels of involved users for each JAD session.

Modeling

Once the interviewing budget has been determined and there is an established understanding of the scope, objectives, constraints, and assumptions of the project, the analyst can begin to determine the time period for modeling the system requirements. Figure 13.3 shows guidelines.

Analysts will need to get a sense during the pre-interviews of the likely number of processes (or data elements with respect to the repository) and how many diagrams might be included. Once this is established, then the budget can be developed. Note that the weight factors are based on the level of integrated automation. Integrated automation refers to the extent of computerization (e.g., a CASE tool) that will be used to develop the models. Non-integrated, which is the non-weighted factor, represents computerized diagramming without intelligent interfaces (which would exist with a CASE product).

Acceptance Test Planning

Acceptance test plan budgeting must take into consideration two key factors: the user interviews and the type of product. The user interview portion should be based on the original budget for user interviews applying a factor based on the modeling budget (Fig. 13.4).

Essentially, Fig. 13.4 reflects that budget hours for acceptance test plans are approximately 10% of the original interview budget hours factored by the estimate of the number of diagrams and the level of automation. The 10% represents the portion of the interview time that is perceived to be spent discussing testing issues

Task: Modeling

Modeling Type	Estimated Hours based on Number of Diagrams or Data Elements	Automation Factor .75 – Integrated CASE 1.00 – Non-Integrated 3.00 – Manual	Factored Hours
Data Flow Diagram			
State Transition			
Data Repository			
Entity Relational Diagrams			
Process Specifications			
Object Orientation			

Fig. 13.3 Modeling budget worksheet

Task: Acceptance Test Plan

Sub-Task	10% of User Interview Weighted Budget Hours	Estimated Hours based on Number of Diagrams or Data Elements (from Modeling budget)	Type of User Interface Factor 2.00 – GUI 1.00 – Character	Estimated Acceptance Test Plan Hours
Individual Meetings				
JAD Sessions				

Fig. 13.4 Acceptance test plan budget worksheet

with the user. The final factor is the GUI. Because of the event-driven nature of GUI screens, the number of tests to be performed is dramatically increased. Many IS professionals would feel that a 2.00 factor is too low, since many favor 3.00.

Problems and Exercises

1. What is the purpose of business specifications?
2. How do functional overview sections relate to the entire business specification?
3. What is the use of a functional flow diagram? Which modeling tool is used?
4. What are the five most common components of the business specification?
5. How does the business specification relate to the programming specification?
6. How does the programming specification interface with DFDs and STDs?
7. How does modeling provide the input for much of the system's documentation?
8. What is an acceptance test plan?
9. Comment on the statement: "Cannot test 100% of everything."
10. How do acceptance test plans facilitate the productivity and quality of programming?
11. Why is it important for the analyst to provide a budget for his/her tasks?

Part III
How to Implement

Project Management

14

Introduction

This chapter provides guidance on system development life cycle methodologies and on best practices for project management of packaged and in-house developed systems. Project organization, including roles and responsibilities, is covered. There are many aspects of package software management that are generic; however, there are certainly unique aspects when managing package software systems. Thus, this chapter provides an understanding of where these unique challenges occur in the life cycle of package software projects. It also focuses on the ongoing support issues that must be addressed to attain best practices.

A project manager who comes from a traditional software development background and understands the phases of software development will perhaps do fine in overseeing the progress of package software projects. Indeed, traditional project managers will focus on budget, the schedule, the resources, and the project plan. Unfortunately, package software systems, because of their widespread involvement with many parts of the business, need to go beyond just watching and managing the software development process. That is, the project management of packaged systems requires much more integration with the internal and external user communities. It must combine traditional development with business creation, and because of the preexisting nature of the package, it also delves into the internal organization structure and requires their participation in every phase of the development and implementation cycle. Listed below are some of the unique components of packaged development projects.

1. *Project managers as complex managers*: package software projects require multiple interfaces that are outside the traditional user community. They can include interfacing with writers, editors, marketing personnel, customers, and consumers, all who might be stakeholders in the success of the system.
2. *Shorter and dynamic development schedules*: due to the dynamic nature of packaged systems, the development is less linear. Because there is less

experience and more stakeholders, there is a tendency to underestimate the time and cost to complete.

3. *New untested technologies*: there is so much new technology offered particularly for Web developers that there is a practice of using new versions of development software that has not matured. The method of obtaining new software is easily distributed over the Web, so it is relatively easy to try new versions as soon as they become available.

4. *Degree of scope changes*: packaged systems because of their involvement with many aspects of the business tend to be much more prone to scope creep. Project managers need to work closely with internal users, customers, and consumers to advise them of the impact of changes on the schedule and the cost of the project. Unfortunately, scope changes that are influenced by changes in market trends may not be avoidable. Thus, part of a good strategy is to manage scope changes rather than attempt to stop them—which might not be realistic.

5. *Costing packaged systems are difficult*: the software industry has always had difficulties in knowing how to cost a project as discussed in Chapter 6. Packaged systems are even more difficult because of the number of variables, unknowns, and use of new technologies and procedures.

6. *Lack of standards*: the software industry continues to be a profession that does not have a governing body. Thus it is impossible to have real enforced standards as other professions enjoy. While there are suggestions and best practices, many of them are unproven and not kept current with new developments. Because of the lack of successful package software projects, there are few success stories to create new and better best practices.

7. *Less specialized roles and responsibilities*: the software development team tends to have staff members who have varying responsibilities. Unlike traditional software projects, separation of roles and responsibilities is more difficult when operating in a Web environment. For example, defining the exact role of an analyst can be very tricky; for example, are analysts programmers, database developers, or content designers? The reality is that all of these roles can be part of a developer's responsibility.

8. *Who bears the cost?* There is general uncertainty as to who should bear the cost of the packaged system. This refers to the internal organization of stakeholders who need to agree on the funding. This becomes even more complex when there are delays and cost overruns, because the constituents cannot easily agree on who is at fault and therefore who should bear the burden of the additional costs.

9. *Project management responsibilities are very broad*: packaged project management responsibilities need to go beyond those of the traditional IT project manager. Packaged project managers are required to provide management services outside the traditional software staff. They need to interact more with internal and external users as well as with non-traditional members of the development team such as content managers. Therefore, there are many more obstacles that can cause project managers to fail at their jobs.

Package Software Projects	Traditional Projects
Project managers are not always trained client managers	Different
Development project schedules tend to be short	Similar
New and untested third-party software are often implemented	Usually never
Changes in scope occur during implementation	Similar
Pricing model does not really exist	Different
Standards for package production do not exist	Similar
Team roles are less specialized	Different
Users have difficulty bearing the costs of development, especially during planning	Different
Project manager responsibilities are broad	Different

Fig. 14.1 Package software and traditional projects compared

10. *The package never ends*: the nature of how packaged systems are built and deployed suggests that they are living systems. This means that they have a long life cycle made up of ongoing maintenance and enhancements. So the traditional begin and end project does not apply to a package software project that inherently must be implemented in ongoing phases.

Figure 14.1 summarizes these differences between traditional and package software projects.

The questions that need to be answered are not only limited to what the process and responsibilities should be, but also who should do them? It is my position that a business analyst takes the responsibility of managing the process from inception to completion. The duties and responsibilities of a business analyst are excellent prerequisites for understanding the intricacies of project management. Their roles as analysts require them to have relationships with the organization and an understanding of the politics and culture that drives the business. I am not suggesting that every analyst should become a project manager, but rather that one of the analysts should also be the project manager. In order to determine the right fit, it is important to define the skill sets that are required for successful project management. These are summarized below:

- Software experience
- Understanding of budgeting, scheduling, and resource allocation
- Excellent written and verbal communication skills
- Ability to hold and lead meeting discussions
- Detailed oriented yet globally motivated (can see the difference between the forest and the trees)
- Pragmatic

- A sense of humor that comes across as a natural personal trait as opposed to an acted one
- Ability to be calm and levelheaded during crisis
- Experience with Web technologies, multimedia, and software engineering

Unfortunately, it is difficult to find the project manager who has all of these traits. In many cases it is wise to promote from within and develop the expertise internally. This is especially effective because an internal individual is a known quantity, and most likely already fits into the culture of the organization. Most important is that the individual is accepted in the culture. On the downside, it takes time to develop internal talent, and sometimes this trained talent leaves the company once they have received their training. There is benefit to bringing in someone from the outside because they can have a fresh view of the project and offer more objective input on what needs to be done to get the project finished on time.

Defining the Project

The first step for the project manager is to develop a mission statement for the project. A mission statement helps managers and users to focus on three core tasks:
1. Identify the project's objectives
2. Identify the users
3. Determine the scope of the project

Identify Objectives

Project objectives are defined as the results that must be attained during the project. According to Lewis (1995), project objectives must be specific, measurable, attainable, realistic, and time-limited. The most difficult of these objectives tends to be "measurable" and "attainable." Ultimately, objectives state the desired outcomes and focus on how the organization will know when it is reached? Objectives are typically devised by the project's stakeholders. These individuals are usually executives and managers who have the most to gain from the successful implementation of the package software system. Unfortunately, while this sounds good, it is difficult to implement. In reality, it is difficult for executives to articulate on what they are looking for. Indeed, the package software paradigm has simply forced many executives to create products because they think it is a competitive advantage for their companies to have one. This, in essence, means that executives might be driven by the fear that they must do something or something is better than nothing.

Package software objectives evolve and cause many iterative events to occur, especially in the early phases of the project. Good and effective objectives tend to be short sentences that are written down. Using this format, objectives can be used by project managers to effectively avoid scope creep. The objectives should be distributed to all stakeholders and project members so that everyone understands them.

Identify Users

Chapter 2 covered the significance of users and their importance to the success of any project. In that chapter, I defined three types of users: internal, customers, and consumers. It is important for project managers to understand the value of the input from each of these users. Indeed, the content of the website will ultimately be determined by the users who access the site. However, managers and developers often disagree on how much input is needed from users. This is further complicated when managing package software projects because of the diversity of the users and the complexity of decisions that must be made. Furthermore, there is always limited time, so package software project managers need to be as productive as possible with how user input is obtained, the types of interviewing that is done, and the method of measuring the value of the user's input.

Since the only way to measure a site's success is to determine whether the objectives have been met, the philosophy of who gets interviewed and how much value their input has should be mapped to the original objectives set forth by management. Thus, besides the internal users, the real obstacle for project managers is to identify which users know best what they want from the package software system. Besides one-on-one interviews and JADs, the project manager can also obtain information from two other sources: market research and focus groups.

There are many firms that provide market research services. Such firms have databases of researched information relating to user preferences and behaviors. They also collect information about packaged solutions and what users expect from them. Every package software system should have a budget using a market research firm so that they can obtain an objective and independent opinion about user preferences, particularly within a certain market segment. Conducting a focus group is a cheaper yet effective way to get objective input from users. It is particularly useful when attempting to assess consumer preferences. Focus groups involve the selection of sample consumers that the project manager feels represents the typical user. The sessions are filmed behind a mirror, and users respond to questions about their preferences when using a package software system. The focus group typically needs a moderator who controls the meeting agenda and ensures that all of the research questions are answered by the participants. During all sessions it is important that the project manager ensures that the objectives of the package software system be clearly defined to the audience. The objectives should be in writing and reviewed before the start and end of each session. In addition, the objectives should be written on a whiteboard or flip chart so participants can be reminded of the scope of the project should certain users start discussions on tangent subjects.

Determining the Scope of the Project

The scope of the project relates to the time and budget of when it needs to be completed. Because there is always a limited amount of time and money to create product, the scope of the project must be negotiated against what can be done with what users want to be done. Thus, scope is the domain of functions and features that will be included in the package software system based on a specific time commitment and cost outlay. The best approach to formulating a scope statement is to first create a work breakdown structure that contains the mission statement, lists the objectives, and formulates the tasks and subtasks to complete each objective. Thus, a work breakdown structure is really a form of functional decomposition of the tasks necessary to meet the objectives. Once stakeholders and the project manager agree on the objectives and what tasks will be done to attain them, then the scope of the project is complete. Figure 14.2 depicts a sample work breakdown structure.

Once tasks and subtasks have been determined, the package software project manager needs to determine the time and cost of completing each component. Thus, the work breakdown structure will eventually contain the costs for each task within each objective for the entire project as proposed. Management and the project manager can then begin the process of negotiating what can be completed on time and on budget by removing subtasks or tasks as appropriate.

Another valuable approach to building package software projects is phasing deliverables. Because package software projects tend never to be finished, it might be advisable to deliver some portion of the system first and then add-on functionality in subsequent releases of the system. Obviously, this might not always be feasible;

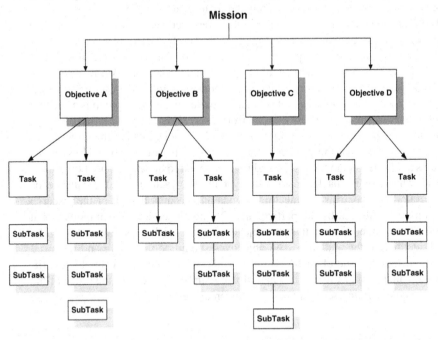

Fig. 14.2 Sample work breakdown structure

ID		Task Name	Duration	Start	Finish	Predecessors	Jul 31, '11	Aug 7, '11	Aug 14, '11	Aug
1		**Package Software Project**	**50 days**	Fri 8/5/11	Thu 10/13/11					
2		General Activities	50 days	Fri 8/5/11	Thu 10/13/11					
3		Planning	12 days	Fri 8/5/11	Mon 8/22/11					
4		Initial Meeting Formulate Scope	1 day	Fri 8/5/11	Fri 8/5/11					
5		Vendor Selection	3.5 days	Fri 8/5/11	Wed 8/10/11					
6		Planning	2 days	Thu 8/11/11	Fri 8/12/11					
7		Planning Packaged Vendor	3 days	Mon 8/15/11	Wed 8/17/11	6				
8		Minutes of Vendor meeting	1 day	Thu 8/18/11	Thu 8/18/11	7				
9		Vendor Meeting	2 days	Fri 8/19/11	Mon 8/22/11	8				
10		Department 1	25 days	Wed 8/24/11	Tue 9/27/11					
11		Planning Meeting	1 day	Wed 8/24/11	Wed 8/24/11					
12		Interviews with Users	5 days	Mon 8/29/11	Fri 9/2/11					
13		Business Specifications	10 days	Mon 9/5/11	Fri 9/16/11	12				
14		Meetings with Users	2 days	Mon 9/19/11	Tue 9/20/11	13				
15		Finalize Specifications	3 days	Fri 9/23/11	Tue 9/27/11					
16		Department 2	24 days	Wed 8/24/11	Mon 9/26/11					
17		Planning Meeting	5 days	Wed 8/24/11	Tue 8/30/11					
18		Interviews with Users	11 days	Mon 8/29/11	Mon 9/12/11					
19		Business Specifications	3 days	Mon 9/5/11	Wed 9/7/11					
20		Meetings with Users	1 day	Mon 9/19/11	Mon 9/19/11					
21		Finalize Specifications	2 days	Fri 9/23/11	Mon 9/26/11					
22		Send out Requirements Document	44 days	Mon 8/15/11	Thu 10/13/11					
23		Prepare Specs	3 days	Wed 9/28/11	Fri 9/30/11					
24		Review with User Dept 1	4 days	Mon 10/3/11	Thu 10/6/11	23				
25		Review with User Dept 2	4 days	Mon 10/10/11	Thu 10/13/11					
26		Finalize Document	5 days	Mon 8/15/11	Fri 8/19/11					

Fig. 14.3 Package software project plan

there are package software systems that cannot be phased, that is, they are all or nothing at all. However, I believe that all projects can have some level of phased development and that such development in the long run benefits the entire scope of the project. Indeed, first releases of a packaged solution typically need revision anyway and the second phase or version might be a better time to add certain features and functions.

I stated that the final work breakdown schedule represents the scope of the project. Typically, the package software project manager will finalize the scope statement by preparing a document that includes the work breakdown structure and articulates how this structure will be formulated into deliverables for the project. In many ways the scope document acts as a management report and reiterates the mission and objectives of the project along with the project plan. Figure 14.3 shows a typical project plan developed in Microsoft Project.

Managing Scope

A project plan can sometimes be referred to as a work breakdown schedule or WBS. As shown in Fig. 14.3, it depicts every step in the project and can enforce dependencies within tasks and subtasks. This is important, because changes to the plan may affect other tasks. A WBS product like Microsoft's Project provides an automated way of tracking changes and determining its effect on the entire project. A popular method of tracking changes is called "critical path analysis." Critical path analysis involves the monitoring of tasks that can have an effect on the entire scope of the project, meaning it can change the time frame and cost of delivery. A critical path is defined as a task that if delayed will cause a delay in the entire project. A task that can delay the project is then called a critical task. The importance of managing critical tasks is crucial for successful management of package software projects. Project

Fig. 14.4 Critical and non-critical tasks using Microsoft Project

managers are often faced with the reality that some task has slipped behind schedule. When faced with this dilemma, the project manager needs to decide whether dedicating more resources to the task might get it back on schedule. However, the first thing that the project manager needs to assess is whether the task can affect the critical path. If the answer is yes, then the project manager must attempt to use other resources to avoid a scope delay. If the task is not critical, then the delay may be acceptable without needing to change the project plan. Figure 14.4 shows a critical task and a non-critical task.

The Budget

Budgeting is one of the most important responsibilities of a project manager. The budget effectively prices the tasks that must be delivered and rolls them up to the project cost level. It is important to recognize that all budgets are estimates. Therefore, they are never 100% accurate—if they were they would not be budgets. The concept behind budgeting is that some tasks will be overbudget and others will be underbudget resulting in an offset that essentially balances out to the assumptions outlined in the original plan. Budgets are typically built on expense categories. Figure 14.5 shows the common budget categories that projects should be tracking.

**Project Budget
Sample**   12/12/2010

Description		Low	High	Comments
Hardware				
Servers	$	150,000	200,000	
Workstations		400,000	600,000	
Modems		25,000	30,000	
Scanners		5,000	20,000	
Total Hardware		580,000	850,000	
Software				
Base Product		250,000	350,000	Cost of vendor base product software
Database		100,000	250,000	Database vendor software license
Office Automation		40,000	100,000	Forms elimination and e-mail intranet
CAD/CAM-Scanning		40,000	100,000	Scanning software
Media Production		90,000	150,000	
Software Modifications		75,000	125,000	Modification costs to vendors product meet needs
Total Software		595,000	1,075,000	
Services				
Network and Software Design		5,000	8,500	Analysis & design of system
Consultants		240,000	285,000	Specialists that may be needed
Scanning Documents		125,000	135,000	Service to put all plans in system
Conversion of Data		120,000	130,000	
Installation		45,000	87,000	low: 300 × 150 high 300 × 250 plus servers
Training		25,000	85,000	Train the trainer all train everyone
Total Services		560,000	730,500	
Total	$	1,735,000	2,655,500	

Fig. 14.5 Sample e-business project budget expense categories

As stated above, a project budget is a set of assumptions. Typical budget assumptions are as follows:
- All content will be provided in machine-readable form
- The content manager will approve content design within 24h
- The Web design team will present two alternate design schemas
- Graphics for the website are finalized and ready for integration

It is not a bad idea for the project manager to create a budget document that includes a list of the assumptions, because it allows the manager to track whether incorrect assumptions caused delays in the scope of the project. Unfortunately, there are also hidden costs that tend not to be included in project budgets. The following is a list of common hidden costs that are missed by the project manager:

- Meetings
- Phone calls
- Research
- Development of documents and status reports
- Project administration
- Review sessions
- Presentations to management

As previously discussed, some project managers add a 10–15% cushion to their budgets to absorb common hidden costs. While I do not support cushions, it is acceptable if actually listed as a budget item, as opposed to a cushion on each budget line item.

The Project Team

The project team is unique from other traditional project organizations. Most of the significant differences are attributable to the addition of the package software responsibilities. Today, the roles and responsibilities for developing and supporting package software team are far more complex and specialized. The project team has evolved because business managers understand the importance of technology in transforming the way business is done. On the other hand, there are certainly traditional roles and responsibilities that have not changed and are generalizable across any software development project.

While the structure of project teams can vary depending on the type of project, the size of the system, and the time to complete, typical organizations contain the following roles and responsibilities:

- *Project manager*: the project manager is responsible for the scope of work, developing the project plan, scheduling, allocating resources, budgeting, managing the team, interfacing with users, and reporting to management on progress. The project manager also deals with politics and other business issues, which include but are not limited to contract negotiations, licensing of third-party products, and staff hiring. In some instances the project manager is responsible for handling customer and consumer needs as it relates to the design and development of the package software system. Perhaps, the most important responsibility of the package software project manager is to know at all times what has been done and what needs to be done.
- *Account manager*: the account manager is usually a senior manager who is responsible for a number of projects. Account managers also serve clients in a number of ways, from selling new products to providing client support. In many ways, the account manager is the representative of the client's needs to the internal development team. Account managers can be called upon to obtain information from customers about their needs and their feedback on how the system supports their needs.

- *Technical manager*: this individual is the senior technologist of the project. He/she is usually from the development team and is the most experienced developer. The technical manger is responsible for ensuring that the correct technology is being used and deployed properly. This individual manages the programmers, database developers, and other system integrators. The technical manger provides feedback on the development status of each task and reports to the project manager.

- *Programmer*: a programmer may be needed to do certain custom modifications if not outsourced. He/she is responsible for coding applications for the project. These applications are coded to spec and can include a myriad of technologies including but not limited to server scripts, database applications, applets, and ActiveX controls. Development languages used on package software projects vary, but the Web uses such languages as Java, JavaScript, Visual Basic, VBScript, SQL, and C/C++. The technical manager usually manages this individual; however, large projects may employ multiple levels of programmers. In certain situations, junior programmers report to senior developers who act as mentors to them.

- *Business analyst*: this individual is responsible for gathering all of the user requirements and designing the logic models and architecture of the system, which include process models, data models, transaction system design, and process specifications. Ultimately, the business analyst is responsible for site architecture, navigation, search and data retrieval, and interaction design. This role is sometimes called an information architect.

- *Designer*: designers create the look and feel of the screens. They use various tools to design template content and overall screen structure. Screen designers report to the project manager who sets the overall project philosophy.

- *Database administrator (DBA)*: the DBA is responsible for all physical database design and development. This individual must also fine-tune the database to ensure efficient operation. Other responsibilities include data partitioning, data warehouse setup, data replication, and report generation.

- *Network engineers*: these individuals are responsible for designing network configurations that support the package software system. Sometimes a network engineer is also a security specialist who is responsible for registering domain names, setting up e-mail servers, and setting up chat rooms.

- *Security expert*: while this might be the network specialist, larger package software projects employ a dedicated security expert who works with encryption formulas, integrates with content systems, and focuses on securing on-line transactions. This individual can also advise the project manager on strategies to implement certain component applications.

- *Quality assurance specialist*: this individual is responsible for creating test scripts to ensure that the package software system operates within spec. The purpose of the test plans, sometimes called acceptance test plans, is to provide the minimal set of tests that must be passed for the site to go into production. The reporting structure for quality assurance personnel varies. Some believe that it is

Type of Project Activity	Staff Organization
Marketing and Media	Account executive, project manager, creative manager, designer, copywriter, production artist, quality assurance specialist
Project transactions	Project manager, technical manager, analyst, creative manager, database administrator, tester
Input/Output data	Project manager, technical manager, creative manager, database administrator, analyst, Web production specialist, quality assurance specialist
Intranet	Project manager, technical manager, creative manager, network engineer, Web production specialist, quality assurance specialist

Fig. 14.6 Project team roles and responsibilities matrix

part of the development team and therefore should report to the technical manager while others believe that it needs to report directly to the project manager. There are still others who believe that the quality assurance staff should report to the chief information officer (CIO). The reporting structure is dependent on how highly the department values the independence of the testing function.

- *Tester*: a tester is simply a person who carries out the test plans developed by the quality assurance staff. These people typically report to quality assurance staff, however, sometimes testers are users who are working with the account manager to assist in the testing of the product. These testers are in a sense a beta test user (beta test means that the software is tested in a live environment).

While this is an exhaustive list of potential positions to have on a project, it is unlikely that every one of these positions will exist in any given package software project. In reality, it is more important that the functionality of each of these positions is carried out, regardless of who takes on the responsibility. In order to provide better insight into the roles and responsibilities of each position, Fig. 14.6 reflects a comparison matrix that compares roles with responsibilities.

Figure 14.7 identifies the necessary skills of each of the critical members of the project team.

Project Team Dynamics

It is not unusual for package software development projects to operate from multiple sites with multiple interfaces. This may require much more organization and communication among the members of the team.

Skill Set	Description
Project Management	Ability to communicate with staff, executives, and users. Keep project on schedule.
Architecture	Ability to design the user interface and interact with technical development personnel
Graphic Design	Ability to transform requirements into visual solutions
Graphic Production	Ability to develop efficient graphics for Web browser use
Content Development	Ability to design and develop text and interactive content
Programming	Ability to use HTML, Javascript, etc.

Fig. 14.7 Necessary project skill sets

Set Rules and Guidelines for Communication

When project members are separated by locations or even by work schedules it is very important that everyone knows what their roles are and what everybody else's responsibilities are to each other. Project managers should establish guidelines on communication and require each member to provide short statuses on where they are in the project. While this might seem like a bother to team members, I have found that it provides immense value to the project manager because it forces each person to discipline themselves and report on where they are in their respective worlds. Furthermore, it forces project staff to articulate in writing what they have accomplished, what is outstanding, and what they plan to get done. Figure 14.8 shows a sample status report that tracks previous objectives with current objectives. It should not take more than 15 minutes to complete.

Extranet Review Sites

Project managers should create extranets that allow project staff to view the work of the project team. This also allows work to be approved virtually over the Web. Furthermore, status reports and general announcements can be viewed by authorized members of the project team as well as by stakeholders and users. Often extranet documents can be coupled with regular conference call sessions where project members can openly discuss reports, website samples, and determine new milestones as appropriate. Unfortunately, managing an extranet review site requires overhead and someone who can do the work. This simply means that someone on the project's staff or some assigned administrative person needs to take on the responsibility. There is also the challenge of dealing with staff who do not comply with procedures or need to be reminded about delivering their status reports on a regular basis. While this is unfortunate, it is a reality. However, it also tells the project manager as to who needs to be watched closer than other team members.

XYZ CORP
Project Plan

Project Status Report

\gprojst Copyright © 1995–2011
A. Langer & Assoc., Inc

Date 1/31/11	Vendor: XSP	Consultant: Art Langer

Previous Objectives: Objective	**Previous Target Date**	**Status**
Send out Software Proposals	1/23/11	Done
Send out Hardware Bids and check labor rates	1/25/11	2/6/11
Get XSP to modify detail design contract to include specifics on deliverables.	1/23/11	Done, waiting approval
Speak with product consultant and contract with him for data and layouts	1/25/11	2/3/11
Finalize Network Design Requirements Document	1/23/11	2/3/11

New Project Objectives: Objective	**Target Date**
Get specification on hardware certification machines from XSP	2/5/11
Get room to do JAD interviews and reviews	2/10/11
Ensure that accounting features are integrated in specs	2/10/11
Art to interview Joe	2/3/11
Check ability of MAS to create output files for display on Web	2/6/11
Identify and meet with brokers as part of interviews	2/3/11
Get prices for Scanning of floor plans for Web browsing	2/10/11

Attendees A. Langer & Assoc. Art Langer	XSP

Fig. 14.8 Sample project status report

Working with User Resources

Users are an interesting yet challenging resource. While they are clearly needed to
perform reviews and quality assurance, they are not officially assigned to the project
and are therefore not under the control of the project manager. Unfortunately, this
can cause problems if a user is not responsive to the needs of the project team.
This can be very damaging because the staff will be dependent on receiving timely
feedback from these resources. Lack of responsiveness from a user can also alienate
them from the project team. Indeed, there is nothing more damaging than a user
who shows disinterest in the project that is being designed to serve them. Therefore,
the package software project manager needs to be careful on what commitments

are made when a user resource is made available to them. Obviously, the project manager would want the individual to report directly to him/her and be a full-time resource. This could also be wishful thinking. It certainly can be dangerous to turn down the help. While this may appear to be a catch-22, it can be managed. First, the package software project manager should establish the need for user assistance early in the project and include it in the requirements documentation (it should be part of the assumptions section). Second, the project manager may need to limit the amount of work assigned to the user if they indeed are just part-time resources.

Outsourcing

As discussed in earlier chapters, not all packaged projects can be completed using internal staff. In fact, most are not. Using outsourced resources makes sense for many projects, especially those that might need very unique and qualified personnel who is not on staff or not deemed worthy of full-time employment. There may also be a lack of talent, which is the usual reason why consultants are hired in the first place. Sometimes, outsourced relationships are managed as strategic partnerships, which means that an outside business provides specific services for the firm on a regular basis. Project strategic partnerships can be made in many different areas or phases of the project. Outsource firms can provide video or audio engineers as needed or network support personnel to assist in installing the packaged solution. On the other hand, the entire project should not be outsourced because there may be a false sense of comfort that the firm's personnel need not be involved in the responsibility. I believe that in the long run this is a mistake. Remember that outsourced firms have their own destiny and growth to manage.

Planning and Process Development

In order to operationalize the project plan and to meet the budget, it is necessary to develop a phased implementation guide that helps members of the team understand where they are in the process. Unfortunately, the project task plan is much too detailed to use, so it is a good idea for the project manager to develop a higher-level document that can be used during the development of project. Such a plan typically contains four phases: (1) strategy, (2) design, (3) development, and (4) testing. Figure 14.9 reflects the major software phases and includes the activities and output of each phase.

1. *Strategy*: this phase requires that the stakeholders, account executive, users, and the project manager all meet to agree on the objectives, requirements, key milestones, and needs of the target audience. The activities in this phase comprise the goals and objectives, feedback from users, research from outside sources, and the project proposal document. The culmination of these steps should be summarized in a document to be used by the project team. This document is sometimes referred to as a creative brief. The creative brief is really a summary

Fig. 14.9 Package software development phases

of the original proposal in template form and created so that project team members can quickly refer to it and obtain the information they need. Figure 14.10 depicts a creative brief template.

Creative briefs allow the project manager to conduct effective brainstorming sessions with staff. The document acts as an agenda and also as a checkpoint to ensure that discussions are not going beyond the objectives of the project and that the products are designed in accordance with the target audience's needs.

2. *Design*: design represents the second major phase. It is composed of all the tasks that participate in the design of the user interface, the analysis and design of technical specifications, and the overall architecture of the package software system. The results of the design phase are the functional specifications, detailed project plan timeline and budget, and website and report prototypes. The design phase typically requires stakeholders and other users to review and sign-off on the specification document before the project can proceed. Of course, the approval process of the design document can be done in phases, that is, portions of the document can be approved so that the implementation can go forward on some limited basis. During the process of designing the packaged system, it is important that the project team has access to the content of all screens and programs. This is especially important for large projects where there can be more than one design group creating content. As stated in the previous chapter, content development is an iterative process; therefore, the team members need to constantly have access to the current site architecture and schematic designs. That is why it is so important to have the technical specifications in a CASE tool and content system so that all members can have instant access to the current state of the project.

3. *Development*: this phase includes all of the activities that are involved with actually building the site. The challenge for project managers is to control changes

---

Creative Brief Template

XYZ, INC

Dates:	Dept:	User:

Project Scope

Objectives:

Target Audiences:

Image: (Explain the image that the system must convey to users)

Current Brand: (Explain the current brand and image of the business to its users)

User Experience: (Explain the most important thing that users should experience from using the system)

\gminutes Copyright © 1995–2011
A. Langer & Assoc., Inc

Fig. 14.10 Sample creative brief

made to the original specifications. This typically occurs after the first proto-type reviews where users begin to change or enhance their original requirements. While it is not impossible to change specifications, it is certainly dangerous and can be a major cause of scope creep.

4. *Testing*: during this phase developers and users are testing the site and reporting errors. Errors are tricky issues; they must be classified in particular areas and levels of severity. For example, some errors cause an application to abort, which would be considered a critical error. Others might be aesthetic in nature and can

Quality Assurance

Acceptance Test Plan

Purpose: To ensure that Contact screens operate properly when supplying new good data. **This plan entry mode with nothing on the screen.**	Product: Contact - Using Enter Key	Page: 1 of 4
		Number:
	Vendor:	
Test Plan #: 1G	QA Technician:	Date:

Test No.	Condition Being Tested	Expected Results	Actual Results	Comply Y/N	Comments
1	Enter LAST NAME for a new contact, press enter key. Repeat and enter FIRST NAME, press enter key	Should accept and prompt for COMPANY SITE			
2	Select COMPANY Site from picklist	Should accept and prompt for next field			
3	Enter LAST NAME and FIRST NAME for a CONTACT that is already in the System.	Should accept and prompt for COMPANY SITE			

Fig. 14.11 QA test plan

be scheduled for fixing, but are not severe enough to holdup going live. Still other errors are not really errors, but rather deficiencies in design. This means that the program is performing to the specification but not in the way the user really expects. All of these issues need to be part of an overall test plan, which identifies what types of errors are critical and how they affect the development process. Figure 14.11 shows a typical test plan.

Technical Planning

Technical planning is the process where the project team develops a working strategy for how they will use the features of the packaged system. These features include all of the components of development including database, programming, transaction systems, multimedia, and scripting. Technical planning is simple in concept; how do all of the technology pieces come together, how do they interface, and what is the schedule of implementation? Because of the object-oriented methods that are employed by package software systems, it is easy to have components developed in separate teams of programmers. However, there comes a time when all components must come together and interface with each other. When the components interface correctly the system works. Project managers never quite know if interfaces will work until they are actually tested. The concept of "working" means many things in software development. The obvious definition is that the program performs its tasks correctly and to specification. There is another part of what "working" means. This relates to performance of the application. While an application might calculate the correct output, it may not do so efficiently.

Application performance problems tend to first show up during component interface testing. Fortunately, this is at a time where applications can be fine-tuned before they go into production. Unfortunately, many interface-oriented performance problems first appear in the production system because the testing environment was not a true representation of the live system. Therefore, it is important for project managers to ensure that the test system correctly matches the live environment. Indeed, many performance problems occur because of the unexpected stress load on the system. Notwithstanding when an application performance problem is discovered, the main challenge is to fix the problem. Sometimes performance interface problems can be a serious problem especially if the solution requires a redesign of the application architecture or substantial changes to the network infrastructure. Any serious problems of this caliber could cause serious setbacks to the project schedule and its cost. In many ways the planning and decision making regarding how applications are designed, which program languages should be used, and what network platforms to choose are crucial steps for the project team to make. The project manager must attempt to surround him/herself with the best knowledge available. This knowledge base of people might not exist in the organization. Therefore, the project manager might need to seek guidance from third-party consultants who can act as specialists during these critical decision times.

Defining Technical Development Requirements

A large part of whether systems are implemented properly has to do with how well the detailed technical requirements are prepared. The technical project team needs to define the technical requirements to implement the logical specifications. Remember that logical specifications do not necessarily specify what hardware or software to use. Thus, the technical team must evaluate the logical specification and make recommendations on how the actual technical specifications are to be built. The project manager can be more effective if they ask some key questions:

- *Are we thinking of using technologies that we have not used before?* Using unknown technologies can be very dangerous. An unknown technology is not only a new product; it is a product that the development team has never used. Because of the extent of new developments in technology, dealing with unknown hardware and software needs to be addressed and risks assessed by the project manager.
- *What benefits will be derived from new technologies?* Implementing new technologies for the sake of new technologies is not a good reason to implement unknowns. This concept gets back to the old cliché: "if it's not broken don't fix it!"
- *What type of coding is being done?* This relates to whether program code is being developed from scratch or via modified software packages. Each has its advantages and disadvantages. Writing code from scratch takes longer, but provides the architecture that best fits the design. Package software is faster to develop, but may not fit well with the overall needs of the company. The rule of thumb

is never to modify packages by more than 20% of their total code. When this percent is exceeded the benefit realized from the package is so minimum that developers might as well start from scratch.

- *Will there be access to production-like testing environments?* This was covered earlier. Project managers must ensure that the proper testing facilities are available to mirror the production environment.

Maintenance

Package software projects should never be implemented without considering how to preserve maintainability. Maintainability is a universal concept that relates to what defines a quality product. Products that work is one thing, those that work and are maintainable is another. In package software systems, product that cannot be maintained easily is problematic. I have previously discussed the power of content management systems and CASE software as vehicles to support maintenance of package software systems. There are other best practices that need to be performed during the planning stage. First, the manner in which code will be developed and the standards to be upheld need to be agreed upon and put in writing. Technical managers should also define how they intend to enforce these standards. Documentation of code should also be addressed in the documents. Furthermore, there needs to be agreement on the database design as well. This involves getting the database administrators to agree on limits to de-normalization, naming standards, and the methods of coding stored procedures and database triggers.

Another important component of maintenance quality is planning for growth. The issue of growth relates more to network infrastructure than to software development. First, the project manager needs to address issues of hardware scalability. This relates to the capacity of the network before the hardware architecture needs to be changed to accommodate new applications. Second, database servers must be configured with real-time backup architecture (no single point of failure concepts) and data warehouses need to be designed to perform at peak times.

Project Management and Communication

Successful project managers communicate well, not only with their staffs, but with vendors, management, and users. Indeed, sometimes communication skills are more important than technical ones. Obviously, a complete project manager has both. However, the advent of package software systems has placed even more emphasis on the importance of communication within the project team. There are many reasons why poor communications occur during project life cycles. According to Burdman (1999), there are 11 leading causes for communication problems in a project team.

1. *People come from different disciplines*: communication is difficult enough among those who work together every day. The influx of many different disciplines on a package software project creates more challenges because staffs are not as familiar with each other. Remember that relationships are very important for team interaction. Many teams need to spend time just getting acclimated to each other's business styles.

2. *Lack of mutual understanding of the technology*: project members do not have consistent understandings of the technology. For example, some staff might use the word "table" to define a logical database entity, while others call it a file. The best solution to this problem is to distribute a list of common technology definitions to all project participants.

3. *Personalities*: this occurs in all projects. Some people have conflicting personalities and do not naturally get along.

4. *Hidden agenda*: there are often political agendas that team members have. They are sometimes difficult to assess, but they definitely cause problems with communication among project staff. These individuals are set in their ways and have questionable dedication to the success of the project, that is, they have a more important political agenda.

5. *Ineffective meetings*: meetings for the sake of meetings is no reason to meet. Sometimes too many meetings can be counterproductive to getting things done. It can sometimes be a false solution to other problems that exist in the project team. Some meetings are necessary but run too long and participants begin to lose focus on the agenda. Project managers need to be cognizant of the time allotments they make to meetings and to respect those time frames.

6. *Proximity*: the demographics of where project team members reside is obviously a factor in hindering communications among the team members. While this is a disadvantage, teleconferencing and video conferencing are all possible anecdotes for managing communication projects at a distance. Communication can be further hindered because of long distances between staff especially when there are time zone changes. In these situations, even conferencing is not feasible. Usually, the best way of communicating is through e-mail and extranets.

7. *Assumptions*: team members can often make assumptions about things that can cause communication breakdowns. Usually, assumptions create problems because things that are believed to be true are not written down.

8. *Poor infrastructure and support*: the severity of this problem is often overlooked. It includes the frustrations of having computer troubles, e-mail incompatibilities, and other hardware failures that contribute to communication problems. The best approach to avoid these frustrations is for the project manager to be very aggressive on having them fixed timely and properly.

9. *Being an expert*: every project has one or two "know-it-allers" who attempt to dominate meetings and want to orchestrate their point of view on the rest of the staff. These individuals spend so much time telling others what to do that they forget what they have to do to make the project successful. Project managers should be very aggressive with these type of participants by making it clear what everyone's role is, including the project manager's responsibilities!

10. *Fear*: fear is a very large barrier with certain staff. These staff members become overwhelmed with the size, complexity, and length of package software project and it can cause them to lose their perspective and creativity. Project managers need to interject and provide assistance to those members who struggle with a package software system.
11. *Lack of good communication structure*: good communication systems fit-in with the culture of the organization and are realistic in what they might accomplish. Many communication problems exist simply because the infrastructure does not relate to the needs of the staff.

Summary

This chapter attempted to provide a project manager with a perspective on the salient issues that can help them be successful. This chapter was not intended to provide a complete step-by-step approach to managing complex projects. I included this chapter because I believe that many analysts can also serve as excellent project managers. Indeed, much of the important issues discussed in this chapter relate to many of the skills that analysts must have to perform in their responsibilities as software engineers. These include

- *Communication skills*: analysts have significant experience in working with users to obtain input so they can develop system requirements properly.
- *Meeting management*: JAD sessions are more complex meetings than typical project meetings. Analysts who have also been JAD facilitators are very well trained on how to control meetings.
- *Politically astute*: analysts are experienced in working with people who have hidden agendas and are driven by politics.
- *Technically proficient*: analysts are educated in logic modeling and are familiar with much of the technical issues that come up during the project life cycle.
- *Project planning*: analysts are used to developing project plans and managing deliverables; each analysis and design task can be seen as a mini-project.
- *Documentation*: analysts are supporters of good documentation and understand the value of having maintainable processes.
- *Executive presence*: analysts work with executive users and understand how to interact with them.
- *Quality assurance*: analysts are familiar with quality assurance test plans and testing methodologies. They are often involved with test plan development.

Problems and Exercises

1. Describe five unique aspects of package software projects.
2. Compare packaged products with traditional ones.
3. What is a mission statement of a project mean? How should a project manager define the project mission?

4. Explain how the scope of a project is determined and how it is controlled.
5. What are the key categories of a project budget?
6. What are the roles and responsibilities of the project team? Who determines the members?
7. Explain the components of a project status report? How often should the report be issued and to whom?
8. What is a creative brief? What are the key components?
9. What are the important aspects of project management communication?

References

Burdman, J. (1999). *Collaborative web development.* New York: Addison-Wesley.
Lewis, V. (1995). *Fundamentals of project management: A worksmart guide.* New York: American Management Association.

ISO 9000 and the Software Development Life Cycle

15

Developing a System of Procedures

Perhaps, one of the most significant challenges in analysis today is its role in the software life cycle. There has been much criticism of the lack of discipline applied to software development projects and personnel in general, and we continue to be an industry that has a poor reputation for delivering quality products on schedule. Although many organizations have procedures, few really follow them and fewer still have any means of measuring the quality and productivity of software development. A system of procedures should first be developed prior to implementing a life cycle that can ensure its adherence to the procedure. These procedures also need to be measured on an ongoing basis. This book restricts its focus to the set of procedures that should be employed in the analysis and design functions.

The process of developing measurable procedures in an organization must start with the people who will be part of its implementation. Standard procedures should not be created by upper management, as the steps will be viewed as a control mechanism as opposed to a quality implementation. How then do we get the implementers to create the standards? When examining this question, one must look at other professions and see how they implement their standards. The first main difference between computer professionals and members of many other professions is that they lack a governing standards board like the American Medical Association (AMA) or the American Institute of Certified Public Accountants (AICPA). Unfortunately, as mentioned in previous chapters, it seems unlikely that any such governing board will exist in the near future. Looking more closely at this issue, however, we need to examine the ultimate value of a governing board. What standards boards really accomplish is to build the moral and professional responsibilities of their trade. Accountants, attorneys, and doctors look upon themselves as professionals who have such responsibilities. This is not to imply that governing boards can resolve every problem, but at least they can help. With or without the existence of a standards board, analysts within an organization must develop the belief that they belong

A.M. Langer, *Guide to Software Development*,
DOI 10.1007/978-1-4471-2300-2_15, © Springer-Verlag London Limited 2012

to a profession. Once this identification occurs, analysts can create the procedures necessary to ensure the quality of their own profession. There simply are not many analysts who view themselves as part of a profession.

If analysts can create this level of self-actualization, then the group can begin the process of developing quality procedures that can be measured for future improvement. The standard procedures should be governed by the group itself and the processes integrated into the software life cycle of the organization. In fact, analysts should encourage other departments to follow the same procedures for implementing their respective quality procedures.

Although not typically required, many firms have elected to employ ISO 9000 as a more formal vehicle to implement the development of measurable procedures. ISO 9000 stands for the International Organization for Standardization, an organization formed in 1947 and based in Geneva, which currently has 91 member countries associated with it. ISO 9000 was founded to establish international quality assurance standards focused on processes rather than on products.

Why ISO 9000?

ISO 9000 offers a method of establishing agreed-upon quality levels through standard procedures in the production of goods and services. Many international companies require that their vendors be ISO 9000 compliant through the certification process. Certification requires an audit by an independent firm that specializes in ISO 9000 compliance. The certification is good for 3 years. Apart from the issue of certification, the benefits of ISO 9000 are in its basis for building a quality program through employee empowerment. It also achieves and sustains specific quality levels and provides consistency in its application. ISO 9000 has a number of subcomponents. ISO 9001, 9002, and 9003 codify the software development process. In particular, 9001 affects the role of the analyst by requiring standards for design specifications and defines 20 different categories of systems. Essentially, ISO 9000 requires three basic things:

1. Say What You Do
2. Do What You Say
3. Prove it

This means that the analyst will need to completely document what should occur during the requirements process to ensure quality. After these procedures are documented, the analyst needs to start implementing based on the standards developed and agreed upon by the organization. The process must be self-documenting, that is, it must contain various control points that can prove at any time that a quality step in the process was not only completed but also done within the quality standard established by the organization. It is important to recognize that ISO 9000 does not establish what the standard should be, but rather simply that the organization can comply with whatever standards it chooses to employ. This freedom is what makes ISO 9000 so attractive. Even if the organization does not opt to go through with the audit, it can still establish an honorable quality infrastructure that:

- creates an environment of professional involvement, commitment, and accountability;
- allows for professional freedom to document the realities of the process itself within reasonable quality measurements;
- pushes down the responsibilities of quality to the implementer as opposed to the executive;
- identifies where the analyst fits in the scope of the software life cycle;
- locates existing procedural flaws;
- eliminates duplication of efforts;
- closes the gap between required procedures and actual practices;
- complements the other quality programs that might exist; and
- requires that the individuals participating in the process be qualified within their defined job descriptions.

How to Incorporate ISO 9000 into Existing Software Life Cycles

The question now is how to incorporate an ISO 9000-type process for the analyst function and incorporate it into the existing software life cycle. Listed below are the nine essential steps to follow:

1. Create and document all the quality procedures for the analyst;
2. Follow these processes throughout the organization and see how they enter and leave the analyst function;
3. Maintain records that support the procedures;
4. Ensure that all professionals understand and endorse the quality policy;
5. Verify that there are no missing processes;
6. Changes or modifications to the procedures must be systematically reviewed and controlled;
7. Have control over all documentation within the process;
8. Ensure that analysts are trained and that records are kept about their training; and
9. Ensure that constant review is carried out by the organization or through third-party audits.

In order for ISO 9000 guidelines to be implemented, it is recommended that the analyst initially provide a work flow diagram of the quality process (Fig. 15.1).

Figure 15.1 reflects some of the steps in a quality process for an analyst. Note that certain steps reflect that there is an actual form that needs to be completed in order to confirm the step's completion (Figs. 15.2, 15.3, and 15.4).

Figures 15.2, 15.3, and 15.4 represent the confirmation of the activities in the quality work flow process outlined by the analyst. At any time during the life cycle, an event can be confirmed by looking at the completed form.

In order to comply with the documentation standards, each form should contain an instruction sheet (Fig. 15.5). This sheet will ensure that users have the appropriate instructions. Confirmation documents can be implemented in different ways. Obviously, if forms are processed manually, the documentation will contain the actual storage of working papers by project. Such working papers are typically

Fig. 15.1 A sample work flow diagram

filed in a documentation storage room similar to a library where the original contents are secure and controlled. Access to the documentation is allowed, but must be authorized and recorded. Sometimes forms are put together using a word-processing package such as Microsoft Word. The blank forms are stored on a central library so that master documents can be accessed by the analyst via a network. Once the forms are completed, they can be stored in a project directory. The most sophisticated method of implementing ISO 9000 is to use a Lotus Notes electronic filing system. Here, forms are filled out and passed to the appropriate individuals automatically. The confirmation documents then become an inherent part of the original work flow. In any event, these types of forms implementation affect only automation, not the concept of ISO 9000 as a whole.

Interfacing IT Personnel

We mentioned earlier that ISO 9000 requires qualified personnel. This means that the organization must provide detailed information about the skill set requirements for each job function. Most organizations typically have job descriptions that are

Fig. 15.2 ISO 9000 project status report

not very detailed and tend to be vague with respect to the specific requirements of the job. In addition, job descriptions rarely provide information that can be used to measure true performance. Questions such as "How many lines of code should a programmer generate per day?" cannot be measured effectively. There is also a question about whether lines of code should be the basis of measurement at all. A solution to this dilemma is to create a job description matrix which provides the specific details of each job responsibility along with the necessary measurement criteria for performance (Fig. 15.6).

Figure 15.6 is a matrix of responsibilities for an analyst. Note that the analyst has a number of efficiency requirements within the managing engagements (projects)

Analysis Acknowledgment

User: _____

Date:	Analyst:	Date of Request	Project #

Confirmation Type	Y/N	Cost	Expected Days	Expected Delivery	Deliverable/Comments
Requirements Definition					
Conceptual Detail Design:					
Development:					
System Tested Enhancements					
User Accepted Enhancements					

\an0050 Rev. 3/21/11

Fig. 15.3 ISO 9000 analysis acknowledgment

Quality Assurance

Acceptance Test Plan

Purpose:		
Test Plan #:	Product:	Number:
	Vendor:	Date:
	QA Technician:	Page: 1 of

Test No.	Condition Being Tested	Expected Results	Actual Results	Comply Y/N	Comments
1					
2					
3					

Fig. 15.4 Quality assurance test plan

responsibility. Efficiency here means that the analyst must perform the task at a certain indicated level to be considered productive at that task. To a degree, efficiency typically establishes the time constraints to deliver the task. Measurement defines the method used to determine whether the efficiency was met. Reports are simply the vehicle in which the analyst proves that the task was completed and on what basis.

The job description matrix represents a subset of the entire job description that strictly focuses on the procedural and process aspects of the individual's position. It not only satisfies ISO 9000, but also represents a healthier way of

Name: Confirmation/Service Acknowledgment	Date Issued: 3/8/11
Form Instructions	Supersedes:
	Revision: 1.00

The purpose of this form is to track the status of various services such as Requirements Definition, Conceptual Detail Design, Development, System Tested Enhancements and User Accepted Enhancements.

The appropriate project # must be attached. The type form must be checked for each type of Confirmation.

\an0050i Rev. 3/8/11

Fig. 15.5 An ISO 9000 form instruction page

Responsibility	PH	Efficiency	Measurement	Reports
MANAGING ENGAGEMENTS	PD	Technical Project Plans are completed and finalized within 2 weeks of Kick-Off Meeting-- 80% compliance	Project plans will be reviewed by Director prior to submission to Client	Technical Project Plan (MG0140)
	PD	Client signs off on Tech Proj Plan within 3 weeks	Director receives copy within 2 days of signing	Project Status Report (MG0010)
	IP	When tech mods are identified up-front attend kick-off meeting with Acc Exec within 2 weeks of sale	Resulting letter to client committing to Project Plan	Kick-Off Meeting (MG0030)
	RQ	Requirements Definition Document on or before due date	Document is delivered within timeframe and signed	Confirmation Letter / Serv Acknow (MG0050) Project Status Report (MG0010)
	CD	Conceptual Detail Design Document on or before due date	Document is delivered within timeframe and signed	Confirmation Letter / Serv Acknow (MG0050) Project Status Report (MG0010)
	D	Development System on or before due date	Document is delivered within timeframe and signed	Confirmation Letter / Serv Acknow (MG0050) Project Status Report (MG0010)
	QA	System Testing Enhancements on or before due date	Document is delivered within timeframe and signed	Confirmation Letter / Serv Acknow (MG0050) Project Status Report (MG0010)

Fig. 15.6 Job description matrix

measuring individual performance in an IS environment. Most individuals should know exactly their performance at any time during the review period. Furthermore, the matrix is an easy tool to use for updating new or changed performance tasks.

Committing to ISO 9000

We have outlined the sequential steps to implement an ISO 9000 organization. Unfortunately, the outline does not ensure success and often just following the suggested steps leads to another software life cycle that nobody really adheres to. In order to be successful, a more strategic commitment must be made. Let's outline these guidelines for the analyst functions:

- A team of analysts should meet to form the governing body that will establish the procedures to follow to reach an ISO 9000 level (this does not necessarily require that certification be accomplished).
- The ISO 9000 team should develop a budget of the milestones to be reached and the time commitments that are required. It is advisable that the budget be forecasted like a project, probably using a Gantt Chart to develop the milestones and time frames.
- The ISO 9000 team should then communicate their objectives to the remaining analysts in the organization and coordinate a review session so that the entire organization can understand the benefits, constraints, and scope of the activity. It is also an opportunity to allow everyone to voice their opinions about how to complete the project. Therefore, the meeting should result in the final schedule for completing the ISO 9000 objective.
- The ISO 9000 team should inform the other IS groups of its objectives, although analysts should be careful not to provoke a political confrontation with other parts of the IS staff. The communication should be limited to helping other departments understand how these analyst quality standards will interface with the entire software life cycle.
- The work flows for the analyst tasks must be completed in accordance with the schedule such that everyone can agree to the confirmation steps necessary to validate each task. It is important that the ISO 9000 processes allow for a percentage of success. This means that not every process must be successful 100% of the time, but rather can be acceptable within some fault tolerance level. For example, suppose that the analyst must have a follow-up meeting with the users within 48 h after a previous step has been completed. It may not be realistic to meet this goal every time such a meeting is necessary. After all, the analyst cannot always force users to attend meetings in a timely way. Therefore, the ISO 9000 step may view this task as successful if it occurs within the 48 h 80% of the time, that is, within a 20% fault tolerance.
- All task steps must have verification. This will require that standard forms be developed to confirm completion. While we have shown samples of these forms earlier, the ISO 9000 team should be aware of producing an unwieldy process

involving too many forms. Many software life cycles have suffered the consequences of establishing too many check points. Remember, ISO 9000 is a professional's standard and should cater to the needs of well-trained professionals. Therefore, the ISO 9000 team should review the initial confirmation forms and begin the process of combining them into a smaller subset. That is, the final forms should be designed to be as generic as possible by confirming multiple tasks. For example, form AN0010 (Fig. 15.2) represents a generic project status report that was used to confirm various types of information attributable to different tasks.

- There should be meetings held with the analysis group that focus on the alternatives for automating the confirmation forms as outlined earlier in this chapter. It is advisable that this topic be confirmed by the group since their full cooperation is needed for the success of the program.

- Allow time for changing the procedures and the forms. Your first effort will not be the final one; therefore, the ISO 9000 team must plan to meet and review the changes necessary to make it work. Analysts should be aware that the opportunity for change always exists as long as it conforms to the essential objectives of ISO 9000.

- The ISO 9000 project should be at least a 1-year plan, from inception of the schedule to actual fulfillment of the processes. In fact, an organization must demonstrate ISO 9000 for at least 18 months prior to being eligible for certification.

- The ISO 9000 group needs to be prepared and authorized to make changes to the job description of the analyst. This may require the submission of requests and authorizations to the executive management team or the human resources department. It is important not to overlook this step, since an inability to change the organization structure could hinder the success of the ISO 9000 implementation.

As we can see from the above steps, establishing an ISO 9000 group is a significant commitment. However, its benefits can include a professional organization that controls its own quality standards. These standards can be changed on an ongoing basis to ensure compliance with the business objectives and requirements of the enterprise. Certification, while not the focus of our discussion, is clearly another level to achieve. Most companies that pursue certification do so for marketing advantage or are required to obtain it by their customers. Implementing ISO 9000 should not require that the entire company conform at once; in fact it is almost an advantage to implement it in a phased approach, department by department. The potential benefits of ISO 9000 concepts may fill the void in many of the IS organizations which lack clearly defined quality standards.

Problems and Exercises

1. Explain why ISO 9000 represents a system of procedures.
2. What are the three fundamental things that ISO 9000 tries to establish?
3. What are the overall benefits of ISO 9000?

4. How is ISO 9000 incorporated into the life cycle?
5. Why are work flows the most critical aspect of developing the ISO 9000 model?
6. Why are forms used in ISO 9000?
7. How are personnel affected by ISO 9000?
8. What is a job description matrix?
9. What steps are necessary for an organization to adopt ISO 9000?
10. Does ISO 9000 need to be implemented in all areas of the business? Explain.

Contract Considerations

16

It becomes increasingly important that contract considerations be included as part of the final selection process of any vendor solution (packaged or customized development). Organizations tend to make the mistake of leaving the contract negotiations toward the end of the selection process as opposed to making it inherently part of the process throughout each phase. That is, the contract is more a "living" document that may change as the needs of the product become more obvious to the stakeholders. In other words, the process feeds the contract needs. Thus, the purpose of this chapter is to provide guidance on the relevant stages, considerations, and content of the contract agreement. It is important to note that the information contained in this chapter is prescriptive in nature and not intended to suggest that technology or business personnel can determine whether a contract should be signed without the assistance of legal counsel, but it does provide a checklist of things to ensure that lawyers are aware about and ensures that the organization is protected.

What everyone wants out of a contract is to be protected, both from the organization (buyer) and from the vendor (seller). The question really becomes how to provide an agreement where both sides feel that it is fair. The core factors typically include

- *Ownership and rights*: this part contains the legal aspects of who owns the product and what rights does each party have in the use of the software.
- *Legal protection and coverage*: this contains various protections such as insurance requirements, indemnifications, and liabilities of each party.
- *Financials*: simply the cost for license of software, cost for development and programming, support and maintenance, and payment schedules.
- *Deliverables and performance*: specific things that the vendor agrees to deliver to the organization.

Each of these components will be defined and analyzed as follows.

A.M. Langer, *Guide to Software Development*,
DOI 10.1007/978-1-4471-2300-2_16, © Springer-Verlag London Limited 2012

Ownership and Rights

The most salient issue of ownership is whether the software is a package owned by another company—in which case it is likely that the product is being licensed for what is known as a "limited" use, that is, the organization is paying a license fee for the right to use the product under the conditions set forth in the agreement. Licensing does not mean ownership even if the source code of the system is delivered for use. Thus it is important to carefully understand the conditions of use, particularly reviewing any limits on use at locations, transferability (if the company is sold, for example), conditions for forfeit of license (usually non-payment), requirements for maintenance, and limits on disclosure of information about the product's source code, etc. Software license agreements are usually standard formats.

The licensed software agreement also includes provisions for the following information:

- *Operating environment*: the software may be restricted to operate within a certain hardware and software environment or platform. Package software license agreements normally require the vendor (or licensor) to be responsible for determining the terms of compatibility.
- *Warrantees*: this relates to safeguards that guarantee certain performance, application runtimes, and specific response times of the product. All warrantees are subject to restrictions on performance based on certain peak periods.
- *License fees*: these can be complex, especially when there are discounts available for volume use or use over a number of physical sites or versions (e.g., Windows, UNIX, and mainframe). Organizations should concentrate on whether there are clauses for increased fees over time, especially relating to maintenance fees for updates and support from the vendor.
- *Refreshment*: this covers bug fixes and patches to software that cannot wait for regularly scheduled maintenance updates. This is a critical clause in that the organization wants to know that serious bugs or needed patches can be fixed timely.
- *Documentation*: almost all licenses come with some form of operating documentation. Today many products have documentation as part of the Help portion of the product itself, but in either case documentation must be available.
- *Source code*: a popular part of third-party licensing is access to source code if not included as part of the license. Organizations have been using attorneys who hold the source code in escrow and will deliver the code to the organization should the vendor default. Default should include failure to perform or that the vendor goes out of business. In this way, an independent agent can judge whether a default has occurred and whether the organization can protect its interests by obtaining the current code. What is also important are the procedures for ensuring that the attorney receives timely updates to the source code. This is most critical if there are customizations being applied to the source during the project.

Legal Protection and Coverage

Agreements for software also contain a myriad of legal items that protect both organizations. These items and clauses are not necessarily unique to software agreements but important to include in any contract. Some key elements are described below:

- *Intellectual property and other indemnification (IPOI)*: IPOI clauses are very common in software license agreements. Essentially, IPOI protects the organization against any third-party lawsuits that have a claim against the vendor's violation of intellectual property rights of another. Thus, the buyer is protected against any suit against a claim that the software being used by the organization violates the rights of another party. The only complication of IPOI is that the laws are different internationally. The laws in many countries may not uphold the same definition of what constitutes violation of intellectual property. It is therefore important in any international indemnity to clearly state that the contract will be upheld based on the Laws of the USA or the UK. In this way, the organization agrees to use *that Law* to resolve matters even if they occur in another country.

- *Limitation of liability*: basically, this clause sets boundaries on an agreed-upon economic exposure to the organization. Specifically, the limitation of liability restricts the amount of damages that can be recovered from the vendor due to contractual breaches and/or negligence. Obviously, the organization should attempt to have a provision of "unlimited" liability that covers all costs, including legal and out-of-pocket expenses should the vendor be found guilty. Such clauses, if enacted could easily bankrupt the vendor. Thus, vendors try to limit their exposure and risk by restricting contractually what can be recovered. Most vendors will suggest that the limit be set to the amount of the vendor's insurance coverage, which means that the amount must be known and possibly increased to an amount that the organization is comfortable with should something occur. Setting a limit on the liability then becomes an organizational risk necessitating analysis from the management team and legal counsel.

- *Waivers*: a waiver clause allows the vendor to be excluded from a responsibility in the contract. It is suggested that no waivers be granted unless they are expressly agreed upon in writing by the organization and that waiver only be given for that specific instance. Effectively, a waiver is an override to a condition in the agreement, like making a payment or delivering product by a certain time.

- *Assignment*: this clause would allow the vendor or the organization to transfer responsibilities to another party. License agreements should not allow the vendor to assign responsibility without expressing written consent of the organization. Assignment gets a bit tricky when a vendor is acquired by another entity. The buyer would likely allow the new firm to assume responsibility.

- *Severability*: this clause is needed in the situation where a particular component of the contract is held illegal. The question becomes, how is the remainder of the contract to be handled? Agreements normally state that the remainder of the contract will continue to be in force. The purpose then of severability is to avoid a complete contract becoming void should one item be found problematic.

- *Notice*: this statement provides information for both the vendor and the organization. It instructs both parties on how notifications are to be communicated between the parties and typically provides a physical address and department where the parties need to be notified. This ensures that both parties are aware should there be a contractual problem.
- *Force Majeure*: stands for "superior force" in French and is used to excuse both parties from contractual obligation when there is an unusual event or as they say, "act of god," like an earthquake and hurricane. The clause does not excuse neglect of duties, however.
- *Confidentiality/privacy*: this clause protects the proprietary information of the entities. It typically states that any information discovered or used during the engagement remains the property of the associated entity (vendor or organization) and that it cannot be shared with any other parties without the written approval of the other party.
- *Proprietary rights/work for hire*: this clause protects the ownership rights of each party. The proprietary rights protect the vendor and the organization. That is, the vendor maintains ownership of the packaged product, but the organization may have ownership of the custom modifications made to the product. This can be a very sticky part of the contract. Certain package software vendors will attempt to absorb any custom modifications into their core product and market it to other organizations. In some cases, this has advantages for both parties in that the customized portion, if part of the base product, must be maintained by the vendor. On the other hand, if the customizations are proprietary to the organizations or are deemed to be competitive advantages, then it is important that such customizations remain under the ownership of the organization. In these cases, the organization should specify these customizations as a "work for hire" which stipulates that the vendor is being paid to develop an application solely for the use by the organization and becomes the exclusive ownership of the paying organization.

Financials

Financials is usually found in a section of the contract called "Fees and Payments." This section provides information about license fees, maintenance fees, programming fees, and any other fees associated with delivery. This section also contains information about payroll tax liabilities, sales tax responsibilities, and invoicing procedures. Details of each of these issues are discussed below:

- *License fees and rates*: this information is usually contained in an exhibit or addendum of the contract. Thus, the body of the agreement "points" to the exhibit which contains specific information regarding license fees, maintenance rates, per diem programming costs, and any other agreed-upon costs such as a fixed price for custom modifications. The reason for having these costs identified in an exhibit is to allow for easier modifications should they arise. These modifications could be the result of an expansion of the original contract which would normally require the re-execution of the agreement. Exhibits, therefore, usually have a separate signature page so that if a change is required, only the Exhibit page needs to be re-signed. This is shown in the sample contract in Fig. 16.1.

- *Sales taxes*: this is an important section to ensure that the organization is NOT responsible for paying the sales tax should the vendor either not collect it or not pay the tax to the appropriate state. Sales taxes can be complicated, since it is collected separately for each state and may depend on where the software is licensed, where the vendor resides, and ultimately where the software is actually used. All of these issues and corresponding liabilities need to be the responsibility of the vendor. Furthermore, the fact that it is part of the agreement discloses the responsibilities of each party.

- *Payroll taxes*: this is another important clause for protecting the organization. Should the vendor use contract labor on the engagement, they may be considered an employee of the vendor by the IRS. IRS rulings in this area can be vague in terms of what constitutes an employee. In either case, you want to protect the organization against any liabilities should the IRS determine that a vendor's consultant must be treated as an employee of that vendor. This section should also address the vendor's employees, that is, that the vendor agrees that they must pay federal, state, and local withholding taxes. While this might seem obvious, government agencies might seek those funds from the organization should the vendor be late or in default of paying.

- *Invoicing*: this section addresses two important issues: (1) where invoices should be sent and (2) net terms of payment. The latter states the number of days before invoices will be paid to the vendor. Some organizations and/or vendors will offer a discount on the amount due if payment is made sooner. Depending on the situation with cash flow and the general philosophy of the organization, discounts can be advantageous for both the vendor and the organization. Some organizations, particularly those that are cash rich, may not want to participate in a discount plan. This should all be addressed in the invoice section.

- *Insurance*: this section requires the vendor to have certain insurance provisions above and beyond just indemnifications. This usually includes comprehensive general liability and property coverage, which protect the organization against any damages that a vendor's employee or consultant does purposefully or inadvertently (e.g., damaging a PC) while on premise. The organization might also require Errors and Omissions (E&O) coverage. E&O protects the organization from any professional errors made by the vendor that can cause problems—such as converting data incorrectly and creating a false representation of information. Other insurance requirements include auto-insurance and inappropriate advertising liability. The organization should require the vendor to provide a "Certificate of Insurance" that evidences the coverage and names the organization as insured.

Deliverables and Performance

This section of the agreement should contain specific information about what the vendor has agreed to deliver to the organization. This should include the product itself, custom modifications, and in general particular features and functions that are deemed critical for the application to be useful to the organization. Another way of stating this is that this section should include critical things about the application that if not delivered would be detrimental to the success of the project. Some key subsections are described below:

- *Warranty*: this clause states that the vendor warrants all of its software and services to the specifications provided to the organization. The specifications should be included in the agreement and/or point to a particular set of documents that provide more detail about what the product/services provide. Typically, such a document could include the vendor's user manual, advertisement materials, and requirements documents prepared by the organization or the vendor's consultants. Often the list of warranty information is contained in an addendum or exhibit of the contract. This type of warranty differs from the warranty of runtime performance but can be included in the same section of the contract.
- *Disputes and remedies*: this subsection addresses the procedures for dealing with problems that arise during the completion of the contract. It could include things that are not specifically addressed in the contract or new things that may be deemed as "implied" in the contract. It could also relate to when something is considered complete and therefore relate when a specific payment is due in the contract.
- *Security*: this section requires the vendor to abide by the organization's internal security requirements. This typically includes access to system policies, on-sight behavior and accommodations, and in general protection of the data that a vendor will have access to during the implementation.

Figure 16.1 provides a sample of how the above provisions are formatted in a contract for software and services.

This SOFTWARE and CONSULTING SERVICES AGREEMENT ("Agreement") is made this ____ day of XXXXXXX, 2011 ("Effective Date") by and between Sample Applications Contract ("SAC"), with a place of business at Xyz Blvd, New York, NY 10026, and the consultant identified below ("Vendor").

Vendor Name: A. Langer & Assoc.

Address: 510A James Hall

City: New York   State: NY   Zip: 10027

Telephone: 914 261-6142   Fax: 212 865-1324

Fig. 16.1 Software and consulting services agreement

VENDOR HAS READ AND AGREES TO THE TERMS AND CONDITIONS ANNEXED
HERETO.

A. Langer & Assoc., Inc	**Sample Application Contract**
By: _____	By: _____
Print Name: __Arthur M. Langer_____	Print Name: _____
Title: _President _____	Title: _____
Date: _____	Date: _____

Fig. 16.1 (continued)

TERMS AND CONDITIONS

Subject to the terms and conditions set forth in Exhibit I executed by SAC and
Vendor, Vendor agrees to perform the consulting services described below.

1. SOFTWARE and SERVICES.

 1.1 Vendor shall, in a professional manner, provide to SAC the software and
  services described in Exhibit I for the fees or compensation set forth
  therein.

 1.2 All rights and benefits granted hereunder to SAC and the terms of this
  Agreement extend to and may be used and/or exercised by SAC, their affil-
  iates, subsidiaries and business divisions (the "SAC Organization"). The
  term "SAC" as used throughout this Agreement includes each entity in
  the SAC Organization. Notwithstanding the foregoing, any modification
  of this Agreement executed by the signatories is binding upon any SAC
  Organization, and any action or consent taken by SAC on its own behalf is
  binding upon any SAC Organization for the purposes of this Agreement.
  This Agreement is not intended to, nor may it be deemed to, create any
  enforceable rights, remedies or performance obligations upon any SAC
  Organization except with respect to Exhibit 1 and Exhibit 2.

2. PROPRIETARY RIGHTS.

 2.1 Vendor acknowledges and agrees that the Services performed hereunder,
  and all materials, products, reports, audio and/or visual works, computer programs (source and object code), documentation, deliverables and
  inventions conceived, developed or prepared for SAC by Vendor in performance of the Services and all elements thereof (the "Work Product") are
  Confidential Information (as defined in Section 3.1 below) and the property

of SAC. All right, title and interest in and to the Work Product vests in SAC and shall be deemed to be a work made for hire, made under the copyright laws of the United States in the course of performing the Services. To the extent that title to any such Work Product does not vest in SAC by operation of law, or such Work Product is not considered a work made for hire under such copyright laws, all right, title and interest therein are hereby irrevocably assigned to SAC. All Work Product belongs exclusively to SAC, with SAC having the right to obtain and to hold in its own name copyright registrations, patents and such other intellectual property protection as may be appropriate to the subject matter, and any extensions and renewals thereof. Vendor agrees to give SAC, and any person designated by SAC, reasonable assistance, at SAC's expense, required to perfect the rights defined in this Section, including, but not limited to, executing and delivering all assignment of copyright and ancillary and confirmatory documents requested by SAC in connection therewith. Alternatively, Vendor irrevocably appoints SAC as Vendor's attorney-in-fact with full powers of substitution and delegation to sign all documents that may be necessary to evidence SAC's ownership rights in the Work Product or any copyright. Vendor waives any moral rights that it may have in the Work Product and represents that it will obtain a waiver of the moral rights of all authors of the Work Product. Vendor may use the Work Product only to perform its obligations under any Engagement Schedule. Unless otherwise directed by SAC, upon the completion of the Services or upon the earlier termination of the engagement, Vendor shall immediately turn over to SAC all Work Product as well as all materials and deliverables developed by Vendor, including, but not limited to, working papers, descriptions, reports, notes and data. All Work Product shall bear SAC's copyright and trade secret notices, as specified by SAC. No rights to the Work Product remain with Vendor.

2.2 Notwithstanding the foregoing, unless otherwise provided for in this agreement, Vendor reserves all rights in and to the tools, utilities and standards developed by Vendor prior to or independent of the Services hereunder and utilized to provide the Services ("Vendor Tools"). Work Product does not include any Vendor owned software or software licensed from any third party, including without limitation, open source software, unless such software is specifically identified in an Engagement Schedule issued hereunder. In the event and to the extent that the Work Product contains any software or other items or elements which may be proprietary to Vendor or a third party, Vendor hereby grants SAC, its agents, consultants and other third parties, an irrevocable, worldwide, royalty free, nonexclusive license to use, execute, reproduce, modify, display, perform, and distribute copies of and prepare derivative works based on the Vendor Tools and/or any Vendor or third party software, items or elements which may be contained in the Work Product, and to authorize others to do any of the foregoing.

3. CONFIDENTIALITY/PRIVACY.

3.1 Vendor acknowledges that in the course of its engagement by SAC, Vendor may receive or have access to confidential and proprietary information about, and Vendor's engagement by SAC may bring it into close contact with confidential and proprietary information of SAC or third parties with whom SAC conducts business. Such information is defined below and collectively referred to as "Confidential Information." In recognition of the foregoing, Vendor covenants and agrees that:

3.1.1 it will keep and maintain all Confidential Information in strict confidence, using such degree of care as is appropriate to avoid unauthorized use or disclosure;

3.1.2 it will use and disclose Confidential Information solely for the purposes for which such information, or access to it, was provided pursuant to the terms of this Agreement, and will not use or disclose Confidential Information for Vendor's own purposes or for the benefit of anyone other than SAC;

3.1.3 it will not, directly or indirectly, disclose Confidential Information to anyone outside SAC, except with SAC's prior written consent as permitted under the terms of this Agreement; and

3.1.4 it shall, upon the earlier of (i) completion of an engagement or termination of this Agreement or the applicable Engagement Schedule; (ii) determination that it has no need for Confidential Information; or (iii) at any time SAC requests, dispose of all records, electronic or otherwise (including all backup records and/or other copies thereof) regarding or including any Confidential Information that Vendor may then possess or control. Disposal may be achieved, at SAC's option, through prompt delivery of the records to SAC or destruction pursuant to Vendor's written policy governing such destruction and in a manner that renders the records unreadable and undecipherable by any means. Upon any occurrence of (i), (ii), or (iii) above, Vendor shall promptly certify in writing to SAC, in a form acceptable to SAC and executed by an authorized officer of Vendor, that all such Confidential Information has been destroyed or returned.

Vendor shall be permitted to disclose Confidential Information only to its employees and permitted subcontractors (individually an "Employee" and collectively, "Employees") having a need to know such information in connection with the performance of the Services, provided that any subcontracting and disclosure of Confidential Information to a subcontractor shall be subject to SAC's prior written consent pursuant to Section 8.1 hereof. Vendor shall instruct all Employees as to their obligations under this Agreement, and shall obtain from each Employee his or her written acknowledgment and agreement to be bound by the terms and conditions of this Agreement prior to such Employee being given access to the Confidential Information. SAC may provide Vendor with a confidentiality agreement to be executed by each Employee providing Services hereunder or Vendor shall otherwise obtain SAC's written consent to Vendor's form. Vendor shall be responsible for all Employees' compliance with the terms of this Agreement. If Vendor is required by law to disclose Confidential Information, Vendor shall promptly notify SAC in writing in advance of such disclosure, and provide SAC with copies of any related information so that SAC may take appropriate action to protect the Confidential Information.

3.2   Confidential Information includes all business and other proprietary information of SAC, written or oral, including without limitation the following:

    3.2.1   information relating to planned or existing businesses or business initiatives; organizational restructuring plans; and actual and projected sales, profits and other financial information;

    3.2.2   information relating to technology, such as computer systems and systems architecture, including, but not limited to, computer hardware, computer software, source code, object code, documentation, methods of processing and operational methods;

    3.2.3   information that describes insurance, annuities and financial services products and strategies, including, but not limited to, actuarial calculations, product designs, product administration and management; tax interpretations, tax positions and treatment of any item for tax purposes;

    3.2.4   confidential information, software and material of third parties with whom SAC conducts business;

    3.2.5   information about SAC employees and personnel;

    3.2.6   "Personal Information," which means information provided by or at the direction of SAC, or to which access was provided in the course of Vendor's performance of this Agreement that (i) identifies an individual (by name, signature, address, telephone number or other unique identifier), or (ii) that can be used to authenticate that individual (including, without limitation, passwords or PINs, biometric data, unique identification numbers, answers to security questions, or other personal identifiers). An individual's social security number, even in isolation, is Personal Information. SAC business contact information is not by itself Personal Information.

Notwithstanding the foregoing, Confidential Information does not include information that (i) is lawfully made available to the general public from federal, state, or local government records, (ii) is or becomes generally known to the public not as a result of a disclosure by Vendor, (iii) is rightfully in the possession of Vendor prior to disclosure by SAC, or (iv) is received by Vendor in good faith and without restriction from a third party not under a confidentiality obligation to SAC and having the right to make such disclosure. The foregoing exceptions do not apply to the disclosure of Personal Information, which shall not be disclosed without SAC's prior written consent unless required by law.

3.3 Vendor agrees to comply with any and all privacy and/or security policies, rules and practices, as SAC may issue, amend, or otherwise make available from time to time pursuant to Section 11.18 of this Agreement.

3.4 Vendor shall notify SAC, promptly and without unreasonable delay, but in no event more than forty-eight (48) hours of learning that unauthorized access to, disclosure of, or breach in the security of Confidential Information may have occurred or been attempted (a "Security Incident"). Thereafter, Vendor shall, at its own cost and expense:

3.4.1 promptly furnish to SAC full details of the Security Incident;

3.4.2 assist and cooperate fully with SAC in SAC's investigation of Vendor, Employees or third parties related to the Security Incident, including but not limited to providing SAC with physical access to the facilities and operations affected, facilitating interviews with Employees and others involved in the matter, and making available all relevant records, logs, files, and data;

3.4.3 cooperate with SAC in any litigation or other formal action against third parties deemed necessary by SAC to protect its rights; and

3.4.4 promptly use its best efforts to prevent a recurrence of any such Security Incident.

In addition to the foregoing, Vendor agrees that in the event of a Security Incident, SAC shall have the sole right to determine (i) whether notice is to be provided to any individuals, regulators, law enforcement agencies, consumer reporting agencies, or others as required by law or regulation, or in SAC's discretion; and (ii) the contents of such notice, whether any type of remediation may be offered to affected persons, and the nature and extent of any such remediation. Any such notice or remediation shall be at Vendor's sole cost and expense.

3.6 Vendor certifies that its treatment of Personal Information is in compliance with applicable laws and/or regulations with respect to privacy and data security and that it has implemented and currently maintains an effective information security program that includes administrative, technical, and physical safeguards to (a) ensure the security and confidentiality of Personal Information; (b) protect against any anticipated threats or hazards to the security or integrity of such Personal Information; and (c) protect against unauthorized access to, destruction, modification, disclosure or use of Personal Information which could result in substantial harm or inconvenience to SAC, or to any person who may be identified by such Personal Information. Vendor shall immediately notify SAC if Vendor is in material breach of this Section. At SAC's request, Vendor agrees to certify in writing to SAC, its compliance with the terms of this Section.

3.7 Notwithstanding any remedy of a material breach of this Section 3, SAC reserves the right to terminate this Agreement within 90 days upon written notice to Vendor should such material breach occur, and SAC may pursue all such remedies as may be available to it at law or in equity.

4. FEES AND PAYMENT.

4.1 Fees and Expenses.

4.1.1 Fees for the Services and payment schedule is specified in Exhibit 2. The fees for Services are fixed for the term of the Agreement or any addendums.

4.1.2 SAC agrees that additional needs above those identified in Exhibit 1 could require more or different Vendor consultants. Such increases or changes in scope shall be negotiated and additional Exhibits or Engagement Schedules will be added to this Agreement as required.

4.1.3 Except as set forth otherwise in Exhibit 1, Vendor is entitled to reimbursement from SAC only for documented "out-of-pocket" expenses that are reasonably incurred and necessary for Vendor's performance of the Services. SAC must pre-approve in writing all expenses for reimbursement. In the event that any travel is required, Vendor shall comply with SAC's travel policies. Under no circumstances will SAC reimburse Vendor for first class or business class travel.

4.2 **Invoices.**

    4.2.1 Vendor shall invoice SAC monthly for all fees due hereunder by submitting each invoice to the address indicated in this Agreement.

4.3 **Taxes.** In addition to the fees payable hereunder:

    4.3.1 Vendor shall specifically state and bill all applicable taxes related to SAC's acquisition of Services in its invoices. Vendor shall indicate on each invoice the jurisdiction, or jurisdictions as the case may be, for which any such tax is being collected. Vendor shall remit all such taxes collected from SAC to the appropriate taxing authority. Vendor shall be responsible for interest and penalties associated with a failure by Vendor to appropriately collect, remit or timely file appropriate tax returns for any such tax to the appropriate tax authority.

    4.3.2 In the event that SAC supplies Vendor with appropriate exemption certificates, the parties agree that the determination of the amount of sales tax, if any, and any other determinations of a substantive or procedural nature relating to such tax, will be the responsibility and prerogative of SAC, in its sole discretion.

    4.3.3 In those states in which Vendor has no obligation to collect sales tax and only in those states in which SAC has an obligation to report and remit sales, use or similar tax, SAC shall be responsible for payment directly to such taxing authority of any sales, use or similar tax imposed in connection with the Services.

    4.3.4 Vendor further agrees that in the event that Vendor has no obligation to collect and remit sales tax, Vendor shall not include any such tax on any invoices or payment requests. Further, if Vendor does erroneously include such tax that SAC is not required to remit, and SAC does remit such tax to Vendor, Vendor shall promptly reimburse SAC for such erroneously charged tax.

    4.3.5 If Vendor is notified by any jurisdiction that it had an obligation to collect sales, use or similar tax from SAC, and Vendor has failed or neglected to include such tax in its invoice to SAC, Vendor shall so advise SAC in a timely manner and Vendor shall allow SAC the right to actively participate in the contest or settlement of such tax. If the resolution of this issue is held to be taxable, SAC shall promptly remit such tax to Vendor or demonstrate that the tax has already been paid by SAC to the taxing authority. Vendor is responsible for interest and penalties where it had an obligation to collect sales, use or similar tax from SAC, and Vendor failed or neglected to include such tax in its invoice to SAC.

4.3.6 Vendor shall be solely responsible for the payment of all withholding taxes for its Employees, including, but not limited to, federal and state income taxes, social security taxes, unemployment insurance taxes and any other applicable taxes.

5. WARRANTIES

5.1 **Warranty.** Vendor warrants that:

5.1.1 it has the expertise to perform the Services in a professional and workmanlike manner and it will perform the Services in accordance with the specifications and description of such Services as set forth in Exhibit I or the applicable Engagement Schedule;

5.1.2 all Work Product conforms to the specifications or descriptions thereof in Exhibit I or the Engagement Schedule;

5.1.3 it will not introduce into any Work Product and the Work Product does not contain any virus or any other contaminant, or disabling devices including, but not limited to, codes, commands or instructions that may have the effect or be used to access, alter, delete, damage or disable the Work Product, other software, SAC information or other SAC property, in a manner other than in accordance with specifications;

5.1.4 all Work Product and Vendor Tools (i) is original to Vendor (or its subcontractors, as the case may be); (ii) is in all respects copyrightable; (iii) does not violate any patent, copyright, trade secret or other property right of any other party; (iv) has been written and developed by Vendor or its subcontractors without referring to or copying lines of code, or the structure, sequence or organization of any software owned by another person or entity or in which another person or entity has a valid and existing copyright;

5.1.5 it has all consents, permissions and/or licenses necessary to perform the Services and Vendor shall comply with all applicable federal, state and local laws, rules and regulations, and shall obtain all applicable permits and licenses required to perform the Services;

5.1.6 Vendor shall not (i) include in any Work Product prepared or provided to SAC, or (ii) use in conjunction with the performance of Services for SAC on SAC's premises, any existing software or materials licensed from any third party, including without limitation open source software, without the prior written consent of SAC. Vendor shall specifically identify any such third-party software or materials for which it seeks SAC's consent in the applicable Engagement Schedule. With respect to any such third party software and materials to be included in Work Product, Vendor warrants and represents that it has all rights necessary to provide such software and materials to, and/or use such software and materials for the benefit of, SAC;

6. INDEMNITIES; LIMITATION ON LIABILITY

6.1 **Vendor Indemnity.** Vendor agrees to indemnify, defend and hold harmless SAC, its assignees, directors, officers, employees and agents, from and against any action brought against same with respect to any claim, loss, demand, cause of action, debt, liability, penalty or fines, including legal fees and expenses, to the limit of WOS' insurance coverage and based upon:

6.1.1 a claim that any Work Product, Services, Vendor Tools or any other software or other material provided, used or delivered by Vendor hereunder infringes or violates any patents, copyrights, trade secrets, licenses, or other property rights of any third party;

6.1.2 personal injury or property damage caused by the fault or negligence of Vendor;

6.1.3 any breach of the terms and warranties provisions contained herein or willful, intentional or negligent actions or failures by Vendor or its agents hereunder;

6.1.4 a claim that any Employee or any person provided to SAC by Vendor to perform services under this Agreement is a SAC employee and not Vendor's employee or an independent contractor, including, but not limited to: (1) any taxes SAC is required to pay on behalf of any Employee; (2) the cost of any employee benefits SAC is required to provide to or pay for on behalf of any Employee; (3) any claim, lawsuit, or proceeding brought by Vendor's Employees against SAC based upon the employer-employee relationship; and (4) breach by any Employee of any of the provisions of this Agreement, including, but not limited to, the provisions regarding subcontractors looking only to Vendor for payment for services which may be rendered.

6.2 **LIMITATIONS ON LIABILITY.**

6.2.1 NEITHER PARTY SHALL BE LIABLE FOR ANY LOST PROFITS, LOST SAVINGS, OR OTHER CONSEQUENTIAL DAMAGES, EVEN IF SUCH PARTY HAS BEEN ADVISED OF THE POSSIBILITY OF OR COULD HAVE FORESEEN SUCH DAMAGES. THE AGGREGATE LIABILITY OF EACH PARTY UNDER THIS AGREEMENT SHALL NOT EXCEED THE TOTAL FEES PAID BY SAC TO VENDOR HEREUNDER.

6.2.2 THE LIMITATIONS ON LIABILITY AND REMEDIES CONTAINED IN SECTION 6.2 ABOVE SHALL NOT APPLY TO:

(a) LIABILITY ARISING UNDER SECTION 6.1 OF THIS AGREEMENT; AND/OR

(b) DAMAGES INCURRED DUE TO INTENTIONAL OR GROSSLY NEGLIGENT ACTS OR NON-PERFORMANCE BY VENDOR; AND/OR

(c) DAMAGES INCURRED DUE TO ABANDONMENT OR DELIBERATE BREACH OF VENDOR'S OBLIGATIONS HEREUNDER; AND/OR

(d) DAMAGES INCURRED DUE TO A BREACH OF VENDOR'S CONFIDENTIALITY OR SYSTEM SECURITY OBLIGATIONS.

7. OTHER RIGHTS AND OBLIGATIONS.

7.1 **Independent Contractor.** Vendor is acting in performance of this Agreement as an independent contractor. Vendor's employees are not employees or agents of SAC, and are not entitled to any of SAC's employee benefits. SAC is not responsible for payment of workers' compensation, disability benefits or unemployment insurance, nor is SAC responsible for withholding or paying employment related taxes for Vendor or its employees. Vendor shall not subcontract the Services, or any part thereof, without the prior written consent of SAC. With respect to any Services which are subcontracted or provided by any third party: (i) Vendor hereby assumes all liability and responsibility for such subcontractors' and third parties' compliance with and breach of the terms of this Agreement and Engagement Schedules, and for all acts and omissions of such subcontractors and third parties; and (ii) Vendor shall include a provision in all of its agreements with subcontractors stating that such subcontractors shall look to Vendor for payment and shall under no circumstances look to any other party, including SAC, for payment.

7.2 **Vendor Resources.** In the event that any Employee assigned to perform Services is found to be unacceptable to SAC, SAC shall notify Vendor of such fact and Vendor shall immediately remove such individual from the engagement, and, if requested by SAC, use diligent efforts to provide replacements acceptable to SAC within three (3) days of said notice, or such other period as may be agreed to by the parties.

7.3 **Security.** Vendor shall comply with SAC's system security policies, procedures and requirements ("Security Regulations") for computer systems and software used to access Confidential Information ("Systems"). Vendor and its Employees will not tamper with, compromise or circumvent any Security Regulations. Vendor shall ensure that only those users who are specifically authorized to gain access to SAC's Systems gain such access. Vendor shall prevent unauthorized destruction, alteration or loss of information contained in SAC's Systems. If at any time SAC or Vendor determines that any Employee has sought to circumvent or has circumvented SAC's Security Regulations or that an unauthorized person has accessed or may access SAC's Systems or a person has engaged in activities that may lead to the unauthorized access, destruction or alteration or loss of data, information or software, Vendor shall immediately terminate any such person's access and immediately notify SAC. If SAC reasonably determines that an Employee has attempted to or has circumvented SAC's Security Regulations, SAC may immediately terminate such person's access to the Systems and shall immediately advise Vendor. SAC may audit Vendor's use of the Systems. Vendor agrees that SAC may review any information, electronic mail communications, or other data stored on or contained in any computer hard drive, disk, or any other storage medium located on SAC's premises to determine whether there has been any breach of security or violation of this Agreement, regardless of whether such computer hard drives, disks, storage media or electronic mail communications are on equipment owned or leased by SAC or are brought or sent onto SAC's premises by Vendor or its Employees. In the event that SAC concludes that there has been any breach of security or violation of this Agreement by Vendor or its Employees, SAC reserves the right to disclose any computer files or electronic mail message to third parties, including (but not limited to) law enforcement officials, as SAC deems appropriate without any prior notice to any individuals who may have written, sent or received such files or message.

7.4 **Consultant Screening.** Prior to placing any Manager or Supervisor level Employee with SAC, Vendor is required to:

7.4.1 allow identified SAC personnel to interview and approve any such placement;

7.4.2 agree that it will not place on assignment at SAC any Employee who has not consented to, and/or satisfied the conditions contained in this Agreement, subject to applicable federal, state or local laws.

7.5 **SAC Policies.** Vendor agrees to comply with SAC's information systems related policies and standards (which include technology, product, and process standards) when delivering Services and Work Products to SAC.

8. TERMINATION.

8.1 This Agreement is effective as of the Effective Date and continues until terminated in accordance with the terms of this Agreement or any applicable Engagement Schedule. SAC, however, may terminate the Services to be provided pursuant to any Engagement Schedule for the reasons set forth in this Section without terminating this Agreement.

8.2 SAC may terminate this Agreement or the Services to be provided under any Engagement Schedule, as follows:

8.2.1 Termination for Cause. SAC may terminate this Agreement or any Engagement Schedule in the event that Vendor or any of its agents breaches any of the terms of this Agreement and said breach is not cured within ten (10) days after written notice thereof to Vendor.

8.2.2 Termination without Cause. SAC may terminate this Agreement or any Engagement Schedule at any time and for any reason upon 90 days' written notice to Vendor.

8.3 If SAC terminates this Agreement without cause, then SAC's sole obligation is to reimburse Vendor for Services satisfactorily performed by Vendor up to the effective date of such termination. If SAC terminates this Agreement or any Engagement Schedule for cause, then SAC has no obligation to make any further payment to Vendor or any third party for any outstanding charges or invoices for Services performed.

9. INSURANCE.

Vendor shall obtain from a company or companies acceptable to SAC, having a current A.M. Best Rating of A- VIII or better, and maintain in force during the term of this Agreement and for not less than two (2) years thereafter, the following insurance coverage in the minimum amounts indicated:

TYPE OF COVERAGE	REQUIRED AMOUNT
Comprehensive General Liability Insurance including Broad Form Contractual, Broad Form Property damage Personal Injury and Advertising Liability, Completed Operation and Products coverage	$1,000,000 combined single limit/general aggregate $2,000,000

Where applicable, the above policies shall name SAC and/or the applicable SAC Organization as additional insureds. Vendor shall, upon request, provide SAC with a Certificate or Certificates of Insurance evidencing that the above insurance requirements have been satisfied and specifying that SAC shall receive a minimum 30-day written advance notice of any cancellation of or reduction in coverage.

10. GENERAL.

10.1 **No Publicity.** Vendor shall not use the name, trademark, service mark, trade name, logo or other commercial or product designations of SAC in any way, in print or electronic format or on a web or internet site, without the prior written consent of SAC in each instance.

10.2 **No Waiver; Remedies.** A party may not waive a right or remedy except pursuant to a writing executed by such party. No failure or delay in exercising any right or remedy or requiring the satisfaction of any condition under this Agreement, and no course of dealing between the parties, operates as a waiver or estoppel of any right, remedy or condition. A waiver made in writing on one occasion is effective only in that instance and only for the purpose that it is given and is not to be construed as a waiver on any future occasion. No single or partial exercise of any right or remedy under this Agreement precludes the simultaneous or subsequent exercise of any other right or remedy. The rights and remedies of the parties set forth in this Agreement are not exclusive of, but are cumulative to, any rights or remedies now or subsequently existing at law, in equity or by statute.

10.3 **Severability.** If a court of competent jurisdiction determines that any provision of this Agreement is invalid, illegal or unenforceable under any applicable statute or rule of law, such provision is to that extent deemed omitted, and the balance of the Agreement remains in full force if the essential terms and conditions of this Agreement for each party remain valid, binding and enforceable.

10.4 **Assignment.** This Agreement is binding upon the parties' respective successors and permitted assigns. Vendor shall not assign any of its rights or delegate any performance under this Agreement, voluntarily or involuntarily, whether by merger, consolidation, dissolution, change of control, operation of law or any other manner, except with the prior written consent of SAC. Any purported assignment by Vendor of rights or delegation of performance without SAC's prior written consent is void, and SAC is entitled to terminate this Agreement effective as of the date SAC obtains knowledge of the purported assignment or delegation without prejudice to SAC's claims for damages. SAC may assign this Agreement in whole or in part and/or any of its rights, licenses, duties and/or obligations hereunder, upon written notice to Vendor and without Vendor's consent, to any SAC Organization, or in connection with a reorganization, demutualization or change of control of SAC, a business unit, division or line of business.

10.5 **Governing Law.** The laws of the State of New York, without giving effect to its choice of law principles, govern all matters arising under or relating to this Agreement and all of the transactions it contemplates, including, without limitation, its validity, interpretation, construction, performance and enforcement. The parties further agree that the Uniform Computer Information Transactions Act (UCITA) does not apply to this Agreement.

10.6 **Forum.** Any party bringing a legal action or proceeding against any other party arising out of or relating to this Agreement shall bring the legal action or proceeding in the United States District Court for the District of New York City. Each party waives, to the fullest extent permitted by law, (a) any objection which it may now or later have to the laying of venue of any action or proceeding arising out of or relating to this Agreement brought in the United States District Court for the District of New York, or any court of the State of New York sitting in New York City; and (b) any claim that any action or proceeding brought in any such court has been brought in an inconvenient forum.

10.7 **Waiver of Trial by Jury.** EACH PARTY, TO THE EXTENT PERMITTED BY LAW, KNOWINGLY, VOLUNTARILY AND INTENTIONALLY WAIVES ITS RIGHT TO A TRIAL BY JURY IN ANY ACTION OR LEGAL PROCEEDING ARISING OUT OF OR RELATING TO THIS AGREEMENT AND THE TRANSACTIONS IT CONTEMPLATES. EACH PARTY ACKNOWLEDGES THAT IT HAS RECEIVED THE ADVICE OF COMPETENT COUNSEL.

10.8 **Notices.** Each party shall deliver any notices required or desired pursuant to this Agreement in writing. Notices are deemed given (i) if by hand delivery, upon receipt thereof; (ii) if mailed, five (5) days after deposit in the U.S. mails, postage prepaid, certified mail, return receipt requested, or (iii) if sent via overnight courier upon receipt. SAC shall address all notices to the Vendor at the address indicated on the first page of this Agreement. Vendor shall address all notices to SAC pursuant to the notice provision contained in the applicable Engagement Schedule.

10.9 **Survival.** All provisions hereof relating to proprietary rights, confidentiality and non-disclosure, indemnification and limitation of liability survive the completion of the Services or any earlier termination, expiration or rescission of this Agreement.

10.10 **EEO Requirements.** To the extent applicable, the equal employment opportunity and affirmative action requirements set forth in 41 C.F.R. Part 60-1.4(a) (women and minorities), 41 C.F.R. Part 60-250.5(a) (covered veterans) and 41 C.F.R. Part 60-741.5(a) (individuals with disabilities) are hereby incorporated by reference into this Agreement.

10.11 **Right to Hire.** SAC shall have the right to hire any Vendor Employee for no additional fee. SAC agrees to provide Vendor with 90 days notice to allow Vendor to replace hired Employee.

10.12 **Further Assurances.** After the Effective Date at SAC's request, Vendor shall execute and deliver to SAC any such additional instruments, documents, conveyances or assurances and take such other actions as are necessary or appropriate to confirm and assure the rights and obligations provided for in this Agreement and consummate the transactions contemplated hereby, or otherwise to effectuate the intent and purposes of this Agreement.

10.13 **Headings.** The section headings are used in this Agreement for reference and convenience only and do not affect this Agreement's construction or interpretation.

10.14 **Subsequent Modifications.** No amendment, alteration or modification of this Agreement is effective or binding unless it is set forth in a writing signed by duly authorized representatives of both parties.

10.15 **Counterparts.** The parties may execute this Agreement in any number of duplicate originals and in multiple counterparts, each of which constitutes an original, and all of which, collectively, constitute only one agreement. The signatures of all of the parties need not appear on the same counterpart, and delivery of an executed counterpart signature page by facsimile is as effective as executing and delivering this Agreement in the presence of the other party to this Agreement. This Agreement is effective upon delivery of one executed counterpart from each party to the other party. Any party delivering an executed counterpart of this Agreement by facsimile shall also deliver a manually executed counterpart of this Agreement as soon as reasonably practicable following transmittal by facsimile, but the failure to do so does not affect the validity, enforceability or binding effect of this Agreement.

10.16 **Entire Agreement.** This Agreement, together with the exhibits and Engagement Schedules, constitutes the entire agreement between the parties in connection with the subject matter hereof and supersedes all prior and contemporaneous agreements, understandings, negotiations and discussions, whether oral or written, of the parties, and there are no warranties, representations and/or agreements between the parties in connection with the subject matter hereof except as set forth in this Agreement. The parties also understand, acknowledge and agree that, unless otherwise specified in a written instrument signed by an officer of each party, no additional terms or changes to these terms are valid or binding on the parties, even if such additional terms or changes contain provisions to the contrary.

EXHIBIT 1

ENGAGEMENT SCHEDULE   Schedule No. _1_

Project Scope

1. License base XYZ enterprise software for 250 users
2. Customized programming per requirements document
3. User training
4. Annual maintenance including 8 hour help desk support

IN WITNESS WHEREOF, the parties have executed this Engagement Schedule by their duly authorized representatives.

A. Langer & Assoc., Inc	Sample Application Contract
By: _____	By: _____
Print Name: Arthur M. Langer	Print Name: _____
Title: President	Title: _____
Date: _____	Date: _____

EXHIBIT 2

FEES

XYZ License Software for 250 users	$250,000
Custom Programming for modifications per requirements document	$ 95,000
Additional Per Diem programming rate	$600 per day
Per diem user training rate	$250 per day
Annual Maintenance on base product	15% of current advertised license fee

---

Problems and Exercises

1. What are the four factors in a software and services contract?
2. What is a proprietary right?
3. What is error and omissions insurance? Who does it favor, the vendor or the organization?
4. What is indemnification? Under what conditions does indemnification apply?
5. What are the key aspects of non-disclosure?
6. How should management handle multinational agreements? What is the best way to protect the organization when dealing in multiple countries?

Going Live and Conclusions   **17**

This chapter deals with the final part of software implementation: going live or moving the system into production. It is also fitting that this chapter contains conclusions about the methods and approaches discussed in this book. There are three major steps that are necessary to move the application into a production environment: user training, IT's role, and the preparation steps for going live.

User Training

This step can often be underestimated, especially with the standardization of help text in products and the perception that software applications are robust. Robust is defined as applications that are "intuitively obvious" to use, so that formal training is not required. Such is likely not the reality with most integrated enterprise-level package software products. Furthermore, user training becomes more complicated when there are custom modifications to the application. Finally, if the product is developed in-house, then training may be a very comprehensive part of rolling out the application into production.

There are a number of steps to develop the right training materials:
1. Focus on the business aspects of the material, that is, what do your users need to know in terms of operating the system.
2. How many users need to be trained?
3. Utilize prototypes during the early stages of training before the product is actually ready. Prototypes are screen pictures that can be populated with data and provide users with an understanding of how data travel through the system. Some of the prototypes need to be done in demo form.
4. Provide exercises for the user groupings. Thus, it is important to develop a strategy on who should be trained and when, and what are the groupings of the users.
5. Training needs to be iterative, do not expect that training will be effective the first time.

A.M. Langer, *Guide to Software Development,*
DOI 10.1007/978-1-4471-2300-2_17, © Springer-Verlag London Limited 2012

Training Step	SDLC Stage
Determine the number of users to be trained, locations, etc.	Feasibility/Analysis and Design
Determine topics	Analysis
Design materials	Design
Determine who will train	Make/Buy
Update and Feedback	QA
Actual training	Prior to Go Live
Training iterations, including feedback	During various phases of production

Fig. 17.1 Training steps in the SDLC

6. Ensure that training includes product setup requirements. New products tend to need tables that are initialized, e.g., user access rights and security.
7. Determine how the training will be delivered, that is, in a traditional classroom, on-line (Internet) and on demand using CBT (computer-based training), packaged delivery, or all of these!
8. Determine who will train. Is the training done by the vendor, or does the vendor train trainers in the organization, or some combination?
9. Where should the training take place? Are there multiple locations? Are there components of the products that are only used in specific businesses within the company?
10. Prepare for feedback from users and common problems that might be discovered during the training.
11. Determine whether certain training sessions should be taped and made available via video.

Clearly many of the above points need to be developed and planned during the SDLC, but most of the actual training must be done as close as possible to going live. If the training takes place too early, users will forget much of the details. Figure 17.1 provides additional guidance on the steps to take and decisions to be made during the SDLC.

The Role of IT

Where and when the IT organization participates in the go live process is another important question. There are some obvious areas where IT personnel are required:

- Placing the application on the servers and general network availability
- Assisting with the review of technical aspects of the license agreement, e.g., runtime licenses
- Ensuring that appropriate security is in place to protect applications and data
- Performance testing both before and during go live
- Appropriate backup and restore procedures are in place
- Help desk personnel are available to handle peak calls during go live

Another important issue is whether IT should be responsible for project management. My experience suggests that most often IT is in charge of the project. This can be both good and bad. The good part is what most would expect—that IT is the experienced organization to perform the project management. The bad part is that IT is not integrated enough in the business units and cannot really manage the project without help from key stakeholders. I have found that the best approach is to form a joint management team, where someone from IT is the project manager, but an associate from the business side provides the business side interface. There might also be a project manager from the vendor. It is this team that ultimately can get the project completed assuming that executive support is available from each of these units. This means that there must be an executive from each business unit that will use the system (or someone who has management over all of them, which is rare), the CIO from the IT side, and a senior executive from the vendor(s).

The IT project manager (IT PM) should provide most of the SDLC supervision; the business project manager (Bus PM) should organize training, plan for "go live," coordinate key events, and most importantly confirm that the requirements are accurate and complete. The Bus PM must also deal with disagreements and escalate as necessary to his/her senior management. Both the IT PM and the Bus PM should jointly manage the vendor project manager. The IT PM should handle the technical and system issues and the Bus PM should ensure that the features and functions of the product are correct.

Perhaps, the most salient role for IT is coordinating the go live administration. This includes ensuring that the systems are ready, parallel systems are in place, help desk people are ready in case of problems, and that the vendor is available to deal with problems that occur during the launch. Additionally, IT should plan to do system fine-tuning in the advent that there are performance problems with the application.

Conclusions

This book has been organized to define the necessary steps in today's SDLC. The premise of the book is that managers need to spend more time ensuring that the requirements are accurate. This may seem like an old story—get the requirements correct before implementing. However, there is little evidence to show that the success rate has changed over the past two decades. Furthermore, the days of developing software from scratch may have come to an end. The library of software routines, packages, and legacy codes are vast, and the key to success is more about selecting the right software partners and managing the process. Indeed, there should be less focus on the actual development and more on the architecture and management. IT and business managers need to finalize the specifications and select the right vendors.

The realities of developing applications today, then, are to create what I call the package software SDLC. This modified SDLC is designed as a *unified* solution to what otherwise has been considered separate SDLCs, depending on whether the software was developed in-house or by a third-party package. It was my intent to dispel any credibility to this notion. The SDLC is now too complex and need to unify all the SDLCs into one cycle. The SDLC is no longer limited to IT, rather it must incorporate a much larger user interface. Business users need to be much more active in the determination of application needs. That is why assessment of needs is more important than feasibility. I also incorporated the build vs. buy and RFI/RFP steps as inherently part of that decision. I included the vendor search and selection as part of the SDLC, as opposed to a precursor or an after thought of analysis and design. Simply put, they are part of the process. Organizations can no longer just do requirements and look for the solution—the solution itself affects the completion of requirements. In addition, I included the budget and ROI as part of the SDLC and at a much later stage than otherwise considered on traditional projects. Specifically, the traditional SDLC had feasibility as the first step. I understand why this was the case, but technology solutions today must be far more agile on spending commitments; it just changes too often during the life cycle. Once the business units know what technology and applications they need, it should not be about whether it is feasible, rather more about how much to spend vs. the cost for not implementing. Budgets today need to be more about control, explanation, and negotiation than about "go" or "no go."

I also explained my driver and supporter theory, which continues to be an effective way of explaining why projects are needed, why they might change, and how to determine costs. All new projects must show why they are a driver, and this alone can help executive managers to better comprehend why the application can change the market, the risks inherently involved in the undertaking, and the importance of providing agile funding when market conditions are dynamic. I emphasize the supporter side as well, since most current applications by definition are legacies that should have been replaced decades ago, but because IT was not positioned to articulate why they needed to be redone, they have now become major impediments to creating new enterprise systems.

This book also integrated project management and quality assurance. These two areas increase the success that projects will be more accountable and delivered on time. Too often project management and quality assurance are treated as separate subjects. Included in the chapter on project management was an emphasis on the importance of vendor contracts and adherence to standards like ISO 9000. I also transformed the balance scorecard into a workable version for package software implementations. The balanced scorecard can be an effective reconciliation tool to understand how the application contributes to the organization. In addition, the strategy map provides the schematic of how learning, support, and users ultimately contribute to the financial performance of the firm.

However, the essence of this book still focuses on the importance of understanding the technical components of analysis and design. Regardless of who reads this book, whether a business user or a systems analyst, a director, or a CIO, the message is that one must know how to do architecture to have success. So everyone involved needs to understand flow diagrams, functional decomposition, pseudocode, logic data modeling, and the object paradigm. They also need to know about test planning and quality assurance as part of how the system is designed, developed, and implemented. Without adherence to the tools of analysis and design, the core of systems development cannot achieve consistent success.

Appendix A
Case Study: The Rainforest Book Company Problem

The following four events are services provided by the Rainforest Book Company:

Event I

A customer wishes to setup an account to purchase books. The Sales Department at the Rainforest Book Company receives the request and sends out a blank Account Request form. The form has space for the following information:

Customer Name
Customer Address
Customer Phone Number
Customer Fax Number
Credit Card Information (if applicable)
Credit Card Number
Type of Credit Card
Expiration Date
Cardholder's Name
Zip or postal code of the billing address for this card

The customer sends back a completed Account Request form. The "for office use only" section is filled out by the Sales Group. This information includes the processor's identification, the date the account is opened, and a customer account number which is assigned. The customer account file is updated and the Account Request form is filed. The Account Processing Department receives notification of the new account and sends the customer a confirmation letter. This letter notifies the customer of their customer account number. This number can be used to expedite the ordering process.

A.M. Langer, *Guide to Software Development*,
DOI 10.1007/978-1-4471-2300-2, © Springer-Verlag London Limited 2012

Event II

A customer makes a book inquiry. The customer can request a book by giving any of the following information: book title and book author or ISBN number. The Sales Department first verifies that the customer has a valid account. If the book is found based upon the information that was given, the customer receives the following information about the book:

Title of the book
Author of the book
Paperback/Hardcover
Price
Date Published
Availability
Reviews

If the book is not available in stock, all of the above information is returned and an out-of-stock notice is sent specifying the approximate date the book will be in stock. If the book is no longer in print and has been discontinued, an out-of-print notice is sent to the customer. This out-of-print notice includes a list of Used-Book Stores in the customer's county.

Event III

A customer decides to purchase books, places the order for the books, and requests a book order form from the Sales Department. A blank book order form is forwarded to the customer. The customer account number and the date the order is being placed are entered. The following information is included in the book order:

Customer Account Number
Date Order is placed
Title of the Book
Author
Paperback or Hardcopy
ISBN, if available

In addition, the customer indicates the shipping option by entering the following information:

Standard Shipping or
Second Day Air or
Next Day Air

Placed orders are sent to the warehouse and the customer account file is updated. The warehouse issues an order confirmation when the books are shipped. The invoice is generated and then sent to the customer. The customer then sends the invoice slip and a payment or authorizes the use of a credit card on file to the Accounting Department. The Accounting Department processes the payment and updates the customer account.

Event IV

The Sales Department generates a monthly sales report and forwards it to Management.

Assignment

1. Create DFDs for the four events.
2. Decompose the four top-level DFDs into their respective functional primitives.
3. Create the data dictionary entries for all the named data flows found in the child diagrams from Step (2). The entries in the resulting data dictionary should be reported in alphabetical order.
4. Write process specifications for all of the functional primitives from Step (2).

Case Study created by Cynthia Hernandez.

Appendix B
Case Study: Northwest General
Practitioner's Office

The following represents information obtained during an interview with the Northwest General Practitioner's office:

Potential patients contact the Northwest General Practitioner's office to make appointments to see a General Practitioner. All patient information is stored in a patient medical history folder.

The patient must provide the following information:

Name
Social Security Number
Address
Home Telephone Number
Work or Mobile Telephone Number

Insurance Provider Name
Insurance Provider ID
Name of Primary Insurance Holder

Reason for Visit
Medical History
Family Medical History
List of Allergies

The office examines the patient medical history file and tries to make an appointment for the patient to see the General Practitioner the patient has specified as his/her "preferred" doctor. If the patient's preference is not available at the time the patient requests for the appointment, then the office provides the patient with a list of practitioners who *are* available at that time.

Additionally, practitioners join the Northwest General Practitioner's office every day. Their information is stored in a practitioner's information folder.

A new practitioner must provide the following information:

Name
Social Security Number
Address
Home Telephone Number
Work or Mobile Telephone Number

Specialty (or list of specialties), if applicable

Hospital Affiliations, if applicable

Seven days before patients are due to come in for their appointments, the office begins to send reminder notices to them. There are three reminder notices sent. The first is sent 7 days beforehand, the second is sent 3 days beforehand, and the third reminder takes place 1 day beforehand, via an automated phone call.

For those patients who are billed for services, a notice is mailed to them 30 days before payment is due.

Assignment

1. Draw one data flow diagram depicting the logical equivalent for the above business process description.
2. Level the diagram to its functional primitives.
3. To the best of your ability, provide the data elements you will need for your data entities. *NOTE*: Pay particular attention to the patient medical history file, the physician information file, any file that keeps track of appointments, and, for extra credit, the invoice file.
4. Create an entity relational diagram depicting the relationship between your tables. *NOTE*: You should end up with at least eight entities, if not more.

Case Study created by Melanie Caffrey.

Appendix C
Case Study: University Student Enrollment Database

The following enrollment form has been obtained from Southeast University's Computer Science Program:

Student Enrollment Form

Last Name: _____
First Name: _____
Social Security Number: _____
Address Line 1: _____
Address Line 2: _____
City: _____
State: _____
Zipcode _____

Course #	Section #	Course Cost
_____	_____	_____
_____	_____	_____
_____	_____	_____
_____	_____	_____
_____	_____	_____

Total Amount Due: _____

The students are choosing their courses from the following Course List:

Course #	Course Name	Section #	Section Time	Course Cost
QC2500	Intro to Programming	1	9:00 AM	800.00
		2	10:30 AM	800.00
		3	3:15 PM	800.00
		4	6:00 PM	800.00
QC2625	Intro to Analysis	1	11:00 PM	910.00
		2	4:00 PM	910.00
		3	5:30 PM	910.00
QC2790	Intro to Web Design	1	12:45 PM	725.00
		2	2:30 PM	725.00
		3	6:00 PM	725.00

Assignment

Using the above form, create a normalized ERD. Make sure you are in 3rd Normal Form.

HINT : You should end up with at least four entities, possibly five.

Case Study created by Melanie Caffrey

Further Reading

Allen, T. J., & Morton, M. S. (1994). *Information technology and the corporation*. New York: Oxford University Press.

Applegate, L. M., McFarlan, F. W., & McKenney, J. L. (1999). *Corporate information systems management: The challenges of managing in an information age*. New York: McGraw-Hill.

Berman, K., & Knight, J. (2008). *Finance intelligence for IT professionals*. Boston: Harvard Business Press.

Blackstaff, M. (1999). *Finance for technology decision makers: A practical handbook for buyers, sellers and managers*. New York: Springer.

Bolman, L., & Deal, T. (2003). *Reframing organizations: Artistry, choice, and leadership* (3rd ed.). San Francisco: Jossey-Bass.

Bysinger, B., & Knight, K. (1997). *Investing in information technology: A decision-making guide for business and technical managers*. New York: Wiley.

Carr, N. G. (2005). *Does it matter? Information technology and the corrosion of competitive advantage*. Cambridge: Harvard Business School.

Chesbrough, H. (2003). *Open innovation: The new imperative for creating and profiting from technology*. Cambridge: Harvard Business School

Chesbrough, H. (2006). *Open business models: How to thrive in the new innovation landscape*. Cambridge: Harvard Business School.

Cortada, J. W. (1997). *Best practices in information technology: How corporations get the most value from exploiting their digital investments*. Paramus, NJ: Prentice Hall.

Edwards, C., Ward, J., & Bytheway, A. (1996). *The essence of information systems* (2nd ed.). Upper Saddle River, NJ: Prentice Hall.

Gardner, C. (2000). *The valuation of information technology*. New York: Wiley.

Goonatilake, S., & Teleaven, P. (1995). *Intelligent systems for finance and business*. New York: Wiley.

Hogbin, G., & Thomas, D. (1994). *Investing in information technology: Managing the decision-making process*. New York: McGraw-Hill.

Langer, A. M. (1997). *The art of analysis*. New York: Springer.

Langer, A. M. (2002). *Applied ecommerce: Analysis and engineering of ecommerce systems*. New York: Wiley.

Langer, A. M. (2004). *IT and organizational learning: Managing change through technology and education*. New York: Routledge.

Laudon, K. C., & Laudon, J. P. (1998). *Management information systems: New approaches to organization and technology*. Upper Saddle River, NJ: Prentice Hall.

Liebowitz, J., & Khosrowpour, M. (1997). *Cases on information technology management in modern organizations*. New York: Idea Group Publishing.

Lientz, B. P., & Larssen, L. (2004). *Manage IT as a business: How to achieve alignment and add value to the company.* Burlington, MA: Elsevier Butterworth-Heinemann.

Lucas, H. C. (2005). *Information technology: Strategic decision making for managers.* New York: Wiley.

Marchand, D. A. (2000). *Competing with information: A manager's guide to creating business value with information content.* New York: Wiley.

McCarthy, E. (1997). *The financial advisor's analytical toolbox.* New York: McGraw-Hill.

McDowell, R., & Simon, W. L. (2004). *In search of business value: Ensuring a return of your technology investment.* New York: SelectBooks, Inc.

Murphy, T. (2002). *Achieving business value from technology: A practical guide for today's executive.* Hoboken, NJ: Wiley.

Rapp, W. V. (2002). *Information technology strategies: How leading firms use IT to gain an advantage.* New York: Oxford University Press.

Remenyi, D., Sherwood-Smith, L., & White, T. (1997). *Achieving maximum value from information systems: A process approach.* New York: Wiley.

Speser, P. L. (2006). *The art and science of technology transfer.* Hoboken, NJ: Wiley.

Stenzel, J. (2007). *CIO best practices: Enabling strategic value with information technology.* Hoboken, NJ: Wiley.

Tushman, M., & Anderson, P. (1997). *Managing strategic innovation and change.* New York: Oxford University Press.

Von Stamm, B. (2003). *Managing innovation, design & creativity.* New York: Wiley.

Weill, P., & Ross, J. W. (2004). *IT governance.* Cambridge: Harvard Business School.

Willcocks, L. P., & Lacity, M. C. (1998). *Strategic sourcing of information systems: Perspectives and practices.* New York: Wiley.

Glossary

Acceptance Test Plans Set of tests that if passed will establish that the software can be used in production.

Alternate Key An attribute that uniquely identifies a row or occurrence in an entity. An alternate key cannot be the primary key.

Attribute A component of an entity or object. An attribute may or may not be an elementary data element.

Business Process Reengineering (BPR) A method to redesign existing applications.

Business Specification A document which reflects the overall requirements of a process or system written in a prose format. The focus of the business specification is to provide the user with enough information so they can authorize the development of the technical requirements.

CASE (Computer-Aided Software Engineering) Products which are used to automate and implement modeling tools and data repositories.

Case A format for developing application logic in a process specification.

Client An application that request services from applications.

Crow's Foot A method of showing the relationship or association between two entities.

CRUD Diagram An association matrix that matches the types of data access between entities and processes. CRUD represents Create, Read, Update, and Delete.

Data Dictionary (DD) A dictionary that defines data. A component of the data repository.

Data Flow Component of a data flow diagram that represents data entering or leaving a process, external, or data store.

Data Flow Diagram (DFD) A tool that shows how data enter and leave a process. A data flow diagram has four possible components: data flow, data store, external, and process.

Data Repository A robust data dictionary that contains information relating to data element behavior.

Data Store Component of a data flow diagram that represents data that can be accessed from a particular area or file. A data store is sometimes called "data-at-rest."

Data Warehousing A de-normalized database created to focus on decision support activities. Data warehouse holds historical information and cannot be used to update data.

Elementary Data Element A functionally decomposed data element.

Entity An object of interest about which data can be collected. Entities can consume a number of attributes.

Entity Relational Diagram (ERD) A diagram that depicts the relationships among the stored data.

Executive Sponsor An individual at an executive level who has responsibility for a business area. The executive sponsor is a defined role in JAD sessions.

External Component of a data flow diagram which represents a provider or user of data who is not part of the system. Externals are therefore boundaries of the system.

Facilitator An impartial individual responsible for controlling the flow of JAD sessions.

Functional Decomposition The process for finding the most basic parts of a system.

Functional Overview A subset view of a specification. The subset usually covers a particular function of the system.

Functional Primitive A functionally decomposed data flow diagram.

Gantt Chart A tool that depicts progress of tasks against time. The Chart was developed by Henry L. Gantt in 1917.

ISO 9000 International Organization for Standardization, quality standard 9000.

Job Description Matrix The portion of an individual's job description that strictly focuses on the procedural and process aspects of the individual's position.

Joint Application Development (JAD) A method of developing the requirements for a system by focusing on group sessions. The sessions are typically under the direction of a facilitator.

Key An attribute of an entity or database that uniquely identifies a row, occurrence, or record.

Key Business Rules Business rules of key attributes that are enforced at the database level (as opposed to the application level).

Legacy System An existing automated system.

Leveling Functional decomposition of a data flow diagram. Each decomposition is called a "level."

Logical Data Modeling (LDM) A set of procedures that examines an entity to ensure that its component attributes should reside in that entity, rather than being stored in another or new entity.

Logical Equivalent An abstraction of the translation from physical requirements to software.

Long Division An abstraction of the relationship of arithmetic formulas to functional decomposition.

Metadata Data about the data being sent or received in a client/server network.

Normalization The elimination of redundancies from an entity.

Open Systems Standards in applications software that allow such software to run across multiple operating system environments.

Pre-Post Conditions A format for developing application logic in a process specification.

Primary Key A key attribute that will be used to identify connections to a particular entity. Normalization requires that every entity contains a primary key. Primary keys can be formed by the concatenation of many attributes.

Process A function in a data flow diagram in which data are transformed from one form to another.

Process Specification A document that contains all of the algorithms and information necessary to develop the logic of a process. Process specifications can be composed of the business and programming requirement documents. Process specifications are sometimes called "minispecs."

Program or Technical Specification A technical algorithm of the requirements of a process or system.

Prototype A sample of a system that does not actually fully operate. Most software prototypes are visual depictions of screens and reports. Prototypes can vary in capability, with some prototypes having limited functional interfaces.

Pseudocode A generic or structured English representation of how real programming code must execute. Pseudocode is a method used in the development of process specifications.

Rapid Application Development (RAD) A method of application development that combines the analysis and design steps through the use of prototypes and CASE tools.

Reverse Engineering The process of analyzing existing applications and database code to create higher-level representations of the code.

Robust Software that operates intuitively and can handle unexpected events.

Scribe A person who is designated in a JAD session to record minutes and decisions made by the group. In certain situations, scribes can also be responsible for data modeling.

Server An application that provides information to a requesting application.

Spiral Life Cycle Life cycle that focuses on the development of cohesive objects and classes. The spiral life cycle reflects a much larger allocation of time spent on design than the waterfall approach.

State Transition Diagram (STD) A modeling tool that depicts time-dependent and event-driven behavior.

Waterfall System Development Life Cycle A life cycle that is based on phased dependent steps to complete the implementation of a system. Each step is dependent on the completion of the previous step.

Index